HOLT SCIENCE & TECHNOLOGY

Cells, Heredity, and Classification

HOLT, RINEHART AND WINSTON

A Harcourt Classroom Education Company

Austin • New York • Orlando • Atlanta • San Francisco • Boston • Dallas • Toronto • London

Acknowledgments

Chapter Writers

Katy Z. Allen
Science Writer and Former Biology Teacher
Wayland, Massachusetts

Linda Ruth Berg, Ph.D.
Adjunct Professor–Natural Sciences
St. Petersburg Junior College
St. Petersburg, Florida

Jennie Dusheck
Science Writer
Santa Cruz, California

Mark F. Taylor, Ph.D.
Associate Professor of Biology
Baylor University
Waco, Texas

Lab Writers

Diana Scheidle Bartos
Science Consultant and Educator
Diana Scheidle Bartos, L.L.C.
Lakewood, Colorado

Carl Benson
General Science Teacher
Plains High School
Plains, Montana

Charlotte Blassingame
Technology Coordinator
White Station Middle School
Memphis, Tennessee

Marsha Carver
Science Teacher and Dept. Chair
McLean County High School
Calhoun, Kentucky

Kenneth E. Creese
Science Teacher
White Mountain Junior High School
Rock Springs, Wyoming

Linda Culp
Science Teacher and Dept. Chair
Thorndale High School
Thorndale, Texas

James Deaver
Science Teacher and Dept. Chair
West Point High School
West Point, Nebraska

Frank McKinney, Ph.D.
Professor of Geology
Appalachian State University
Boone, North Carolina

Alyson Mike
Science Teacher
East Valley Middle School
East Helena, Montana

C. Ford Morishita
Biology Teacher
Clackamas High School
Milwaukie, Oregon

Patricia D. Morrell, Ph.D.
Assistant Professor, School of Education
University of Portland
Portland, Oregon

Hilary C. Olson, Ph.D.
Research Associate
Institute for Geophysics
The University of Texas
Austin, Texas

James B. Pulley
Science Editor and Former Science Teacher
Liberty High School
Liberty, Missouri

Denice Lee Sandefur
Science Chairperson
Nucla High School
Nucla, Colorado

Patti Soderberg
Science Writer
The BioQUEST Curriculum Consortium
Beloit College
Beloit, Wisconsin

Phillip Vavala
Science Teacher and Dept. Chair
Salesianum School
Wilmington, Delaware

Albert C. Wartski
Biology Teacher
Chapel Hill High School
Chapel Hill, North Carolina

Lynn Marie Wartski
Science Writer and Former Science Teacher
Hillsborough, North Carolina

Ivora D. Washington
Science Teacher and Dept. Chair
Hyattsville Middle School
Washington, D.C.

Academic Reviewers

Renato J. Aguilera, Ph.D.
Associate Professor
Department of Molecular, Cell, and Developmental Biology
University of California
Los Angeles, California

David M. Armstrong, Ph.D.
Professor of Biology
Department of E.P.O. Biology
University of Colorado
Boulder, Colorado

Alissa Arp, Ph.D.
Director and Professor of Environmental Studies
Romberg Tiburon Center
San Francisco State University
Tiburon, California

Russell M. Brengelman
Professor of Physics
Morehead State University
Morehead, Kentucky

John A. Brockhaus, Ph.D.
Director of Mapping, Charting, and Geodesy Program
Department of Geography and Environmental Engineering
United States Military Academy
West Point, New York

Linda K. Butler, Ph.D.
Lecturer of Biological Sciences
The University of Texas
Austin, Texas

Barry Chernoff, Ph.D.
Associate Curator
Division of Fishes
The Field Museum of Natural History
Chicago, Illinois

Donna Greenwood Crenshaw, Ph.D.
Instructor
Department of Biology
Duke University
Durham, North Carolina

Hugh Crenshaw, Ph.D.
Assistant Professor of Zoology
Duke University
Durham, North Carolina

Joe W. Crim, Ph.D.
Professor of Biology
University of Georgia
Athens, Georgia

Peter Demmin, Ed.D.
Former Science Teacher and Chair
Amherst Central High School
Amherst, New York

Joseph L. Graves, Jr., Ph.D.
Associate Professor of Evolutionary Biology
Arizona State University West
Phoenix, Arizona

William B. Guggino, Ph.D.
Professor of Physiology and Pediatrics
The Johns Hopkins University School of Medicine
Baltimore, Maryland

David Haig, Ph.D.
Assistant Professor of Biology
Department of Organismic and Evolutionary Biology
Harvard University
Cambridge, Massachusetts

Roy W. Hann, Jr., Ph.D.
Professor of Civil Engineering
Texas A&M University
College Station, Texas

Acknowledgments (cont.)

John E. Hoover, Ph.D.
Associate Professor of Biology
Millersville University
Millersville, Pennsylvania

Joan E. N. Hudson, Ph.D.
Associate Professor of Biological Sciences
Sam Houston State University
Huntsville, Texas

Laurie Jackson-Grusby, Ph.D.
Research Scientist and Doctoral Associate
Whitehead Institute for Biomedical Research
Massachusetts Institute of Technology
Cambridge, Massachusetts

George M. Langford, Ph.D.
Professor of Biological Sciences
Dartmouth College
Hanover, New Hampshire

Melanie C. Lewis, Ph.D.
Professor of Biology, Retired
Southwest Texas State University
San Marcos, Texas

V. Patteson Lombardi, Ph.D.
Research Assistant Professor of Biology
Department of Biology
University of Oregon
Eugene, Oregon

Glen Longley, Ph.D.
Professor of Biology and Director of the Edwards Aquifer Research Center
Southwest Texas State University
San Marcos, Texas

William F. McComas, Ph.D.
Director of the Center to Advance Science Education
University of Southern California
Los Angeles, California

LaMoine L. Motz, Ph.D.
Coordinator of Science Education
Oakland County Schools
Waterford, Michigan

Nancy Parker, Ph.D.
Associate Professor of Biology
Southern Illinois University
Edwardsville, Illinois

Barron S. Rector, Ph.D.
Associate Professor and Extension Range Specialist
Texas Agricultural Extension Service
Texas A&M University
College Station, Texas

Peter Sheridan, Ph.D.
Professor of Chemistry
Colgate University
Hamilton, New York

Miles R. Silman, Ph.D.
Assistant Professor of Biology
Wake Forest University
Winston-Salem, North Carolina

Neil Simister, Ph.D.
Associate Professor of Biology
Department of Life Sciences
Brandeis University
Waltham, Massachusetts

Lee Smith, Ph.D.
Curriculum Writer
MDL Information Systems, Inc.
San Leandro, California

Robert G. Steen, Ph.D.
Manager, Rat Genome Project
Whitehead Institute—Center for Genome Research
Massachusetts Institute of Technology
Cambridge, Massachusetts

Martin VanDyke, Ph.D.
Professor of Chemistry, Emeritus
Front Range Community College
Westminister, Colorado

E. Peter Volpe, Ph.D.
Professor of Medical Genetics
Mercer University School of Medicine
Macon, Georgia

Harold K. Voris, Ph.D.
Curator and Head
Division of Amphibians and Reptiles
The Field Museum of Natural History
Chicago, Illinois

Mollie Walton
Biology Instructor
El Paso Community College
El Paso, Texas

Peter Wetherwax, Ph.D.
Professor of Biology
University of Oregon
Eugene, Oregon

Mary K. Wicksten, Ph.D.
Professor of Biology
Texas A&M University
College Station, Texas

R. Stimson Wilcox, Ph.D.
Associate Professor of Biology
Department of Biological Sciences
Binghamton University
Binghamton, New York

Conrad M. Zapanta, Ph.D.
Research Engineer
Sulzer Carbomedics, Inc.
Austin, Texas

Safety Reviewer

Jack Gerlovich, Ph.D.
Associate Professor
School of Education
Drake University
Des Moines, Iowa

Teacher Reviewers

Barry L. Bishop
Science Teacher and Dept. Chair
San Rafael Junior High School
Ferron, Utah

Carol A. Bornhorst
Science Teacher and Dept. Chair
Bonita Vista Middle School
Chula Vista, California

Paul Boyle
Science Teacher
Perry Heights Middle School
Evansville, Indiana

Yvonne Brannum
Science Teacher and Dept. Chair
Hine Junior High School
Washington, D.C.

Gladys Cherniak
Science Teacher
St. Paul's Episcopal School
Mobile, Alabama

James Chin
Science Teacher
Frank A. Day Middle School
Newtonville, Massachusetts

Kenneth Creese
Science Teacher
White Mountain Junior High School
Rock Springs, Wyoming

Linda A. Culp
Science Teacher and Dept. Chair
Thorndale High School
Thorndale, Texas

Georgiann Delgadillo
Science Teacher
East Valley Continuous Curriculum School
Spokane, Washington

Alonda Droege
Biology Teacher
Evergreen High School
Seattle, Washington

Michael J. DuPré
Curriculum Specialist
Rush Henrietta Junior-Senior High School
Henrietta, New York

Rebecca Ferguson
Science Teacher
North Ridge Middle School
North Richland Hills, Texas

Susan Gorman
Science Teacher
North Ridge Middle School
North Richland Hills, Texas

Gary Habeeb
Science Mentor
Sierra-Plumas Joint Unified School District
Downieville, California

Karma Houston-Hughes
Science Mentor
Kyrene Middle School
Tempe, Arizona

Roberta Jacobowitz
Science Teacher
C. W. Otto Middle School
Lansing, Michigan

Kerry A. Johnson
Science Teacher
Isbell Middle School
Santa Paula, California

M. R. Penny Kisiah
Science Teacher and Dept. Chair
Fairview Middle School
Tallahassee, Florida

Kathy LaRoe
Science Teacher
East Valley Middle School
East Helena, Montana

Jane M. Lemons
Science Teacher
Western Rockingham Middle School
Madison, North Carolina

Scott Mandel, Ph.D.
Director and Educational Consultant
Teachers Helping Teachers
Los Angeles, California

Thomas Manerchia
Former Biology and Life Science Teacher
Archmere Academy
Claymont, Delaware

Maurine O. Marchani
Science Teacher and Dept. Chair
Raymond Park Middle School
Indianapolis, Indiana

Jason P. Marsh
Biology Teacher
Montevideo High School and Montevideo Country School
Montevideo, Minnesota

Edith C. McAlanis
Science Teacher and Dept. Chair
Socorro Middle School
El Paso, Texas

Kevin McCurdy, Ph.D.
Science Teacher
Elmwood Junior High School
Rogers, Arkansas

Kathy McKee
Science Teacher
Hoyt Middle School
Des Moines, Iowa

Acknowledgments continue on page 215.

C Cells, Heredity, and Classification

Skills Development

Process Skills

QuickLabs

Chapter Labs

Skills Development

Research and Critical Thinking Skills

Apply

Feature Articles

Across the Sciences

Health Watch

Science, Technology, and Society

Scientific Debate

Eye on the Environment

Science Fiction

Careers

Weird Science

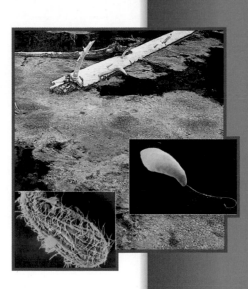

Connections

Chemistry Connection

Meteorology Connection

Geology Connection

Environment Connection

Mathematics

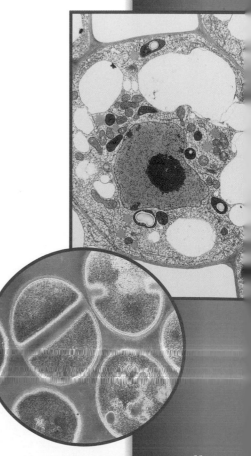

To the Student

This book was created to make your science experience interesting, exciting, and fun!

Go for It!

Science is a process of discovery, a trek into the unknown. The skills you develop using *Holt Science & Technology*— such as observing, experimenting, and explaining observations and ideas— are the skills you will need for the future. There is a universe of exploration and discovery awaiting those who accept the challenges of science.

Science & Technology

You see the interaction between science and technology every day. Science makes technology possible. On the other hand, some of the products of technology, such as computers, are used to make further scientific discoveries. In fact, much of the scientific work that is done today has become so technically complicated and expensive that no one person can do it entirely alone. But make no mistake, the creative ideas for even the most highly technical and expensive scientific work still come from individuals.

Activities and Labs

The activities and labs in this book will allow you to make some basic but important scientific discoveries on your own. You can even do some exploring on your own at home! Here's your chance to use your imagination and curiosity as you investigate your world.

Keep a ScienceLog

In this book, you will be asked to keep a type of journal called a ScienceLog to record your thoughts, observations, experiments, and conclusions. As you develop your ScienceLog, you will see your own ideas taking shape over time. You'll have a written record of how your ideas have changed as you learn about and explore interesting topics in science.

Know "What You'll Do"

The "What You'll Do" list at the beginning of each section is your built-in guide to what you need to learn in each chapter. When you can answer the questions in the Section Review and Chapter Review, you know you are ready for a test.

Check Out the Internet

You will see this logo throughout the book. You'll be using *sci*LINKS as your gateway to the Internet. Once you log on to *sci*LINKS using your computer's Internet link, type in the *sci*LINKS address. When asked for the keyword code, type in the keyword for that topic. A wealth of resources is now at your disposal to help you learn more about that topic.

In addition to *sci*LINKS you can log on to some other great resources to go with your text. The addresses shown below will take you to the home page of each site.

---

internet **connect**

This textbook contains the following on-line resources to help you make the most of your science experience.

go. hrw .com	*sci*LINKS NSTA	 Smithsonian Institution® Internet Connections	 CNN fyi.com
Visit **go.hrw.com** for extra help and study aids matched to your textbook. Just type in the keyword HST HOME.	Visit **www.scilinks.org** to find resources specific to topics in your textbook. Keywords appear throughout your book to take you further.	Visit **www.si.edu/hrw** for specifically chosen on-line materials from one of our nation's premier science museums.	Visit **www.cnnfyi.com** for late-breaking news and current events stories selected just for you.

Contents   **1**

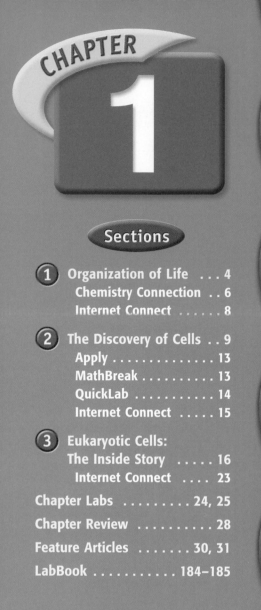

CHAPTER 1

Cells: The Basic Units of Life

Pre-Reading Questions

1. What is a cell, and where are cells found?
2. Why are there cells, and why are they so small?

TINY DEFENDERS

Invading bacteria have entered your body. These foreign cells are about to make you sick. But wait—your white blood cells come to the rescue! In this microscopic image, a white blood cell is reaching out its "arm" (called a *pseudopod*) to destroy a bacterium. In this chapter, you will learn about bacteria, blood cells, and other cells in your body.

START-UP Activity

WHAT ARE PLANTS MADE OF?

All living things, including plants, are made of cells. What do plant cells look like? Do this activity to find out.

Procedure

1. Tear off a small leaf near the tip of an *Elodea* sprig.

2. Using **tweezers,** place the whole leaf in a drop of **water** on a **microscope slide.**

3. Place a **coverslip** on top of the water drop. Put one edge on the slide, then slowly lower the coverslip over the drop to prevent air bubbles.

4. Place the slide on your **microscope.** Find the cells. You may have to use the highest powered lens to see them.

5. Draw a picture of what you see.

Analysis

6. Describe the shape of the *Elodea* cells. Are they all the same?

7. Do you think your cells look like *Elodea* cells? Explain your answer.

Terms to Learn

tissue	multicellular
organ	population
organ system	community
organism	ecosystem
unicellular	

What You'll Do

♦ Explain how life is organized, from a single cell to an ecosystem.

♦ Describe the difference between unicellular organisms and multicellular organisms.

Organization of Life

Imagine that you are going on a trip to Mars. In your suitcase, you should pack everything you will need in order to survive. What would you pack? To start, you'd need food, oxygen, and water. And that's just the beginning. You would probably need a pretty big suitcase, wouldn't you? Actually, you have all of these items inside your body's cells. A cell is smaller than the period at the end of this sentence, yet a single cell has all the items necessary to carry out life's activities.

Every living thing has at least one cell. Many living things exist as a single cell, while others have trillions of cells. To get an idea of what a living thing with nearly 100 trillion cells looks like, just look in the mirror!

Cells: Starting Out Small

Most cells are too small to be seen without a microscope, but you might have one of the world's largest cells in your refrigerator. To find out what it is, see **Figure 1.** The first cell of a chicken is yellow with a tiny white dot in it, and it is surrounded by clear, jellylike fluid called egg white. The white dot divides over and over again to form a chick. The yellow yolk (from the first cell) and the egg white provide nutrients for the developing chick's cells. Like a chicken, you too began as a single egg cell. Look at **Figure 2** to see some of the early stages of your development.

Not all of your cells look or act the same. You have about 200 different kinds of cells, and each type is specialized to do a particular job. Some are bone cells, some are blood cells, and others are skin cells. When someone looks at all of those cells together, they see you.

Figure 1 *The first cell of a chicken is one of the largest cells in the world.*

Figure 2 *You began as a single cell. But after many cell divisions, you are now made of about 100 trillion cells.*

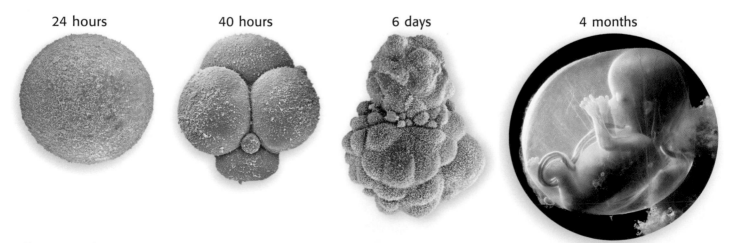

24 hours	40 hours	6 days	4 months

Tissues: Cells Working in Teams

When you look closely at your clothes, you can see that threads have been grouped together (woven) to make cloth that has a function. In the same way, cells are grouped together to make a tissue that has a function. A **tissue** is a group of cells that work together to perform a specific job in the body. The material around and between the cells is also part of the tissue. Some examples of tissues in your body are shown in **Figure 3**.

Organs: Teams Working Together

When two or more tissues work together to perform a specific job, the group of tissues is called an **organ.** Some examples of organs are your stomach, intestines, heart, lungs, and skin. That's right; even your skin is an organ because it contains different kinds of tissues. To get a closer look, see **Figure 4.**

Plants also have different kinds of tissues that work together. A leaf is a plant organ that contains tissue that traps light energy to make food. Other examples of plant organs are stems and roots.

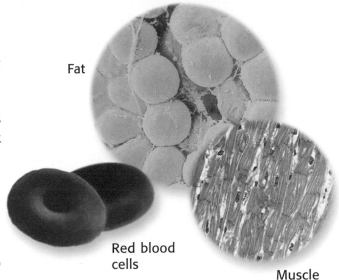

Fat

Red blood cells

Muscle

Figure 3 *Blood, fat, and muscle cells are just a few of the many cells that make tissues in your body.*

Figure 4 *The skin is the body's largest organ. An average-sized person's skin has a mass of about 4.5 kg.*

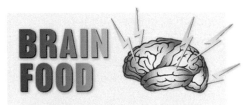

BRAIN FOOD

The part of the skin, hair, and nails that you can see is dead tissue! Isn't it strange to think that we put so much effort into making sure our dead cells look nice?

Organ Systems: A Great Combination

Organs work together in groups to perform particular jobs. These groups are called **organ systems.** Each system has a specific job to do in the body. For example, your digestive system's job is to break down food into very small particles so it can be used by all of your body's cells. Your nervous system's job is to transmit information back and forth between your brain and the other parts of your body. Organ systems in plants include leaf systems, root systems, and stem systems.

Your body has several organ systems. The digestive system is shown in **Figure 5.** Each organ in the digestive system has a job to do. A particular organ is able to do its job because of the different tissues within it.

The organs in an organ system depend on each other. If any part of the system fails, the whole system is affected. And failure of one organ system can affect other organ systems. Just think of what would happen if your digestive system stopped converting food to energy. None of the other organ systems would have energy to function.

Activity

A school system's job is to educate students at all levels. The different schools (elementary, middle, and high school) are like the different organs within an organ system. Groups of teachers at each school work together to teach a specific grade level. If each group of teachers can be thought of as tissue, what would that make each individual teacher? What other examples can you use to represent the parts of an organ system? Explain your answer.

Try at Home

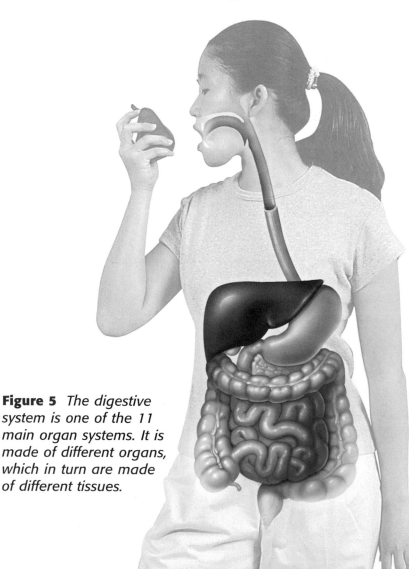

Figure 5 *The digestive system is one of the 11 main organ systems. It is made of different organs, which in turn are made of different tissues.*

Organisms: Independent Living

Anything that can live on its own is called an **organism.** All organisms are made up of at least one cell. If a single cell is living on its own, it is called a **unicellular** organism. Most unicellular organisms are so small that you need to use a microscope to see them. Some different kinds of unicellular organisms are shown in **Figure 6.**

You are a **multicellular** organism. This means that you can exist only as a group of cells and that most of your cells can survive only if they remain a part of your body. When you fall down on a sidewalk and scrape your knee, the cells you leave behind on the sidewalk are not able to live on their own. **Figure 7** shows how your cells work together to make a multicellular organism.

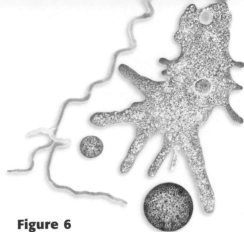

Figure 6
Unicellular organisms come in a wide variety of shapes and sizes.

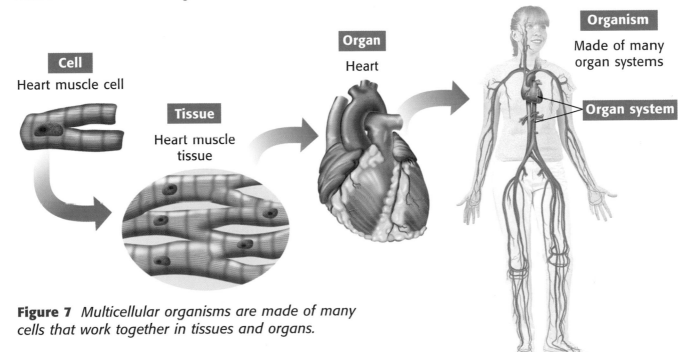

Cell
Heart muscle cell

Tissue
Heart muscle tissue

Organ
Heart

Organism
Made of many organ systems

Organ system

Figure 7 *Multicellular organisms are made of many cells that work together in tissues and organs.*

The Big Picture

Although unicellular organisms and multicellular organisms can live on their own, they usually do not live alone. Organisms interact with each other in many different ways.

Populations A group of organisms that are of the same kind and that live in the same area make up a **population.** All of the ladybird beetles living in the forest shown in **Figure 8** make up the ladybird beetle population of that forest. All of the red oak trees make up the forest's red oak population.

Figure 8 *A population is made up of all of the individuals of the same kind that live in the same area.*

Figure 9 *The fox, flowers, and trees are all part of a forest community.*

Communities Two or more different populations living in the same area make up a **community.** The populations of foxes, oak trees, lizards, flowers, and other organisms in a forest are all part of a forest community, as shown in **Figure 9.** Your hometown is a community that includes all of the people, dogs, cats, and other organisms living there.

Ecosystems The community and all of the nonliving things that affect it, such as water, soil, rocks, temperature, and light, make up an **ecosystem.** Ecosystems on land are called *terrestrial* ecosystems, and they include forests, deserts, prairies, and your own backyard. Ecosystems in water are called *aquatic* ecosystems, and they include rivers, ponds, lakes, oceans, and even aquariums. The community in Figure 9 lives in a terrestrial ecosystem.

SECTION REVIEW

1. Complete the following sentence: *Cells* are related to __?__ in the same way that __?__ are related to *organ systems.*

2. How do the cells of unicellular organisms differ from the cells of multicellular organisms?

3. **Applying Concepts** Use the picture of an aquarium below to answer the following questions:

   a. How many *different* kinds of organisms are visible?

   b. How many populations are visible?

   c. How many communities are visible?

Terms to Learn

cell membrane   prokaryotic
organelles   eukaryotic
cytoplasm   bacteria
nucleus

What You'll Do

◆ State the parts of the cell theory.
◆ Explain why cells are so small.
◆ Calculate a cell's surface-to-volume ratio.
◆ List the advantages of being multicellular.
◆ Explain the difference between prokaryotic cells and eukaryotic cells.

The Discovery of Cells

Most cells are so tiny that they are not visible to the naked eye. So how did we find out that cells are the basic unit of all living things? What would make someone think that a rabbit or a tree or a person is made up of tiny parts that cannot be seen? Actually, the first person to see cells was not even looking for them.

Seeing the First Cells

In 1665, a British scientist named Robert Hooke was trying to find something interesting that he could show to other scientists at a meeting. Earlier, he had built a crude microscope that allowed him to look at very tiny objects. One day he decided to look at a thin slice of cork, a soft plant tissue found in the bark of trees like the ones shown in **Figure 10.** To his amazement, the cork looked like hundreds of little boxes, which he described as looking like a honeycomb. He named these tiny boxes *cells,* which means "little rooms" in Latin.

Although Hooke did not realize it, these boxes were actually the outer layers of the cork cells that were left behind after the cells died. Later, he looked at thin slices of plants and saw that they too were made of tiny cells. Some of them were even filled with "juice" (those were living cells). Hooke's microscope and drawings of cork cells are shown in **Figure 11.**

Hooke also used his microscope to look at feathers, fish scales, and the eyes of house flies, but he spent most of his time looking at plants and fungi. Since plant and fungal cells had walls that were easier to see, Hooke thought that cells were found only in those types of organisms and not in animals.

Figure 10 *Cork is a soft material found in trees. Cork cells were the first cells seen with a microscope.*

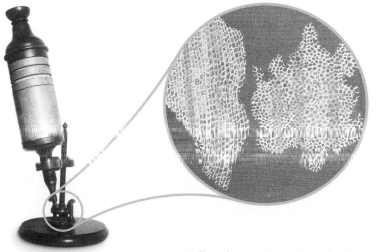

Figure 11 *This is the compound microscope that Hooke used to see the first cells. Hooke made a drawing of the cork cells that he saw.*

Cells: The Basic Units of Life   **9**

Seeing Cells in Other Life-Forms

In 1673, a few years after Hooke made his observations, a Dutch merchant named Anton van Leeuwenhoek (LAY vuhn hook) used one of his own handmade microscopes to get a closer look at pond scum, similar to that shown in **Figure 12.** He was amazed to see many small creatures swimming around in the slimy ooze; he named the creatures *animalcules,* which means "little animals."

Leeuwenhoek also looked at blood he took from different animals and tartar he scraped off their teeth and his own. He observed that blood cells in fish, birds, and frogs are oval-shaped, while those in humans and dogs are flatter. He was the first person to see bacteria, and he discovered that the yeasts used to make bread dough rise are actually unicellular organisms.

Figure 12 *Leeuwenhoek saw unicellular organisms similar to these, which are found in pond scum.*

The Cell Theory

After Hooke first saw the cork cells, almost two centuries passed before anyone realized that cells are present in *all* living things. Matthias Schleiden, a German scientist, looked at many slides of plant tissues and read about what other scientists had seen under the microscope. In 1838, he concluded that all plant parts are made of cells.

The next year, Theodor Schwann, a German scientist who studied animals, stated that all animal tissues are made of cells. Not long after that, Schwann wrote the first two parts of what is now known as the *cell theory:*

- **All organisms are composed of one or more cells.**

- **The cell is the basic unit of life in all living things.**

About 20 years later, in 1858, Rudolf Virchow, a German doctor, saw that cells could not develop from anything except other cells. He then wrote the third part of the cell theory:

- **All cells come from existing cells.**

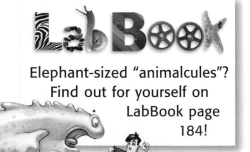

LabBook

Elephant-sized "animalcules"? Find out for yourself on LabBook page 184!

Cell Similarities

Cells come in many different shapes and sizes and perform a wide variety of functions, but they all have the following things in common:

Cell Membrane All cells are surrounded by a **cell membrane.** This membrane acts as a barrier between the inside of the cell and the cell's environment. It also controls the passage of materials into and out of the cell. **Figure 13** shows the outside of a cell.

Figure 13 *The cell membrane holds the contents of the cell together.*

Hereditary Material Part of the cell theory states that all cells are made from existing cells. When new cells are made, they receive a copy of the hereditary material of the original cells. This material is *DNA* (deoxyribonucleic acid). It controls all of the activities of a cell and contains the information needed for that cell to make new cells.

Cytoplasm and Organelles All cells have chemicals and structures that enable the cell to live, grow, and reproduce. The structures are called **organelles.** Although all cells have organelles, they don't all have the same kind. Some organelles are surrounded by membranes, but others are not. The cell in **Figure 14** has membrane-covered organelles. The chemicals and structures of a cell are surrounded by fluid. This fluid and almost everything in it are collectively called the **cytoplasm** (SIET oh PLAZ uhm).

Small Size Almost all cells are too small to be seen with the naked eye. You are made up of 100 trillion cells, and it would take 50 of these cells just to cover up the dot on the letter *i*.

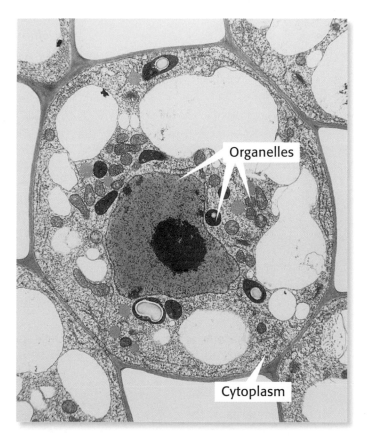

Figure 14 *This cell has many organelles. These organelles are surrounded by membranes.*

Self-Check

Why do all cells need DNA? *(See page 216 to check your answer.)*

Giant Amoeba Eats New York City

This is not a headline you are likely to ever see. Why not? Amoebas consist of only a single cell. Most amoebas can't even grow large enough to be seen without a microscope. That's because as a cell gets larger, it needs more food and produces more waste. Therefore, more materials must be able to move into and out of the cell through the cell membrane.

Surface-to-Volume Ratio To keep up with these demands, a growing cell needs a larger surface area through which to exchange materials. As the cell's volume increases, its outer surface grows too. But the volume of a cell (the amount a cell will hold) increases at a faster rate than the area of its outer surface. If a cell gets too large, its surface will have too few openings to allow enough materials into and out of it.

To understand why the volume of a cell increases faster than its surface area, look at the table below. The *surface-to-volume ratio* is the area of a cell's outer surface in relation to its volume. The surface-to-volume ratio decreases as cell size increases. Increasing the number of cells but not their size maintains a high surface-to-volume ratio.

Surface-to-Volume Ratio

Each side of this cell is 1 unit long.	Each side of this cell is 2 units long.	The sides of each of these 8 cells are 1 unit long.
The surface area of one side is **1 square unit.** (1 × 1 = 1)	The surface area of one side is **4 square units.** (2 × 2 = 4)	The combined surface area of these 8 cells is **48 square units.** (8 × 6 square units = 48)
The surface area of the cell is **6 square units.** (1 × 1 × 6 = 6)	This cell has a surface area of **24 square units.** (2 × 2 × 6 = 24)	The combined volume of these cells is **8 cubic units.** (8 × 1 cubic unit = 8)
The volume of this cell is **1 cubic unit.** (1 × 1 × 1 = 1)	The volume of this larger cell is **8 cubic units.** (2 × 2 × 2 = 8)	The surface-to-volume ratio of the combined cells is 48:8, or **6:1.**
The surface-to-volume ratio of this cell is **6:1.**	The surface-to-volume ratio of this cell is 24:8, or **3:1.**	

The Benefits of Being Multicellular Do you know now why you are made up of many tiny cells instead of one large cell? A single cell as big as you are would have an incredibly small surface-to-volume ratio. The cell could not survive because its outer surface would be too small to allow in the materials it would need. Multicellular organisms grow by producing more small cells, not larger cells. The elephant in **Figure 15** has cells that are the same size as yours.

Many Kinds of Cells In addition to being able to grow larger, multicellular organisms are able to do lots of other things because they are made up of different kinds of cells. Just as there are teachers who are specialized to teach and mechanics who are specialized to work on cars, different cells are specialized to perform different jobs. A single cell cannot do all the things that many different cells can do. Having many different cells that are specialized for specific jobs allows multicellular organisms to perform more functions than unicellular organisms.

The different kinds of cells can form tissues and organs with different functions. People have specialized cells, such as muscle cells, eye cells, and brain cells, so they can walk, run, watch a movie, think, and do many other activities. If you enjoy doing many different things, be glad you are not a single cell.

Figure 15 *An elephant is larger than a human because it has more cells, not larger cells.*

MATH BREAK

Surface-to-Volume Ratio

The shape of a cell can affect its surface-to-volume ratio. Examine the cells below, and answer the questions that follow:

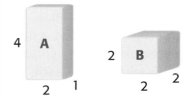

1. What is the surface area of Cell A? of Cell B?
2. What is the volume of Cell A? of Cell B?
3. Which of the two cells pictured here has the greater surface-to-volume ratio?

A Pet *Paramecium*

Imagine that you have a pet *Paramecium,* a type of unicellular organism. In order to properly care for your pet, you have to figure out how much you need to feed it. The dimensions of your *Paramecium* are roughly 125 μm × 50 μm × 20 μm. If seven food molecules can enter through each square micrometer of surface every minute, how many molecules can it eat in 1 minute? If your pet needs one food molecule per cubic micrometer of volume every minute to survive, how much would you have to feed it every minute?

Self-Check

1. As a cell grows larger, what happens to its surface-to-volume ratio?

2. What does a eukaryotic cell have that a prokaryotic cell does not?

(See page 216 to check your answer.)

QuickLab

Do Bacteria Taste Good?

If they're the kind found in yogurt, they taste great! Using a **cotton swab,** put a small dot of **yogurt** on a **plastic microscope slide.** Add a drop of **water,** and use the cotton swab to stir. Add a **plastic coverslip,** and examine the slide using a **microscope.** Draw what you see.

The masses of rod-shaped bacteria feed on the sugar in milk (lactose) and convert it into lactic acid. Lactic acid causes milk to thicken, which makes yogurt!

Two Types of Cells

The many different kinds of cells that exist can be divided into two groups. As you have already learned, all cells have DNA. In one group, cells have a **nucleus,** which is a membrane-covered organelle that holds the cells' DNA. In the other group, the cells' DNA is not contained in a nucleus. Cells that do not have a nucleus are **prokaryotic** (proh KAR ee AH tik), and cells that have a nucleus are **eukaryotic** (yoo KAR ee AH tik).

Prokaryotic Cells Prokaryotic cells are also called **bacteria.** They are the world's smallest cells, and they do not have a nucleus. A prokaryotic cell's DNA is one long, circular molecule shaped sort of like a rubber band.

Bacteria do not have any membrane-covered organelles, but they do have tiny, round organelles called *ribosomes.* These organelles work like little factories to make proteins.

Most bacteria are covered by a hard cell wall outside a softer cell membrane. Think of the membrane pressing against the wall as an inflated balloon pressing against the inside of a glass jar. But unlike the balloon and jar, the membrane and the wall allow food and waste molecules to pass through. **Figure 16** shows a generalized view of a prokaryotic cell.

Bacteria were probably the first type of cells on Earth. The oldest fossils ever found are of prokaryotic cells. Scientists have estimated these fossils to be 3.5 billion years old.

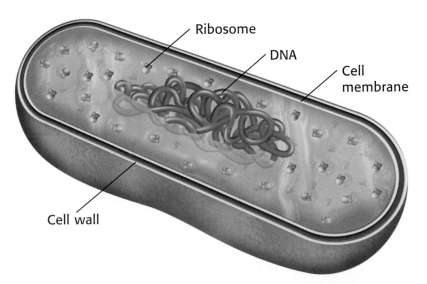

Figure 16 *Prokaryotic cells do not have a nucleus or any other membrane-covered organelles. The circular DNA is bunched up in the cytoplasm.*

Eukaryotic Cells Eukaryotic cells are more complex than prokaryotic cells. Although most eukaryotic cells are about 10 times larger than prokaryotic cells, they still have a high enough surface-to-volume ratio to survive. Fossil evidence suggests that eukaryotic cells first appeared about 2 billion years ago. All living things that are not bacteria are made of one or more eukaryotic cells. This includes plants, animals, fungi, and protists.

Eukaryotic cells have a nucleus and many other membrane-covered organelles. An advantage of having the cell divided into compartments is that it allows many different chemical processes to occur at the same time. A generalized eukaryotic cell is shown in **Figure 17.**

There is more DNA in eukaryotic cells than in prokaryotic cells, and it is stored in the nucleus. Instead of being circular, the DNA molecules in eukaryotic cells are linear.

All eukaryotic cells have a cell membrane, and some of them have a cell wall. Those that have cell walls are found in plants, fungi, and some unicellular organisms. The tables below summarize the differences between eukaryotic and prokaryotic cells.

Nucleus

Figure 17 *Eukaryotic cells contain a nucleus and many other organelles.*

Prokaryotic Cells	Eukaryotic Cells
No nucleus	Nucleus
No membrane-covered organelles	Membrane-covered organelles
Circular DNA	Linear DNA
Bacteria	All other cells

Science CONNECTION

A new way to cure sick cells? See page 30.

SECTION REVIEW

1. What are the three parts of the cell theory?

2. What do all cells have in common?

3. What are two advantages of being multicellular?

4. If a unicellular organism has a cell wall, ribosomes, and circular DNA, is it eukaryotic or prokaryotic?

5. **Applying Concepts** Which has the greater surface-to-volume ratio, a tennis ball or a basketball? Explain your answer. What could be done to increase the surface-to-volume ratio of both?

internetconnect

SCiLINKS
NSTA

TOPIC: Prokaryotic Cells
GO TO: www.scilinks.org
sciLINKS NUMBER: HSTL065

Terms to Learn

cell wall
ribosome
endoplasmic
  reticulum
mitochondria

chloroplast
Golgi complex
vesicle
vacuole
lysosome

What You'll Do

◆ Explain the function of each part of a eukaryotic cell.
◆ Describe the differences between animal cells and plant cells.

Eukaryotic Cells: The Inside Story

For a long time after the discovery of cells, scientists did not really know what cells were made of. Cells are so small that the details of their structure could not be seen until better methods of magnifying and staining were developed. We now know that cells are very complex, especially eukaryotic cells. Everything, from the structures covering the cells to the organelles inside them, performs a task that helps to keep the cells alive.

Holding It All Together

All cells have outer coverings that separate what is inside the cell from what is outside. One kind of covering, called the cell membrane, surrounds all cells. Some cells have an additional layer outside the cell membrane called the cell wall.

Cell Membrane   All cells are covered by a cell membrane. The job of the cell membrane is to keep the cytoplasm inside, to allow nutrients in and waste products out, and to interact with things outside the cell. In **Figure 18,** you can see a close-up view of the cell membrane of a cell that has had its top half cut away.

Phospholipids

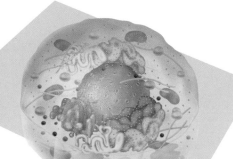

Figure 18 *A cell membrane surrounds all cells. Phospholipid molecules form the cell membrane.*

Cell Wall The cells of plants and algae have a hard cell wall made of cellulose. The **cell wall** provides strength and support to the cell membrane. When too much water enters or leaves a plant cell, the cell wall can prevent the membrane from tearing. The strength of billions of cell walls in plants enables a tree to stand tall and its limbs to defy gravity. When you are looking at dried hay, sticks, and wooden boards, you are seeing the cell walls of dead plant cells. The cells of fungi, such as mushrooms, toadstools, mold, and yeasts, have cell walls made of a chemical similar to that found in the hard covering of insects. **Figure 19** shows a cross section of a generalized plant cell and a close-up view of the cell wall.

The Cell's Library

The largest and most visible organelle in a eukaryotic cell is the nucleus. The word *nucleus* means "kernel" or "nut" (maybe it does look sort of like a nut inside a piece of candy). As you can see in **Figure 20,** the nucleus is covered by a membrane through which materials can pass.

The nucleus has often been called the control center of the cell. As you know, it stores the DNA that has information on how to make all of the cell's proteins. Almost every chemical reaction that is important to the cell's life involves some kind of protein. Sometimes a dark spot can be seen inside the nucleus. This spot is called a *nucleolus,* and it looks like a small nucleus inside the big nucleus. The nucleolus stores the materials that will be used later to make ribosomes in the cytoplasm.

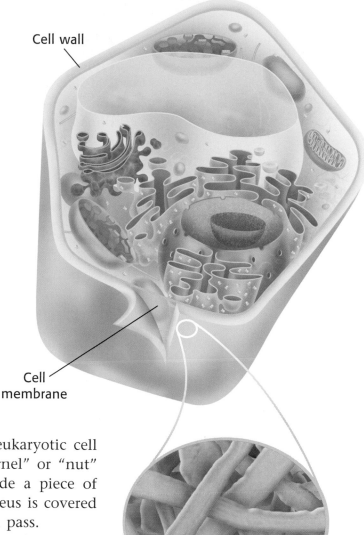

Cell wall

Cell membrane

Figure 19 *The cell wall surrounds the cell membrane. In plant cells, the cell wall is made of cellulose fibers.*

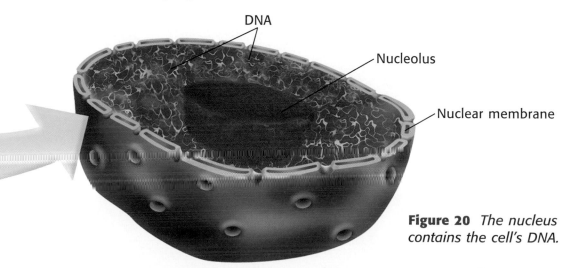

DNA

Nucleolus

Nuclear membrane

Figure 20 *The nucleus contains the cell's DNA.*

Cells: The Basic Units of Life   **17**

Protein Factories

Proteins, the building blocks of all cells, are made up of chemicals known as *amino acids*. These amino acids are hooked together to make proteins at very small organelles called **ribosomes.** Ribosomes are the smallest but most abundant organelles. *All* cells have ribosomes because all cells need protein to live. Unlike most other organelles, ribosomes are not covered with a membrane.

✓ Self-Check

What is the difference between a cell wall and a cell membrane? *(See page 216 to check your answer.)*

The Cell's Delivery System

Eukaryotic cells have an organelle called the endoplasmic (EN doh PLAZ mik) reticulum (ri TIK yuh luhm), which is shown in **Figure 21.** The **endoplasmic reticulum,** or ER, is a membrane-covered compartment that makes lipids and other materials for use inside and outside the cell. It is also the organelle that breaks down drugs and certain other chemicals that could damage the cell. The ER is the internal delivery system of a cell. Substances in the ER can move from one place to another through its many tubular connections, sort of like cars moving through tunnels.

The ER looks like flattened sacks stacked side by side or a cloth folded back and forth. Some ER may be covered with ribosomes that make its surface look rough. The proteins made at those ribosomes pass into the ER. Later the proteins are released from the ER for use elsewhere.

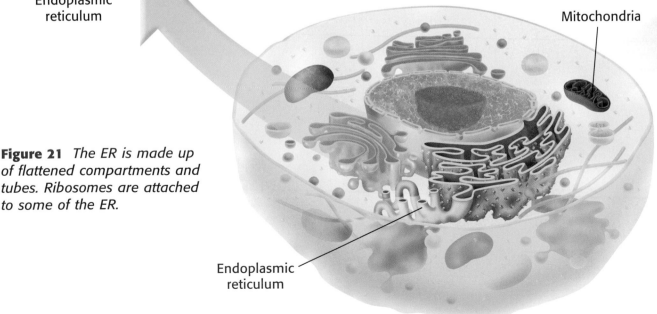

Ribosome

Endoplasmic reticulum

Mitochondria

Figure 21 *The ER is made up of flattened compartments and tubes. Ribosomes are attached to some of the ER.*

Endoplasmic reticulum

The Cell's Power Plants

In today's world, we use many sources of energy, such as oil, gas, and nuclear power. We need this energy to heat our homes, fuel our cars, and cook our food. Cells also need energy to function. Where do they get it?

Mitochondria Inside all cells, food molecules are "burned" (broken down) to release energy. The energy is transferred to a special molecule that the cell uses to get work done. As you learned earlier, this molecule is called ATP.

ATP can be made at several locations in eukaryotic cells, but most of it is produced at bean-shaped organelles called **mitochondria** (MIET oh KAHN dree uh), shown in **Figure 22.** These organelles are surrounded by two membranes. The inner membrane, which has many folds in it, is where most of the ATP is made.

Mitochondria can work only if they have oxygen. The reason you breathe air is to make sure your mitochondria have the oxygen they need to make ATP. Highly active cells, such as those in the heart and liver, may have thousands of mitochondria, while other cells may have only a few.

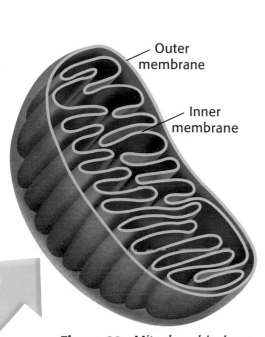

Outer membrane

Inner membrane

Figure 22 *Mitochondria have two membranes. The inner membrane has many folds.*

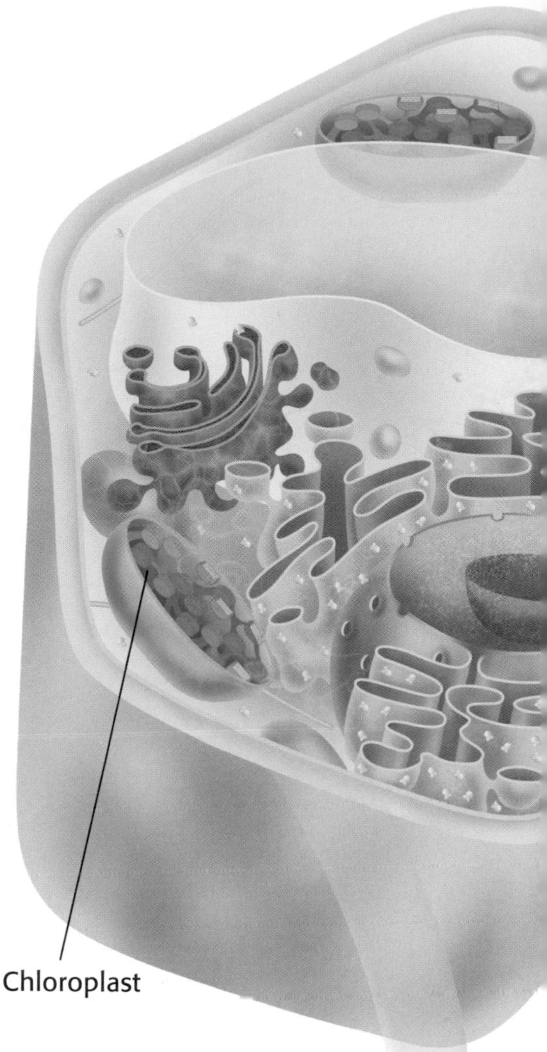

Chloroplast

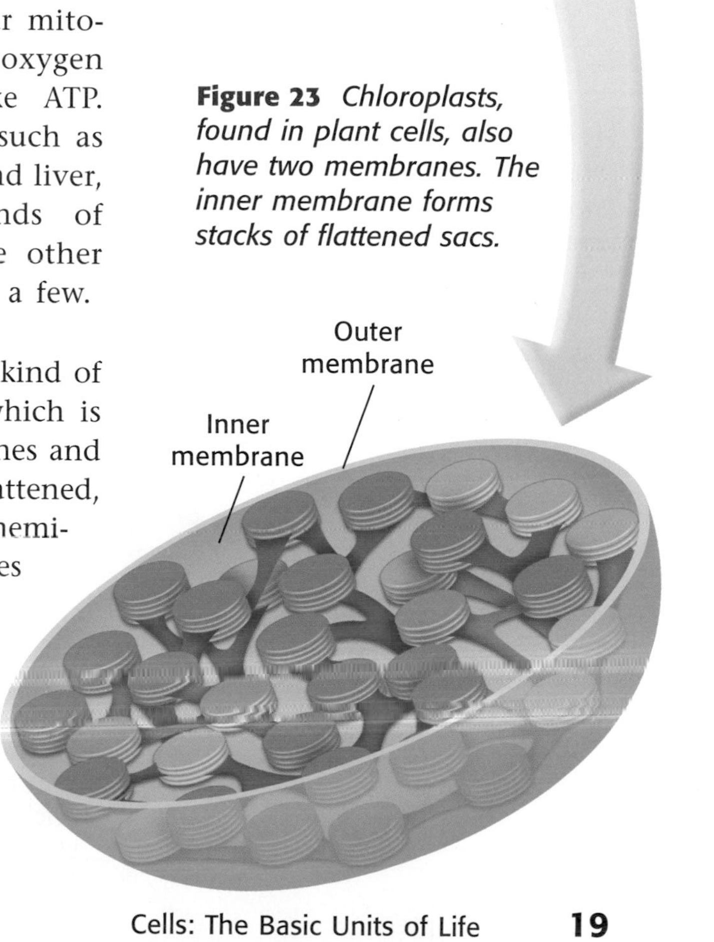

Figure 23 *Chloroplasts, found in plant cells, also have two membranes. The inner membrane forms stacks of flattened sacs.*

Outer membrane

Inner membrane

Chloroplasts Plants and algae have an additional kind of energy-converting organelle, called a **chloroplast,** which is shown in **Figure 23.** Chloroplasts have two membranes and structures that look like stacks of coins. These are flattened, membrane-covered sacs that contain an important chemical called chlorophyll. Chlorophyll is what makes chloroplasts green. The energy of sunlight is trapped by chlorophyll and used to make sugar. This process is called *photosynthesis.* The sugar that is produced is used by mitochondria to make ATP. You will learn more about photosynthesis in a later chapter.

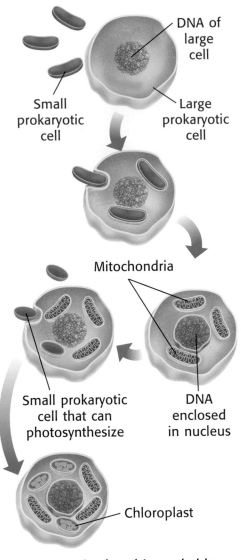

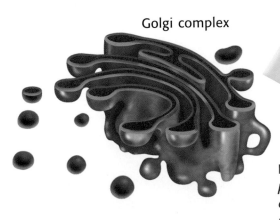

Golgi complex

Figure 24 *Mitochondria and chloroplasts may have originated from energy-producing ancestors that were engulfed by larger cells.*

Where Did They Come From? Many scientists believe that mitochondria and chloroplasts originated as prokaryotic cells that were "eaten" by larger cells. Instead of being digested, the bacteria survived. **Figure 24** shows how bacteria might have become the ancestors of mitochondria and chloroplasts.

What evidence do scientists have that this theory is correct? The first piece of evidence is that mitochondria and chloroplasts are about the same size as bacteria. The second is that both are surrounded by *two membranes*. If the theory is correct, the outer membrane was created when the bacteria were engulfed by the larger cells. Other evidence supports this theory. Mitochondria and chloroplasts have the same kind of ribosomes and circular DNA as bacteria. They also divide like bacteria.

The Cell's Packaging Center

When proteins and other materials need to be processed and shipped out of a eukaryotic cell, the job goes to an organelle called the **Golgi complex.** This structure is named after Camillo Golgi, the Italian scientist who first identified it.

The Golgi complex looks like the ER, but it is located closer to the cell membrane. The Golgi complex of a cell is shown in **Figure 25.** Lipids and proteins from the ER are delivered to the Golgi complex, where they are modified for different functions. The final products are enclosed in a piece of the Golgi complex's membrane that pinches off to form a small compartment. This small compartment transports its contents to other parts of the cell or outside of the cell.

Figure 25 *The Golgi complex processes, packages, and transports materials sent to it from the ER.*

The Cell's Storage Centers

All eukaryotic cells have membrane-covered compartments called **vesicles.** Some of them form when part of the membrane pinches off the ER or Golgi complex. Others are formed when part of the cell membrane surrounds an object outside the cell. This is how white blood cells engulf other cells in your body, as shown in **Figure 26.**

Vacuoles Most plant cells have a very large membrane-covered chamber called a **vacuole,** as shown in **Figure 27.** Vacuoles store water and other liquids. Vacuoles that are full of water help support the cell. Some plants wilt when their cell vacuoles lose water. If you want crispy lettuce for a salad, all you need to do is fill up the vacuoles by leaving the lettuce in water overnight. Have you ever wondered what makes roses red and violets blue? It is a colorful liquid stored inside vacuoles. Vacuoles also contain the juices you associate with oranges and other fruits.

Some unicellular organisms that live in freshwater environments have a problem with too much water entering the cell. They have a special structure called a contractile vacuole that can squeeze excess water out of the cell. It works in much the same way that a pump removes water from inside a boat.

Figure 26 *The smaller cell is a yeast cell that is being engulfed by a white blood cell.*

Vacuole

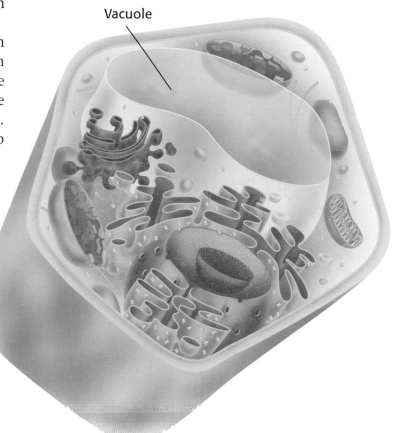

Figure 27 *This plant cell's vacuole is the large structure in the middle of the cell shown in blue. Vacuoles are usually the largest organelles in a plant cell.*

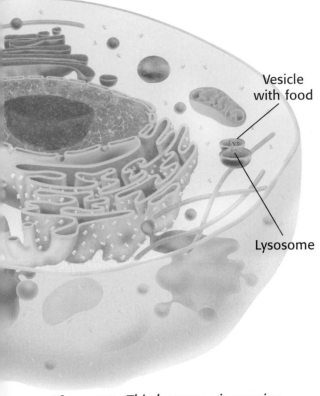

Vesicle
with food

Lysosome

Figure 28 *This lysosome is pouring enzymes into a vesicle that contains food particles. The digested food molecules are released into the cytoplasm for use by the cell.*

Packages of Destruction

What causes most of the cells of a caterpillar to dissolve into ooze inside a cocoon? What causes the tail of a tadpole to shrink and then disappear? Lysosomes, that's what!

Lysosomes are special vesicles in animal cells that contain enzymes. When a cell engulfs a particle and encloses it in a vesicle, lysosomes bump into these vesicles and pour enzymes into them. This is illustrated in **Figure 28.** The particles in the vesicles are digested by the enzymes.

Lysosomes destroy worn-out or damaged organelles. They also get rid of waste materials and protect the cell from foreign invaders.

Sometimes lysosome membranes break, and the enzymes spill into the cytoplasm, killing the cell. This is what must happen for a tadpole to become a frog. Lysosomes cause the cells in a tadpole's tail to die and dissolve as the tadpole becomes a frog. Lysosomes played a similar role in your development! Before you were born, lysosomes caused the destruction of cells that formed the webbing between your fingers. Lysosome destruction of cells may also be one of the factors that contribute to the aging process in humans.

Organelles and Their Functions

	Nucleus contains the cell's DNA and is the control center of the cell		**Chloroplasts** make food using the energy of sunlight
	Ribosomes the site where amino acids are hooked together to make proteins		**Golgi complex** processes and transports materials out of the cell
	Endoplasmic reticulum makes lipids, breaks down drugs and other substances, packages up proteins for release from the cell		**Vacuole** stores water and other materials
	Mitochondria break down food molecules to make ATP		**Lysosomes** digest food particles, wastes, cell parts, and foreign invaders

Plant or Animal?

How can you tell the difference between a plant cell and an animal cell? They both have a cell membrane, and they both have nuclei, ribosomes, mitochondria, endoplasmic reticula, Golgi complexes, and lysosomes. But plant cells have things that animal cells do not have: a cell wall, chloroplasts, and a large vacuole. You can see the differences between plant and animal cells in **Figure 29.**

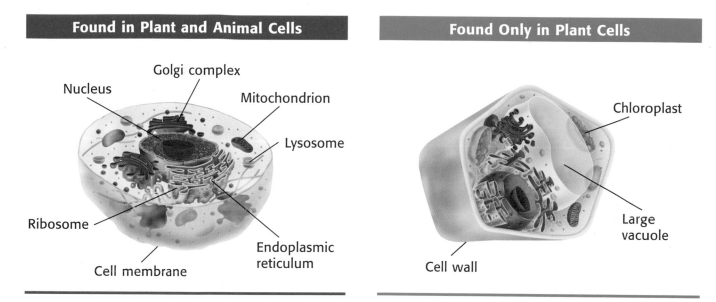

Found in Plant and Animal Cells

Golgi complex

Nucleus

Mitochondrion

Lysosome

Ribosome

Cell membrane

Endoplasmic reticulum

Found Only in Plant Cells

Chloroplast

Large vacuole

Cell wall

Figure 29 *Animal and plant cells have some structures in common, but they also have some that are unique.*

SECTION REVIEW

1. How does the nucleus control the cell's activities?

2. Which of the following would not be found in an animal cell: mitochondria, cell wall, chloroplast, ribosome, endoplasmic reticulum, Golgi complex, large vacuole, DNA, chlorophyll?

3. Use the following words in a sentence: oxygen, ATP, breathing, and mitochondria.

4. **Applying Concepts** You have the job of giving new names to different things in a city. The new names have to be parts of a eukaryotic cell. Write down some things you would see in a city. Assign the name of a cell part that is most appropriate to their function. Explain your choices.

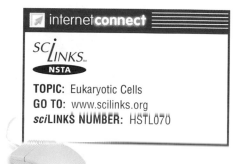

internet**connect**

SC*i*LINKS.
NSTA

TOPIC: Eukaryotic Cells
GO TO: www.scilinks.org
*sci*LINKS NUMBER: HSTL070

Discovery Lab

Cells Alive!

You probably have used a microscope to look at single-celled organisms such as those shown on this page. Single-celled organisms can be found in pond water. In the following exercise, you will look at *Protococcus*—algae that form a greenish stain on tree trunks, wooden fences, flowerpots, and buildings.

MATERIALS

- *Protococcus* (or other algae)
- microscope
- eyedropper
- water
- microscope slide and coverslip

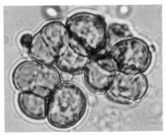
Protococcus

Procedure

1 Locate some *Protococcus*. Scrape a small sample into a container. Bring the sample to the classroom, and make a wet mount of it as directed by your teacher. If you can't find *Protococcus* outdoors, look for algae on the glass in an aquarium. Such algae may not be *Protococcus*, but they will be a very good substitute.

Euglena   *Amoeba*   *Paramecium*

2 Set the microscope on low power to examine the algae. Draw the cells that you see.

3 Switch to high power to examine a single cell. Draw the cell.

4 You probably will notice that each cell contains several chloroplasts. Label a chloroplast on your drawing. What is the function of the chloroplast?

5 Another structure that should be clearly visible in all the algae cells is the nucleus. Find the nucleus in one of your cells, and label it on your drawing. What is the function of the nucleus?

6 What does the cytoplasm look like? Describe any movement you see inside the cells.

Analysis

7 Are *Protococcus* single-celled organisms or multi-cellular organisms?

8 How are *Protococcus* different from amoebas?

Skill Builder Lab

Name That Part!

Plant cells and animal cells have many organelles and other parts in common. For example, both plant and animal cells contain a nucleus and mitochondria. But plant cells and animal cells differ in several ways. In this exercise, you will investigate the similarities and differences between animal cells and plant cells.

MATERIALS

- colored pencils or markers
- white, unlined paper

Procedure

1 Using colored pencils or markers and white, unlined paper, trace or draw the plant cell and the animal cell shown below. Draw each cell on a separate sheet of paper. You may color each organelle a different color.

2 Label the parts of each cell.

3 Below each drawing, list all the parts that you labeled and describe their function.

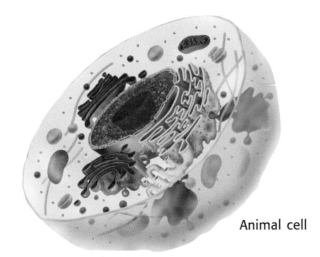

Animal cell

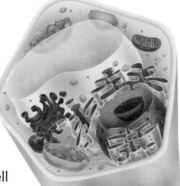

Plant cell

Analysis

4 List at least four structures that plant cells and animal cells have in common.

5 List three structures that plant cells have that animal cells do not have.

Chapter Highlights

SECTION 1

Vocabulary

tissue *(p. 5)*

organ *(p. 5)*

organ system *(p. 6)*

organism *(p. 7)*

unicellular *(p. 7)*

multicellular *(p. 7)*

population *(p. 7)*

community *(p. 8)*

ecosystem *(p. 8)*

Section Notes

- The cell is the smallest unit of life on Earth. Organisms can be made up of one or more cells.

- In multicellular organisms, groups of cells can work together to form tissue. Organs are formed from different tissues and work together with other organs in organ systems.

- The same kind of organisms living together in the same place at the same time make up a population. Different populations living together in the same area make up a community. An ecosystem includes the community and an area's nonliving parts, such as the water and soil.

SECTION 2

Vocabulary

cell membrane *(p. 11)*

organelles *(p. 11)*

cytoplasm *(p. 11)*

nucleus *(p. 14)*

prokaryotic *(p. 14)*

eukaryotic *(p. 14)*

bacteria *(p. 14)*

Section Notes

- The cell theory states that all organisms are made of cells, the cell is the basic unit of life, and all cells come from other cells.

- All cells have a cell membrane, DNA, cytoplasm, and organelles. Most cells are too small to be seen with the naked eye.

☑ Skills Check

Math Concepts

SURFACE-TO-VOLUME RATIO You can determine the surface-to-volume ratio of a cell or other object by dividing surface area by the volume. To determine the surface-to-volume ratio of the rectangle at left, you must first determine the surface area. Surface area is the total area of all the sides. This rectangle has two sides with an area of 6 cm × 3 cm, two sides with an area of 3 cm × 2 cm, and two sides with an area of 6 cm × 2 cm.

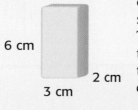

6 cm

2 cm

3 cm

surface area = 2(6 cm × 3 cm) + 2(3 cm × 2 cm) + 2(6 cm × 2 cm) = 72 cm^2

Next you need to find the volume. The volume is determined by multiplying the length of the three sides.

volume = 6 cm × 3 cm × 2 cm = 36 cm^3

To find surface-to-volume ratio, you divide the surface area by the volume:

$$\frac{72}{36} = 2$$

So the surface-to-volume ratio of this rectangle is 2:1.

SECTION 2

- Materials that cells need to take in or release must pass through the cell membrane.

- The surface-to-volume ratio is a comparison of the cell's outer surface to the cell's volume. A cell's surface-to-volume ratio decreases as the cell grows.

- Eukaryotes have linear DNA enclosed in a nucleus and membrane-covered organelles. Prokaryotic cells have circular DNA and organelles that are not covered by membranes.

Labs

Elephant-Sized Amoebas?
(p. 184)

SECTION 3

Vocabulary

cell wall *(p. 17)*

ribosome *(p. 18)*

endoplasmic reticulum *(p. 18)*

mitochondria *(p. 19)*

chloroplast *(p. 19)*

Golgi complex *(p. 20)*

vesicle *(p. 21)*

vacuole *(p. 21)*

lysosome *(p. 22)*

Section Notes

- All cells have a cell membrane that surrounds the contents of the cell. Some cells have a cell wall outside their membrane.

- The nucleus is the control center of the eukaryotic cell. It contains the cell's DNA.

- Ribosomes are the sites where amino acids are strung together to form proteins. Ribosomes are not covered by a membrane.

- The endoplasmic reticulum (ER) and the Golgi complex are membrane-covered compartments in which materials are made and processed before they are transported to other parts of the cell or out of the cell.

- Mitochondria and chloroplasts are energy-producing organelles.

- Vesicles and vacuoles are membrane-covered compartments that store material. Vacuoles are found in plant cells. Lysosomes are vesicles found in animal cells.

---

internet connect

GO TO: go.hrw.com

Visit the **HRW** Web site for a variety of learning tools related to this chapter. Just type in the keyword:

KEYWORD: HSTCEL

GO TO: www.scilinks.org

Visit the **National Science Teachers Association** on-line Web site for Internet resources related to this chapter. Just type in the **sci**LINKS number for more information about the topic:

TOPIC: Organization of Life	**sci**LINKS NUMBER: HSTL055
TOPIC: Populations, Communities, and Ecosystems	**sci**LINKS NUMBER: HSTL060
TOPIC: Prokaryotic Cells	**sci**LINKS NUMBER: HSTL065
TOPIC: Eukaryotic Cells	**sci**LINKS NUMBER: HSTL070

Chapter Review

USING VOCABULARY

To complete the following sentences, choose the correct term from each pair of terms listed below:

1. The cell wall of plant cells is made of ___?___. (*lipids* or *cellulose*)

2. Having membrane-covered organelles is a characteristic of ___?___ cells. (*prokaryotic* or *eukaryotic*)

3. The information for how to make proteins is located in the ___?___. (*Golgi complex* or *nucleus*)

4. The two organelles that can generate ATP in a plant cell are ___?___ and ___?___. (*chloroplasts/ER* or *mitochondria/ chloroplasts*)

5. Vesicles that will transport materials out of the cell are formed at the ___?___. (*Golgi complex* or *cell membrane*)

UNDERSTANDING CONCEPTS

Multiple Choice

6. Which of the following is *not* found in animal cells?
   a. cell wall
   c. lysosomes
   b. cell membrane
   d. vesicle

7. Different ___?___ work together in an organ.
   a. organ systems
   b. tissues
   c. organisms
   d. prokaryotes

8. Which of the following refers to all of the organisms in a particular area?
   a. population
   b. ecosystem
   c. community
   d. organelles

9. The scientist who said that all cells come from cells was named
   a. Virchow.
   b. Schleiden.
   c. Hooke.
   d. Schwann.

10. Which of the following are *not* covered by a membrane?
    a. Golgi complex
    b. mitochondria
    c. ribosomes
    d. none of the above

11. Which of the following contain enzymes that can break down particles in vesicles?
    a. mitochondria
    b. endoplasmic reticulum
    c. lysosomes
    d. none of the above

Short Answer

12. Why are most cells so small?

13. What five characteristics of mitochondria suggest that they may have originated as bacteria?

14. In your own words, list the three parts of the cell theory.

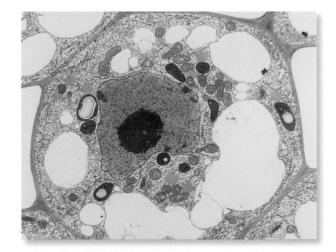

Concept Mapping

15. Use the following terms to create a concept map: ecosystem, cells, organisms, Golgi complex, organ systems, community, organs, endoplasmic reticulum, nucleus, population, tissues.

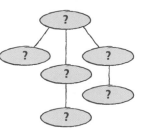

CRITICAL THINKING AND PROBLEM SOLVING

Write one or two sentences to answer the following questions:

16. Explain how the nucleus can control what happens in a lysosome.

17. Even though cellulose is not made at ribosomes, explain how ribosomes in a plant cell are important to the formation of a cell wall.

MATH IN SCIENCE

18. Assume that three food molecules per cubic unit of volume per minute is required for the cell below to survive. If one molecule can enter through each square unit of surface per minute, this cell is
    a. too big and would starve.
    b. too small and would starve.
    c. at a size that would allow it to survive.

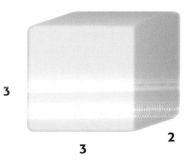

3
3
2

INTERPRETING GRAPHICS

Look at the cell diagrams below, and answer the questions that follow:

Cell A

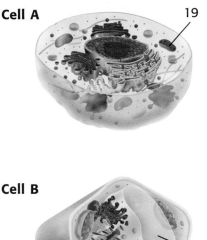

19

Cell B

21

19. Name the organelle labeled "19" in Cell A.

20. Is Cell A a bacterial cell, a plant cell, or an animal cell? Explain your answer.

21. What is the name and function of the organelle labeled "21" in Cell B?

22. Is Cell B a prokaryotic cell or a eukaryotic cell? Explain your answer.

Reading Check-up

Take a minute to review your answers to the Pre-Reading Questions found at the bottom of page 2. Have your answers changed? If necessary, revise your answers based on what you have learned since you began this chapter.

Battling Cancer with Pigs' Blood and Laser Light

What do you get when you cross pigs' blood and laser beams? Would you believe a treatment for cancer? Medical researchers have developed an effective new cancer treatment called *photodynamic therapy,* or PDT. It combines high-energy laser beams with a light-sensitive drug derived from pigs' blood to combat the deadly disease.

▲ Blood from pigs provides substances used to help treat cancer.

Pigs' Blood to the Rescue

The first step in PDT involves a light-sensitive substance called *porphyrin.* Porphyrins are natural chemicals found in red blood cells that bind to lipoproteins, which carry cholesterol in our blood. All cells use lipoproteins in their cell membranes. But cells that divide quickly, like cancer cells, make membranes faster than normal cells. Since they use more lipoproteins, they also accumulate more porphyrins.

Scientists have developed a synthetic porphyrin, called Photofrin®, made from natural porphyrins found in pigs' blood. Photofrin can absorb energy from light. When Photofrin is injected into a patient's bloodstream, it acts the same way natural porphyrins do—it becomes part of the cell membranes formed by cancer cells. A short time later, the patient visits a surgeon's office for step two of PDT, zapping the diseased tissue with a laser beam.

Hitting the Target

A surgeon threads a long, thin laser-tipped tube into the cancerous area where the Photofrin has accumulated. When the laser beam hits the cancerous tissue, Photofrin absorbs the light energy. Then, in a process similar to photosynthesis, Photofrin releases oxygen. The type of oxygen released damages the proteins, lipids, nucleic acids, and other components of cancer cells. This damage kills off cancer cells in the treated area but doesn't kill healthy cells. Photofrin is more sensitive to certain wavelengths of light than are natural porphyrins. And the intense beam of laser light can be precisely focused on the cancerous tissue without affecting nearby healthy tissue.

An Alternative?

PDT is an important medical development because it kills cancer cells without many of the harmful side effects caused by other cancer therapies, such as chemotherapy. However, PDT does have some side effects. Until the drug wears off, in about 30 days, the patient is susceptible to severe sunburn. Researchers are working to develop a second-generation drug, called BPD (benzoporphyrin derivative), that will have fewer side effects and respond to different wavelengths of lasers. BPD is also being tested for use in certain eye diseases and as a treatment for psoriasis.

Find Out for Yourself

▶ Do some research to find out why scientists used pigs' blood to create Photofrin.

Health

The Scrape of the Future

What did you do the last time you scraped your knee? You probably put a bandage on it, and before you realized it your knee was as good as new. Bandages serve as barriers that help prevent infection and further injury. But what if there were such a thing as a living bandage that actually helped your body heal? It sounds like science fiction, but it's not!

▲ Dr. Daniel Smith holds the GEBB that he designed.

The Main Factor

An injury to the skin, such as a scraped knee, triggers skin cells to produce and release a steady stream of proteins that heal the injury. These naturally occurring proteins are called *human growth factors,* or just *growth factors.* Growth factors specialize in rebuilding the body. Some reconstruct connective tissue that provides structure for new skin, some help rebuild blood vessels in a wounded area, and still others stimulate the body's immune system. Thanks to growth factors, scraped skin usually heals in just a few days.

Help from a Living Bandage

Unfortunately, healing isn't always an easy, natural process. Someone with a weakened immune system may be unable to produce enough growth factors to heal a wound properly. For example, someone with severe burns may have lost the ability in the burned area to produce the proteins necessary to rebuild healthy tissues. In these cases, using manufactured human growth factors can greatly assist the healing process.

Recent advances in bio-engineering can help people whose immune system prevents them from healing naturally. The Genetically Engineered Biological Bandage (GEBB) is a special bandage that is actually a bag of living skin cells taken from donors. The cells' DNA is manipulated to produce human growth factors. The GEBB is about 1 cm thick and consists of three layers: a thin gauze layer; a thin, permeable membrane; and a dome-shaped silicone bag containing the growth factors. The bandage is applied to the wound just as a normal bandage is, with the gauze layer closest to the injury. The growth factors leave the silicone bag through the membrane and pass through the gauze into the wound. There they act on the wound just as the body's own growth factors would.

Time-Release Formula

The GEBB also helps heal wounds more quickly. It maximizes the effectiveness of growth hormones by releasing them at a constant rate over 3 to 5 days.

Because the GEBB imitates the body's own healing processes, other versions of the living bandage will likely be used in the future to treat a variety of wounds and skin conditions, such as severe acne.

Think About It

▶ Can you think of other advances in medical technology, such as eyeglasses or a hearing aid, that mimic or enhance what the human body does naturally?

The Cell in Action

Pre-Reading
Questions

1. How do water, food, and wastes get into and out of a cell?

2. How do cells use food molecules?

3. How does one cell produce many cells?

A COPIER MACHINE

These cells are from the growing tip of a plant root. In order to grow, the plant is producing many new cells. When plant cells divide, the cell copies its genetic material. The cell then undergoes mitosis. Mitosis is the process that ensures that each new cell ends up with the correct complement of chromosomes. All the different stages of mitosis can be seen in this tissue.

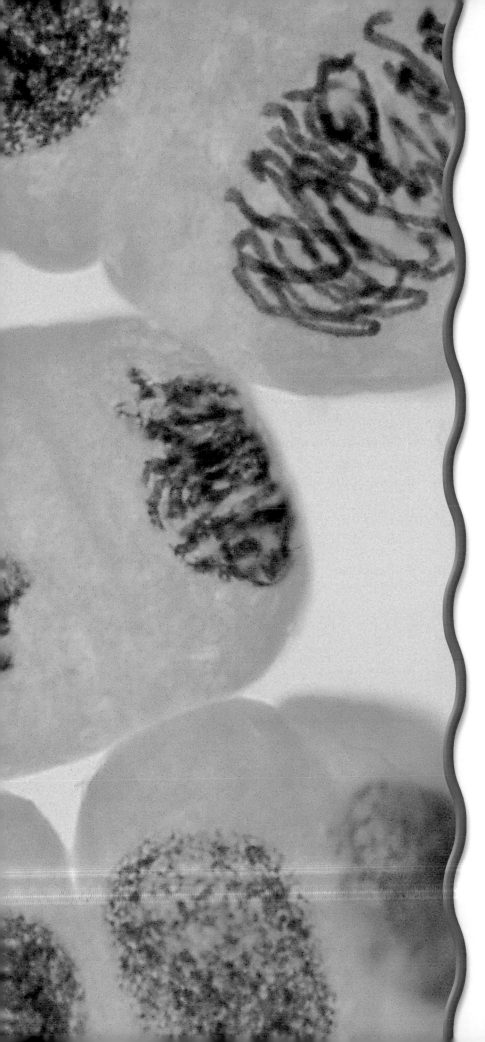

START-UP
Activity

CELLS IN ACTION

Yeasts are fungi that are used in baking. Yeast cells break down sugar molecules to release energy. In the process, a gas called carbon dioxide (CO_2) is produced. Bubbles of CO_2 cause the bread dough to rise. The amount of CO_2 produced depends on how much sugar is broken down.

Procedure

1. Pour **4 mL of a sugar solution** into **a cup** that contains **10 mL of** a **yeast-and-water mixture.** Mix the two liquids with a **stirring rod.**

2. Pour the contents into a **small test tube.**

3. Place a slightly **larger test tube** over the small test tube. The top of the small test tube should touch the bottom of the larger test tube. Quickly turn both test tubes over. Use a **ruler** to measure the height of the fluid in the large test tube.

4. Place the test tubes in a **test-tube rack** and do not disturb them. After 20 minutes, measure the height of the liquid in the larger test tube again.

Analysis

5. What is the difference between the first height measurement and the second?

6. What do you think caused the change in the height of the fluid?

Terms to Learn

diffusion   active transport

osmosis   endocytosis

passive transport   exocytosis

What You'll Do

◆ Explain the process of diffusion.

◆ Describe how osmosis occurs.

◆ Compare passive transport with active transport.

◆ Explain how large particles get into and out of cells.

Exchange with the Environment

What would happen to a factory if its power were shut off or its supply of raw materials never arrived? What if it couldn't get rid of its garbage? The factory would stop functioning. Like a factory, a cell must be able to obtain energy and raw materials and get rid of wastes.

The exchange of materials between a cell and its environment takes place at the cell's membrane. To understand how materials move into and out of the cell, you need to know about diffusion, a process that affects the movement of particles.

What Is Diffusion?

What happens if you pour dye into a container of solid gelatin? At first, it is easy to see where the gelatin ends and the dye begins. But over time the line between the two layers will become blurry, as shown in **Figure 1.** Why? Dye and gelatin, like all matter, are made up of tiny particles. The particles are always moving and colliding with each other. The mixing of the different particles causes the layers to blur. This occurs whether matter is in the form of a gas, liquid, or solid.

Bead Diffusion

Arrange three groups of **colored beads** on the bottom of a **plastic bowl.** Each group should have five beads of the same color. Stretch some **clear plastic wrap** tightly over the top of the bowl. Gently shake the bowl for 10 seconds while watching the beads. How is the scattering of the beads like the diffusion of particles? How is it different from the diffusion of particles?

Figure 1 *The particles of the dye and the gelatin slowly begin to mix because of diffusion.*

Particles naturally travel from areas where they are crowded to areas where they are less crowded. **Diffusion** is the movement of particles from an area where their concentration is high to an area where their concentration is low. This movement can occur across cell membranes or outside of cells. Cells do not need to use any energy for diffusion of particles to occur.

Diffusion of Water All organisms need water to live. The cells of living organisms are surrounded by and filled with fluids that are made mostly of water. The diffusion of water through the cell membrane is so important to life processes that it has been given a special name—**osmosis.**

Water, like all matter, is made up of small particles. Pure water has the highest possible concentration of water particles. To lower this concentration, you simply mix water with something else, such as food coloring, sugar, or salt. **Figure 2** shows what happens when osmosis occurs between two different concentrations of water.

Figure 2 *This container is divided by a barrier. Particles of water are small enough to pass through the barrier, but the particles of food coloring are not.*

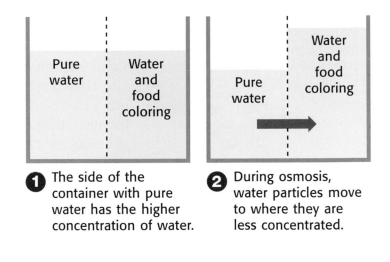

1 The side of the container with pure water has the higher concentration of water.

2 During osmosis, water particles move to where they are less concentrated.

The Cell and Osmosis As you have learned, water particles will move from areas of high concentration to areas of lower concentration. This concept is especially important when you look at it in relation to your cells.

For example, **Figure 3** shows the effects of different concentrations of water on a red blood cell. As you can see, osmosis takes place in different directions depending on the concentration of water surrounding the cell. Fortunately for you, your red blood cells are normally surrounded by blood plasma, which is made up of water, salts, sugars, and other particles in the same concentration as they exist inside the red blood cells.

The cells of plants also take in and release water by osmosis. This is why a wilted plant or even a wilted stalk of celery will become firm again if given water.

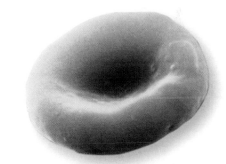

This cell has a normal shape because the concentration of water in the cell is the same as the concentration outside the cell.

This cell is in pure water. It is gaining water because the concentration of water particles is lower inside the cell than outside.

✓ Self-Check

What would happen to a grape if you placed it in a dish of pure water? in water mixed with a large amount of sugar? (See page 216) to check your answer.)

Figure 3 *The shape of these red blood cells is affected by the concentration of water outside the cell.*

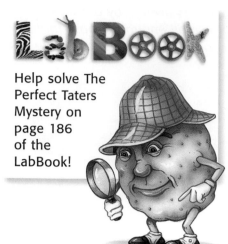

Help solve The Perfect Taters Mystery on page 186 of the LabBook!

Moving Small Particles

Many particles, such as water and oxygen, can diffuse directly through the cell membrane, which is made of phospholipid molecules. These particles can slip through the molecules of the membrane in part because of their small size. However, not all of the particles a cell needs can pass through the membrane in this way. For example, sugar and amino acids aren't small enough to squeeze between the phospholipid molecules, and they are also repelled by the phospholipids in the membrane. They must travel through protein "doorways" located in the cell membrane in order to enter or leave the cell.

Particles can travel through these proteins either by passive transport or by active transport. **Passive transport,** shown in **Figure 4,** is the diffusion of particles through the proteins. The particles move from an area of high concentration to an area of low concentration. The cell does not need to use any energy to make this happen.

Active transport, shown in **Figure 5,** is the movement of particles through proteins against the normal direction of diffusion. In other words, particles are moved from an area of low concentration to an area of high concentration. The cell must use energy to make this happen. This energy comes from the molecule ATP, which stores energy in a form that cells can use.

Passive Transport

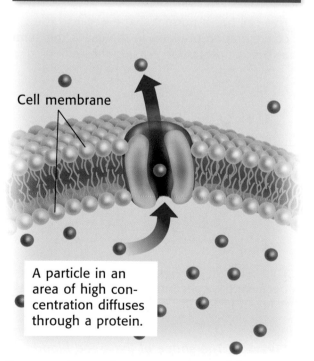

Cell membrane

A particle in an area of high concentration diffuses through a protein.

Figure 4 *In passive transport, particles travel through proteins from areas of high concentration to areas of low concentration.*

Active Transport

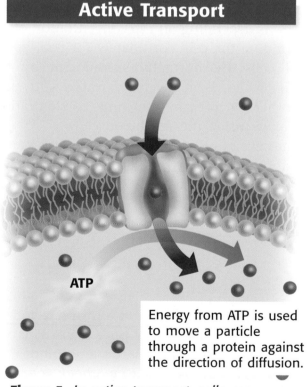

ATP

Energy from ATP is used to move a particle through a protein against the direction of diffusion.

Figure 5 *In active transport, cells use energy to move particles from areas of low concentration to areas of high concentration.*

Moving Large Particles

Diffusion, passive transport, and active transport are good methods of moving small particles into and out of cells, but what about moving large particles? The cell membrane has two ways of accomplishing this task: *endocytosis* and *exocytosis*.

Endocytosis In **endocytosis,** the cell membrane surrounds a particle and encloses it in a vesicle. This is how large particles, such as other cells, can be brought into a cell, as shown in **Figure 6.**

① The cell comes into contact with a particle.

② The cell membrane begins to wrap around the particle.

③ Once the particle is completely surrounded, a vesicle pinches off.

Figure 6 Endocytosis *means "within the cell."*

Exocytosis When a large particle must be removed from the cell, the cell uses a different process. In **exocytosis,** vesicles are formed at the endoplasmic reticulum or Golgi complex and carry the particles to the cell membrane, as shown in **Figure 7.**

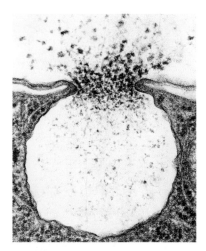

① Large particles that must leave the cell are packaged in vesicles.

② The vesicle travels to the cell membrane and fuses with it.

③ The cell releases the particles into its environment.

Figure 7 Exocytosis *means "outside the cell."*

SECTION REVIEW

1. During diffusion, how do particles move?

2. How does a cell take in large particles? How does a cell expel large particles?

3. **Making Inferences** The transfer of glucose into a cell does not require ATP. What type of transport supplies a cell with glucose? Explain your answer.

Terms to Learn

photosynthesis
cellular respiration
fermentation

What You'll Do

◆ Describe photosynthesis and cellular respiration.
◆ Compare cellular respiration with fermentation.

Cell Energy

Why do you get hungry? Feeling hungry is your body's way of telling you that your cells need energy. Your cells and the cells of all organisms use energy to carry out the chemical activities that allow them to live, grow, and reproduce.

From Sun to Cell

Nearly all of the energy that fuels life comes from the sun. Plants are able to capture light energy from the sun and change it into food through a process called **photosynthesis.** The food that plants make supplies them with energy and also becomes a source of energy for the organisms that eat the plants. Without plants and other producers, consumers would not be able to live.

Photosynthesis Plants have molecules in their cells that absorb the energy of light. These molecules are called *pigments.* Chlorophyll, the main pigment used in photosynthesis, gives plants their green color. In the cells of plants, chlorophyll is found in chloroplasts, which are shown in **Figure 8.**

Plants use the energy captured by chlorophyll to change carbon dioxide (CO_2) and water (H_2O) into food, the simple sugar glucose ($C_6H_{12}O_6$). Glucose is a carbohydrate. When plants make glucose, they are converting the sun's energy into a form of energy that can be stored. The energy in glucose is used by the plant's cells, and some of it may be stored in the form of other carbohydrates or lipids. Photosynthesis also produces oxygen (O_2). Photosynthesis can be summarized by the following equation:

Plant Cell

Chloroplast

$$6CO_2 + 6H_2O + \text{light energy} \longrightarrow C_6H_{12}O_6 + 6O_2$$

Carbon dioxide   Water   Glucose   Oxygen

Figure 8 *During photosynthesis, plant cells use the energy in sunlight to make food (glucose) from carbon dioxide and water. Photosynthesis takes place in chloroplasts.*

Getting Energy from Food

The food you eat has to be broken down so that the energy it contains can be converted into a form your cells can use. In fact, all organisms must break down food molecules in order to release the stored energy. There are two ways to do this. One way uses oxygen and is called **cellular respiration.** The other way does not use oxygen and is called **fermentation.**

Cellular Respiration The word *respiration* means "breathing," but cellular respiration is not the same thing as breathing. Breathing supplies your cells with the oxygen they need to perform cellular respiration. Breathing also rids your body of carbon dioxide, which is a waste product of cellular respiration.

Most organisms, such as the cow in **Figure 9,** use cellular respiration to obtain energy from food. During cellular respiration, food (glucose) is broken down into CO_2 and H_2O, and energy is released. A lot of the energy is stored in the form of ATP. ATP is the molecule that supplies energy to fuel the activities of cells. Most of the energy released, however, is in the form of heat. In some organisms, including yourself, this heat helps to maintain the body's temperature.

In the cells of eukaryotes, cellular respiration takes place in mitochondria. The process of cellular respiration is summarized in the equation below. Does this equation remind you of the equation for photosynthesis? The diagram on the next page shows how photosynthesis and respiration are related.

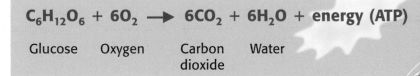

$$C_6H_{12}O_6 + 6O_2 \longrightarrow 6CO_2 + 6H_2O + energy\ (ATP)$$

| Glucose | Oxygen | Carbon dioxide | Water |

Mitochondria

Animal Cell

Figure 9 *The mitochondria in the cells of this cow will use cellular respiration to release the energy stored in the grass.*

The Cell in Action   **39**

Photosynthesis and Respiration: What's the Connection?

ATP

Photosynthesis
Light energy, carbon dioxide, and water are used to make glucose in chloroplasts. Oxygen is released.

Light Energy

$CO_2 + H_2O$

Chloroplast

Mitochondrion

$C_6H_{12}O_6 + O_2$

Cellular Respiration
Oxygen and the energy in glucose are used to make ATP. ATP is a molecule that stores energy in a form that cells can use. ATP is produced by mitochondria. Carbon dioxide and water are also released. Cellular respiration occurs in both plant and animal cells.

Fermentation Have you ever run so far that you started to feel a burning sensation in your muscles? Well, sometimes your muscle cells can't get the oxygen they need to produce ATP by cellular respiration. When this happens, they use the process of fermentation. Fermentation leads to the production of a small amount of ATP and products from the partial breakdown of glucose.

There are two major types of fermentation. The first type occurs in your muscles. It produces lactic acid, which contributes to muscle fatigue after strenuous activity. This type of fermentation also occurs in the muscle cells of other animals and in some types of fungi and bacteria. The second type of fermentation occurs in certain types of bacteria and in yeast. This type of fermentation is described in **Figure 10.**

Figure 10 *Yeast cells make carbon dioxide and alcohol during the fermentation of sugar. The carbon dioxide causes bubbles to form in bread.*

Fantasy Island

You have been given the assignment of restoring life to a barren island. What types of organisms would you put on the island? If you want to have animals on the island, what other organisms must be on the island as well? Explain your answer.

SECTION REVIEW

1. Why are producers important to the survival of all other organisms?

2. How do the processes of photosynthesis and cellular respiration relate to each other?

3. What does breathing have to do with cellular respiration?

4. How are respiration and fermentation similar? How are they different?

5. **Identifying Relationships** In which cells would you expect to find the greater number of mitochondria: cells that are very active or cells that are not very active? Why?

internet**connect**

*SCi*LINKS.

NSTA

TOPIC: Cell Energy, Photosynthesis
GO TO: www.scilinks.org
*sci*LINKS NUMBER: HSTL080, HSTL085

The Cell Cycle

Terms to Learn

cell cycle
chromosome
binary fission
homologous
  chromosomes

chromatids
centromere
mitosis
cytokinesis

What You'll Do

- Explain how cells produce more cells.
- Discuss the importance of mitosis.
- Explain how cell division differs in animals and plants.

MATH BREAK

Cell Multiplication

It takes Cell *A* 6 hours to complete its cell cycle and produce two cells. The cell cycle of Cell *B* takes 8 hours. How many more cells would be formed from Cell *A* than from Cell *B* in 24 hours?

In the time that it takes you to read this sentence, your body will have produced millions of new cells! Producing new cells allows you to grow and replace cells that have died. For example, the environment in your stomach is so acidic that the cells lining it must be replaced every few days!

The Life of a Cell

As you grow, you pass through different stages in life. Similarly, your cells pass through different stages in their life cycle. The life cycle of a cell is known as the **cell cycle.**

The cell cycle begins when the cell is formed and ends when the cell divides and forms new cells. Before a cell divides, it must make a copy of its DNA. DNA contains the information that tells a cell how to make proteins. The DNA of a cell is organized into structures called **chromosomes.** In some organisms, chromosomes also contain protein. Copying chromosomes ensures that each new cell will be able to survive.

How does a cell make more cells? Well, that depends on whether the cell is prokaryotic or eukaryotic.

Making More Prokaryotic Cells Prokaryotic cells (bacteria) and their DNA are not very complex. Bacteria have ribosomes and a single, circular molecule of DNA, but they don't have any membrane-covered organelles. Because of this, cell division in bacteria is fairly simple. It is called **binary fission,** which means "splitting into two parts." Each of the resulting cells contains one copy of the DNA. Some of the bacteria in **Figure 11** are undergoing binary fission.

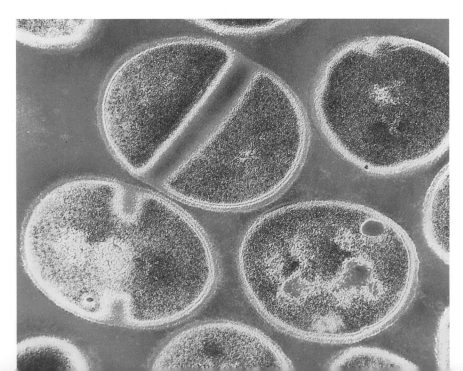

Figure 11 *Bacteria reproduce by pinching in two.*

Eukaryotic Cells and Their DNA Eukaryotic cells are usually much larger and more complex than prokaryotic cells. Because of this, eukaryotic cells have a lot more DNA. The chromosomes of eukaryotes contain DNA and proteins.

The number of chromosomes in the cells of eukaryotes differs from one kind of organism to the next and has nothing to do with the complexity of an organism. For example, fruit flies have 8 chromosomes, potatoes have 48, and humans have 46. **Figure 12** shows the 46 chromosomes of a human body cell lined up in pairs. These pairs are made up of similar chromosomes known as **homologous** (hoh MAHL uh guhs) **chromosomes.**

Making More Eukaryotic Cells The eukaryotic cell cycle includes three main stages. In the first stage, the cell grows and copies its organelles and chromosomes. During this time, the strands of DNA and proteins are like loosely coiled pieces of thread. After each chromosome is duplicated, the two copies are called **chromatids.** Chromatids are held together at a region called the **centromere.** The chromatids each twist and coil and condense into an X shape, as shown in **Figure 13.** After this happens, the cell enters the second stage of the cell cycle.

In the second stage, the chromatids separate. The complicated process of chromosome separation is **mitosis.** Mitosis ensures that each new cell receives a copy of each chromosome. Mitosis can be divided into four phases, as shown on the following pages.

In the third stage of the cell cycle, the cell divides and produces two cells that are identical to the original cell. Cell division will be discussed after mitosis has been described.

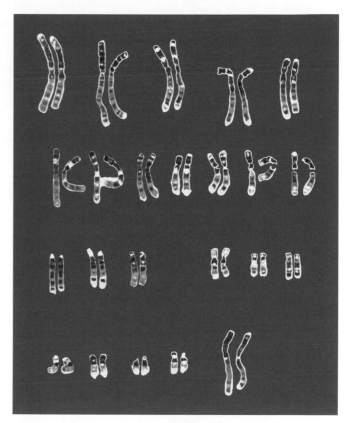

Figure 12 *Human body cells have 46 chromosomes, or 23 pairs of homologous chromosomes.*

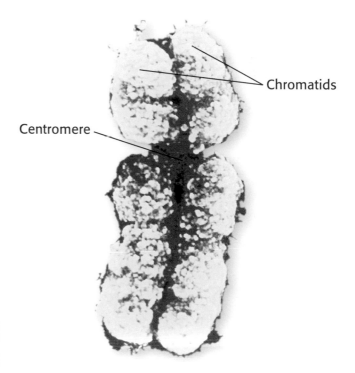

Figure 13 *Two strands of DNA and protein coiled together to form this duplicated chromosome, which consists of two chromatids.*

> ## ✔Self-Check
>
> After duplication, how many chromatids are there in a pair of homologous chromosomes? *(See page 216 to check your answer.)*

Mitosis and the Cell Cycle

The diagram below shows the cell cycle and the phases of mitosis in an animal cell. Although mitosis is a continuous process, it can be divided into the four phases that are shown and described. As you know, different types of living things have different numbers of chromosomes. In this diagram, only four chromosomes are shown to make it easier to see what's happening.

Before mitosis begins, the chromosomes and other cell materials are copied. The pair of *centrioles*, which are two cylindrical structures, are also copied. Each chromosome now consists of two chromatids.

Mitosis Phase 1

Mitosis begins. The nuclear membrane breaks apart. Chromosomes condense into rodlike structures. The two pairs of centrioles move to opposite sides of the cell. Fibers form between the two pairs of centrioles and attach to the centromeres.

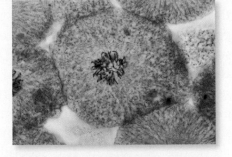

Mitosis Phase 2

The chromosomes line up along the equator of the cell.

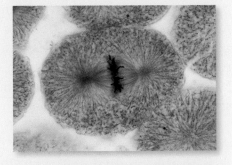

Mitosis Phase 3

The chromatids separate and are pulled to opposite sides of the cell by the fibers attached to the centrioles.

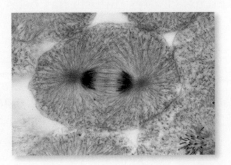

Mitosis Phase 4

The nuclear membrane forms around the two sets of chromosomes, and they unwind. The fibers disappear. Mitosis is completed.

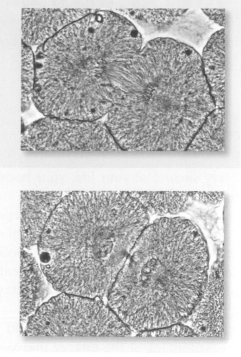

Once mitosis is completed, the cytoplasm splits in two. This process is called **cytokinesis.** The result is two identical cells that are also identical to the original cell from which they were formed. After cytokinesis, the cell cycle is complete, and the new cells are at the beginning of their next cell cycle.

More About Cytokinesis In animal cells and other eukaryotes that do not have cell walls, division of the cytoplasm begins at the cell membrane. The cell membrane begins to pinch inward to form a groove, which eventually pinches all the way through the cell, and two daughter cells are formed. Cytokinesis in an animal cell is shown above.

Eukaryotic cells that have a cell wall, such as the cells of plants, algae, and fungi, do things a little differently. In these organisms, a *cell plate* forms in the middle of the cell and becomes the new cell membranes that will separate the two new cells. After the cell is split in two, a new cell wall forms between the two membranes. Cytokinesis in a plant cell is shown in **Figure 14.**

Cell plate

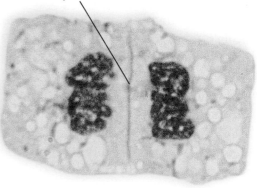

Figure 14 *When plant cells divide, a cell plate forms and the cell is split in two.*

SECTION REVIEW

1. How are binary fission and mitosis similar? How are they different?

2. Why is it important for chromosomes to be copied before cell division?

3. How does cytokinesis differ in animals and plants?

4. **Applying Concepts** What would happen if cytokinesis occurred without mitosis?

internet**connect**

SC*L*INKS
NSTA

TOPIC: The Cell Cycle
GO TO: www.scilinks.org
SciLINKS NUMBER: HOTL090

Staying Alive!

Every second of your life, your body's trillions of cells take in, use, and store energy. They repair themselves, reproduce, and get rid of waste. Together, these processes are called metabolism. Your cells use the food that you eat to provide the energy you need to stay alive.

Your basal metabolic rate (BMR) is a measurement of the energy that your body needs to carry out all the basic life processes while you are at rest. These processes include breathing, keeping your heart beating, and keeping your body's temperature stable. Your BMR is influenced by your gender, your age, and many other things. Your BMR may be different from everyone else's, but it is normal for you. In this activity, you will find the amount of energy, measured in Calories, you need every day in order to stay alive.

MATERIALS

- bathroom scale
- tape measure

Procedure

1 Find your weight on a bathroom scale. If the scale measures in pounds, convert your weight in pounds to your mass in kilograms. To convert your weight in pounds (lb) to mass in kilograms (kg), multiply the number of pounds by 0.454 kg/lb.

Example: If Carlos weighs 125 lb, his mass in kilograms is:

$$125 \text{ lb} \times \frac{0.454 \text{ kg}}{\text{lb}} = 56.75 \text{ kg}$$

2 Use a tape measure to find your height. If the tape measures in inches, convert your height in inches to height in centimeters. To convert your height in inches (in.) to your height in centimeters (cm), multiply the number of inches by 2.54 cm/in.

Example: If Carlos is 62 in. tall, his height in centimeters is:

$$62 \text{ in.} \times \frac{2.54 \text{ cm}}{\text{in.}} = 157.48 \text{ cm}$$

3 Now that you know your height and mass, use the appropriate formula on the next page to get a close estimate of your BMR. Your answer will give you an estimate of the number of Calories your body needs each day just to stay alive.

Calculating Your BMR	
Females	**Males**
65 + (10 × your mass in kilograms) + (1.8 × your height in centimeters) − (4.7 × your age in years)	66 + (13.5 × your mass in kilograms) + (5 × your height in centimeters) − (6.8 × your age in years)

4 Your metabolism is also influenced by how active you are. Talking, walking, and playing games all take more energy than being at rest. To get an idea of how many Calories your body needs each day to stay healthy, select the lifestyle that best describes yours from the table below. Then multiply your BMR by the activity factor.

Activity Factors		
Activity	**Activity lifestyle**	**Factor**
Moderately inactive	normal, everyday activities	1.3
Moderately active	exercise 3 to 4 times a week	1.4
Very active	exercise 4 to 6 times a week	1.6
Extremely active	exercise 6 to 7 times a week	1.8

Analysis

5 In what way could you compare your whole body to a single cell? Explain your answer.

6 Does an increase in activity increase your BMR? Does an increase in activity increase your need for Calories? Explain your answers.

7 If you are moderately inactive, how many more Calories would you need if you began to exercise every day?

Going Further

The best energy sources are those that supply the correct amount of Calories for your lifestyle and also provide the nutrients you need. Research in the library or on the Internet to find out which kinds of foods are the best energy sources for you. How does your list of best energy sources compare with your diet?

List everything you eat and drink in one day. Find out how many Calories are in each item, and find the total number of Calories you have consumed. How does this number of Calories compare with the number of Calories you need each day for all your activities?

Chapter Highlights

SECTION 1

Vocabulary

diffusion *(p. 34)*

osmosis *(p. 35)*

passive transport *(p. 36)*

active transport *(p. 36)*

endocytosis *(p. 37)*

exocytosis *(p. 37)*

Section Notes

- A cell can survive only if food molecules are taken into the cell and waste materials are removed. Materials enter and leave the cell by passing through the cell membrane. The cell membrane allows some materials to pass through but prevents others.

- A cell does not need to use energy to move particles from regions of high concentration to regions of low concentration. This type of movement is called diffusion.

- Osmosis is the diffusion of water through a membrane.

- Some substances enter and leave a cell by passing through proteins. During passive transport, substances diffuse through proteins. During active transport, substances are moved from areas of low concentration to areas of high concentration. The cell must supply energy for active transport to occur.

- Particles that are too large to pass easily through the membrane can enter a cell by a process called endocytosis. Large particles can leave a cell by exocytosis.

Labs

The Perfect Taters Mystery *(p. 186)*

☑ Skills Check

Math Concepts

CELL CYCLE It takes 4 hours for a cell to complete its cell cycle and produce 2 cells. How many cells can be produced from this cell in 12 hours? First you must determine how many cell cycles will occur in 12 hours:

12 hours/4 hours = 3

The number of cells doubles after each cycle:

Cycle 1	1 cell × 2 = 2 cells
Cycle 2	2 cells × 2 = 4 cells
Cycle 3	4 cells × 2 = 8 cells

Therefore, after 3 cell cycles (12 hours), 8 cells will have been produced from the original cell.

Visual Understanding

MITOSIS The process of mitosis can be confusing, but looking at illustrations can help. Look at the illustrations of the cell cycle on pp. 44 and 45. Read the label for each phase, and look at the illustrations and photographs for each. Look for the cell structures that are described in the label. Trace the movement of chromosomes through each step. By carefully studying the labels and pictures, you can better understand mitosis.

SECTION 2

Vocabulary

photosynthesis *(p. 38)*

cellular respiration *(p. 39)*

fermentation *(p. 39)*

Section Notes

- The sun is the ultimate source of almost all energy needed to fuel the chemical activities of organisms. Most producers use energy from sunlight to make food during the process known as photosynthesis. This food then becomes a source of energy for the producers and for the consumers that eat the producers.

- Cells use cellular respiration or fermentation to release the energy from food to make ATP. Cellular respiration requires oxygen, but fermentation does not.

SECTION 3

Vocabulary

cell cycle *(p. 42)*

chromosome *(p. 42)*

binary fission *(p. 42)*

homologous chromosomes *(p. 43)*

chromatids *(p. 43)*

centromere *(p. 43)*

mitosis *(p. 43)*

cytokinesis *(p. 45)*

Section Notes

- The life cycle of a cell is called the cell cycle. The cell cycle begins when the cell is formed and ends when the cell divides to produce two new cells. Prokaryotic cells produce new cells by binary fission. Eukaryotic cells produce new cells by mitosis and cytokinesis.

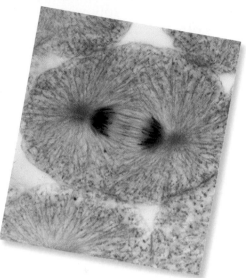

- Before mitosis, the chromosomes are copied. During mitosis, chromatids separate, and two new nuclei are formed. During cytokinesis, the cell divides.

Chapter Review

To complete the following sentences, choose the correct term from each pair of terms listed below:

1. The diffusion of water through the cell membrane is called __?__. *(osmosis or active transport)*

2. A cell can remove large particles during __?__. *(exocytosis or endocytosis)*

3. Plants use __?__ to make glucose. *(cellular respiration or photosynthesis)*

4. During __?__, food molecules are broken down to form CO_2 and H_2O and release large amounts of energy. *(cellular respiration or fermentation)*

5. In eukaryotes, __?__ creates two nuclei, and __?__ creates two cells. *(cytokinesis or mitosis)*

UNDERSTANDING CONCEPTS

Multiple Choice

6. When particles are moved through a membrane from a region of low concentration to a region of high concentration, the process is called
   a. diffusion.
   b. passive transport.
   c. active transport.
   d. fermentation.

7. An organism with chloroplasts is a
   a. consumer.   c. producer.
   b. prokaryote.   d. centromere.

8. What is produced by mitosis?
   a. two identical cells
   b. two nuclei
   c. chloroplasts
   d. two different cells

9. Before the energy in food can be used by a cell, it must first be transferred to molecules of
   a. proteins.
   b. carbohydrates.
   c. DNA.
   d. ATP.

10. Which one of the following does not perform mitosis?
   a. prokaryotic cell
   b. human body cell
   c. eukaryotic cell
   d. plant cell

11. Which of the following would form a cell plate during the cell cycle?
   a. human cell
   b. prokaryotic cell
   c. plant cell
   d. all of the above

Short Answer

12. What cell structures are needed for photosynthesis? for respiration?

13. How many chromatids are present in a chromosome at the beginning of mitosis?

14. What are the three stages of the cell cycle in a eukaryotic cell?

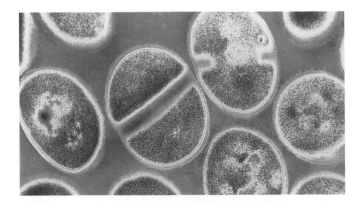

Concept Mapping

15. Use the following terms to create a concept map: chromosome duplication, cytokinesis, prokaryote, mitosis, cell cycle, binary fission, eukaryote.

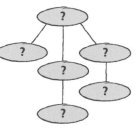

Write one or two sentences to answer the following questions:

16. Which one of the plants below was given water mixed with salt, and which one was given pure water? Explain how you know, and be sure to use the word *osmosis* in your answer.

17. Why would your muscle cells need to be supplied with more food when there is a lack of oxygen than when there is plenty of oxygen present?

18. A parent cell has 10 chromosomes before dividing.
 a. Will the cell go through binary fission or mitosis and cytokinesis to produce new cells?
 b. How many chromosomes will each new cell have after the parent cell divides?

19. A cell has six chromosomes at the beginning of its cell cycle. How many chromatids will line up at the equator of the cell during mitosis?

Look at the cell below to answer the following questions:

20. Is the cell prokaryotic or eukaryotic?

21. In what stage of the cell cycle is this cell?

22. How many chromatids are present? How many pairs of homologous chromosomes are present?

23. How many chromosomes will be present in each of the new cells after the cell divides?

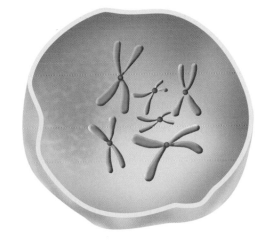

Reading Check-up

Take a minute to review your answers to the Pre-Reading Questions found at the bottom of page 32. Have your answers changed? If necessary, revise your answers based on what you have learned since you began this chapter.

Electrifying News About Microbes

Your car is out of fuel, and there isn't a service station in sight. No problem! Your car's motor runs on electricity supplied by trillions of microorganisms—and they're hungry. You pop a handful of sugar cubes into the tank along with some fresh water, and you're on your way. The microbes devour the food and produce enough electricity to get you home safely.

A "Living" Battery

Sound far-fetched? Peter Bennetto and his team of scientists at King's College, in London, don't think so. Chemists there envision "living" batteries that will someday operate everything from wristwatches to entire towns. Although cars won't be using batteries powered by bacteria anytime soon, the London scientists have demonstrated that microorganisms can convert food into usable electrical energy. One test battery that is smaller than 0.5 cm^2 kept a digital clock operating for a day.

Freeing Electrons

For nearly a century, scientists have known that living things produce and use electric charges. But only in the last few decades have they figured out the chemical processes that produce these tiny electric charges. As part of their normal activities, living cells break down starches and sugars, and these chemical reactions release electrons. Scientists produce electricity by harvesting these free electrons from single-celled organisms, such as bacteria.

Bennetto and his colleagues have developed a list of foods that matches the carbohydrates, such as table sugar and molasses, with the microorganisms that digest them the most efficiently. Bennetto explains that there are lazy bacteria and efficient bacteria. An efficient microbe can convert more than 90 percent of its food into compounds that will fuel an

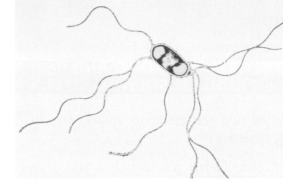

▲ *Bacteria like this can convert carbohydrates to electrical energy.*

electric reaction. A less efficient microbe converts 50 percent or less of its food into electron-yielding compounds.

Feed Them Leftovers

One advantage that batteries powered by microbes have over generators is that microbes do not require nonrenewable resources, such as coal or oil. Microbes can produce electricity by consuming pollutants, such as certain byproducts from the milk and sugar industries. And since the microorganisms reproduce constantly, no battery charging is necessary; just give the battery a bacteria change from time to time. For now, the London scientists are content to speculate on the battery's potential. Other specialists, such as electrical engineers, are needed to make this technology practical.

Project Idea

▶ Imagine that you manage a government agency and you are asked to provide funds for research on batteries powered by microbes. Think of some of the benefits of developing "living batteries." Are there any problems you can think of? As a class, decide whether you would fund the research.

Science Fiction

"Contagion"

by Katherine MacLean

A quarter mile from their spaceship, the *Explorer,* a team of doctors walk carefully along a narrow forest trail. Around them, the forest looks like an Earth forest in the fall—the leaves are green, copper, purple, and fiery red. But it isn't fall. And the team is not on Earth.

Minos is enough like Earth to be the home of another colony of humans. But Minos might also be home to unknown organisms that could cause severe illness or death among the *Explorer*'s crew. These diseases might be enough like Earth diseases to be contagious, yet just different enough to be extremely difficult to treat.

Something large moves among the shadows —it looks like a man. When he suddenly steps out onto the trail, he is taller than any of them, lean and muscled, and darkly tanned with bright red hair. Even more amazing, he speaks.

"Welcome to Minos. The mayor sends greetings from Alexandria."

And so we, and the crew of the *Explorer,* meet red-haired Patrick Mead. According to Patrick, there was once a colony of humans on Minos. About two years after the colony arrived, a terrible plague swept through the colony and killed everyone except the Mead family. But, Patrick tells them, the plague has never come back and there are no other contagions on Minos.

Or are there? What has Patrick hidden from the crew of the *Explorer*? Read Katherine MacLean's "Contagion" in the *Holt Anthology of Science Fiction* to find out.

Heredity

Pre-Reading
Questions

1. Why don't all humans
   look exactly alike?
2. What determines whether
   a human baby will be a
   boy or a girl?

INDIAN PAINTBRUSHES

What do you notice about the red and yellow flowers in this photo? Besides their color, these flowers look very much alike. This similarity is because the flowers are of the same kind of plant, called Indian Paintbrush. Many things about the way a plant looks, including flower color, is determined by the plant's genes. These plants have different genes for flower color. In this chapter, you will learn about genes and about how differences in genes are important to evolution.

CLOTHING COMBOS

In this activity, your class will investigate how traits from parents can be joined to make so many different combinations in children.

Procedure

1. The entire class should use **three boxes.** One box contains **five hats.** One box contains **five gloves,** and one box contains **five scarves.**

2. Without looking in the boxes, five of your classmates will select one item from each box. Lay the items on the table. Repeat this process, five students at a time, until the entire class has picked "an outfit." Record what hat, scarf, and glove each student chose.

Analysis

3. Were any two outfits exactly alike? Do you think you saw all of the possible combinations? Explain your answer.

4. Choose a partner. Using the pieces of clothing you and your partner selected from the box, how many different combinations could you make by giving a third person one hat, one glove, and one scarf?

5. How is step 4 like parents passing traits to their children?

6. Based on this activity, why do you think parents often have children who look very different from each other?

Mendel and His Peas

Terms to Learn

heredity   alleles
dominant trait   genotype
recessive trait   phenotype
genes   probability

What You'll Do

◆ Explain the experiments of Gregor Mendel.
◆ Explain how genes and alleles are related to genotypes and phenotypes.
◆ Use the information in a Punnett square.

There is no one else in the world exactly like you. You are unique. But what sets you apart? If you look around your classroom, you'll see that you share many physical characteristics with your classmates. For example, you all have skin instead of scales and a noticeable lack of antennae. You are a human being very much like all of your fellow human beings.

Yet you are different from everyone else in many ways. The people you most resemble are your parents and your brothers and sisters. But you probably don't look exactly like them either. Read on to find out why this is so.

Why Don't You Look Like a Rhinoceros?

The answer to this question seems simple: Neither of your parents is a rhinoceros. But there's more to this answer than meets the eye. As it turns out, **heredity,** or the passing of traits from parents to offspring, is a very complicated subject. For example, you might have curly hair, while both of your parents have straight hair. You might have blue eyes, even though both of your parents have brown eyes. How does this happen? People have investigated this question for a long time. About 150 years ago, some very important experiments were performed that helped scientists begin to find some answers. The person who performed these experiments was Gregor Mendel.

Who Was Gregor Mendel?

Gregor Mendel was born in 1822 in Heinzendorf, Austria. Growing up on his family's farm, Mendel learned a lot about cultivating flowers and fruit trees. After completing his studies at a university, he entered a monastery. He worked in the monastery garden, where he was able to use plants to study the way traits are passed from parents to offspring. **Figure 1** shows an illustration of Mendel in the monastery garden.

Activity

Imagine that you are planning to meet your pen pal at the airport, but you have never met. How would you describe yourself? Would you say that you are tall or short, have curly hair or straight hair, have brown eyes or green eyes? Make a list. Put a check mark next to traits you think you inherited.

TRY at HOME

Figure 1 Gregor Mendel

Unraveling the Mystery

From his experiences breeding plants, Mendel knew that sometimes the patterns of inheritance seemed simple and sometimes they did not. Mendel wanted to find out why.

Mendel was interested in the way traits are passed from parents to offspring. For example, sometimes a trait that appeared in one generation did not show up in any of the offspring in the next generation. In the third generation, though, the trait showed up again. Mendel noticed similar patterns in people, plants, and many other living things.

To simplify his investigation, Mendel decided to study only one kind of organism. He had already done studies using the garden pea plant, so he chose this as his subject.

How Do You Like Your Peas?   Garden peas were a good choice for several reasons. These plants grow quickly, they are usually self-pollinating, and they come in many varieties. A *self-pollinating plant* contains both male and female reproductive structures, like the flower in **Figure 2.** Therefore, pollen from one flower or plant can fertilize the eggs of the same flower or the eggs of another flower on the same plant. **Figure 3** illustrates the parts of a flower and how fertilization takes place in plants.

Figure 2 *This photograph of a flower shows the male and female reproductive structures.*

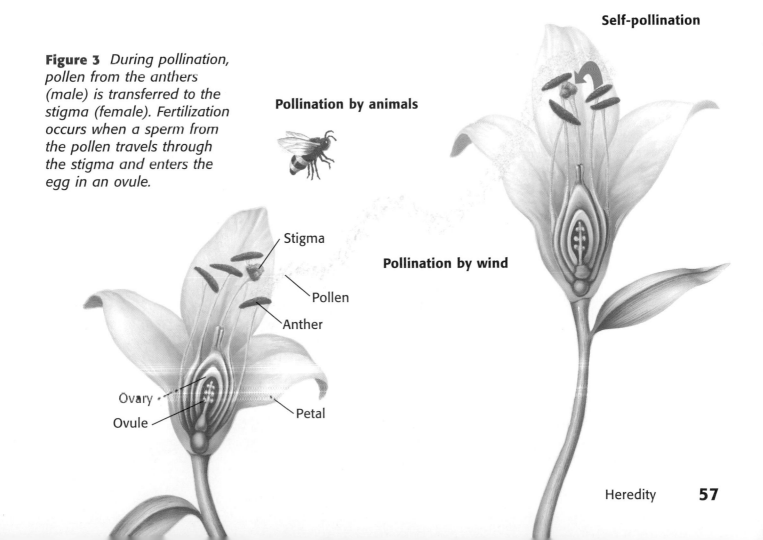

Figure 3 *During pollination, pollen from the anthers (male) is transferred to the stigma (female). Fertilization occurs when a sperm from the pollen travels through the stigma and enters the egg in an ovule.*

Pollination by animals

Pollination by wind

Self-pollination

Stigma

Pollen

Anther

Ovary

Ovule

Petal

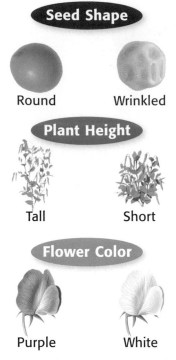

Seed Shape

Round   Wrinkled

Plant Height

Tall   Short

Flower Color

Purple   White

Figure 4 *These are some of the plant characteristics that Mendel studied.*

Peas Be My Podner

Mendel chose to study only one characteristic, such as plant height or pea color, at a time. That way, he could understand the results. Mendel chose plants that had two forms for each of the characteristics he studied. For example, for the characteristic of plant height, one form always produced tall plants, and the other form always produced short plants. Some of the characteristics investigated by Mendel are shown in **Figure 4.** The two different traits of each characteristic are also shown.

True-Breeding Plants Mendel was very careful to use plants that were true breeding for each of the traits he was studying. When a *true-breeding plant* self-pollinates, it will always produce offspring with the same trait the parent plant has. For example, a tall true-breeding plant will always produce offspring that are tall.

Mendel decided to find out what would happen if he crossed two plants that had different forms of a single trait. To do this, he used a method known as *cross-pollination*. In cross-pollination, the anthers of one plant are removed so that the plant cannot self-pollinate. Then pollen from another plant is used to fertilize the plant without anthers. This way, Mendel could select which pollen would fertilize which plant. This technique is illustrated in **Figure 5.**

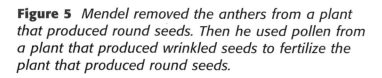

Pollen is transferred.

Anther

A plant that produces wrinkled seeds

A plant that produces round seeds

Stigma

Anthers are removed.

Figure 5 *Mendel removed the anthers from a plant that produced round seeds. Then he used pollen from a plant that produced wrinkled seeds to fertilize the plant that produced round seeds.*

Mendel's First Experiment

In his first experiment, Mendel performed crosses to study seven different characteristics. Each of the crosses was between the two traits of each characteristic. The results of the cross between plants that produce round seeds and plants that produce wrinkled seeds are shown in **Figure 6.** The offspring from this cross are known as the *first generation.* Do the results surprise you? What do you think happened to the trait for wrinkled seeds?

Mendel got similar results for each of the crosses that he made. One trait always appeared, and the other trait seemed to vanish. Mendel chose to call the trait that appeared the **dominant trait.** The other trait seemed to recede into the background, so Mendel called this the **recessive trait.** To find out what might have happened to the recessive trait, Mendel decided to perform another experiment.

Mendel's Second Experiment

Mendel allowed the first generation from each of the seven crosses to self-pollinate. This is also illustrated in Figure 6. This time the plant with the dominant trait for seed shape (which is round) was allowed to self-pollinate. As you can see, the recessive trait for wrinkled seeds showed up again.

Mendel performed this same experiment on the two traits of each of the seven characteristics. No matter which characteristic Mendel investigated, when the first generation was allowed to self-pollinate, the recessive trait reappeared.

Figure 6 *A plant that produces wrinkled seeds is fertilized with pollen from a plant that produces round seeds.*

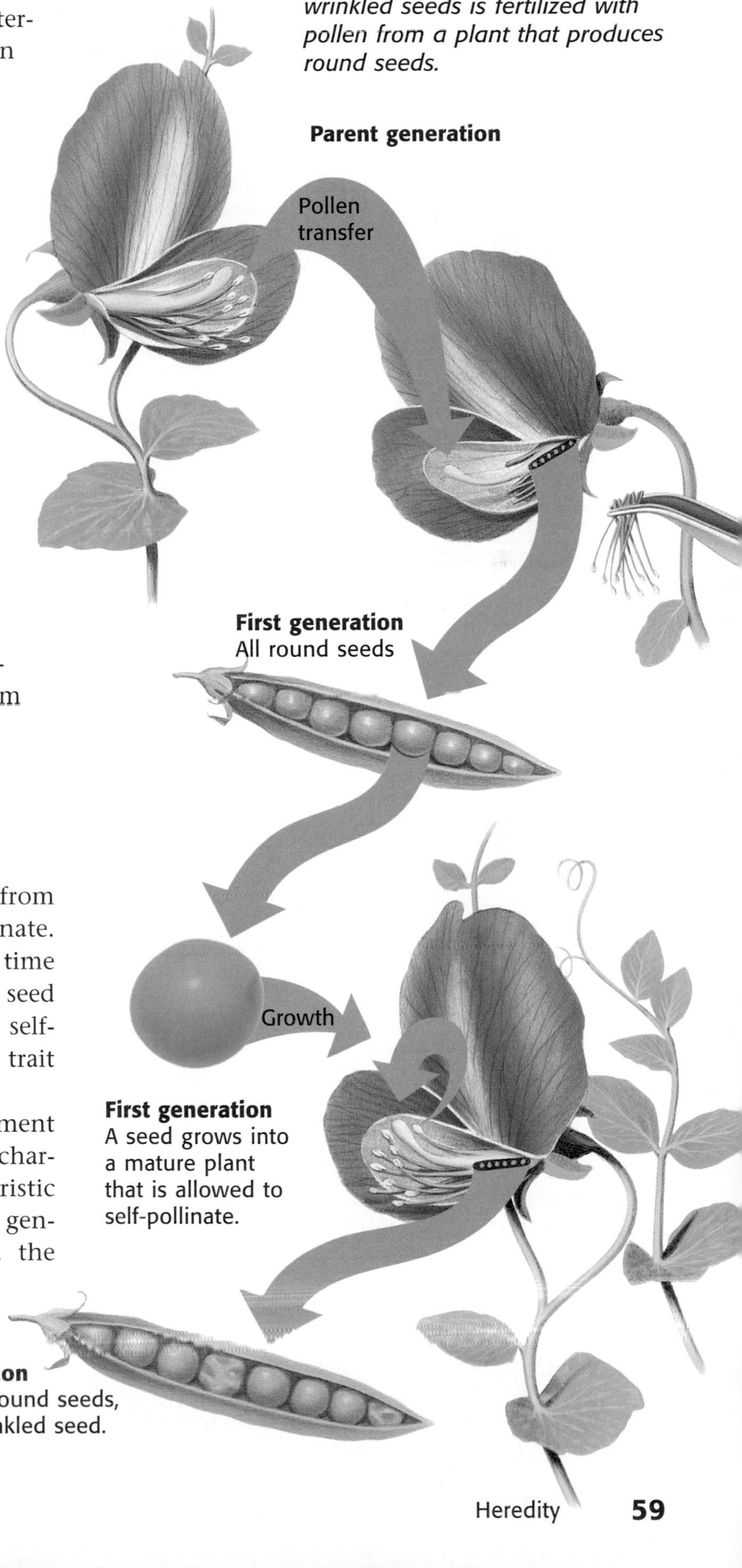

Parent generation

Pollen transfer

First generation
All round seeds

Growth

First generation
A seed grows into a mature plant that is allowed to self-pollinate.

Second generation
For every three round seeds, there is one wrinkled seed.

A Different Point of View

Mendel then did something that no one else had done before: He decided to count the number of plants with each trait that turned up in the second generation. He hoped that this might help him explain his results. Take a look at Mendel's actual results, shown in the table below.

Characteristic	Dominant trait		Recessive trait		Ratio
Mendel's Results					
Flower color	705 purple		224 white		3.15:1
Seed color	6,002 yellow		2,001 green		?
Seed shape	5,474 round		1,850 wrinkled		?
Pod color	428 green		152 yellow		?
Pod shape	882 smooth		299 bumpy		?
Flower position	651 along stem		207 at tip		?
Plant height	787 tall		277 short		?

MATH BREAK

Understanding Ratios

A ratio is a way to compare two numbers by using division. The ratio of plants with purple flowers to plants with white flowers can be written as 705 to 224 or 705:224. This ratio can be reduced, or simplified, by dividing the first number by the second as follows:

$$\frac{705}{224} = \frac{3.15}{1}$$

which is the same thing as a ratio of 3.15:1. For every three plants with purple flowers, there will be roughly one plant with white flowers. Try this problem:

> In a box of chocolates, there are 18 nougat-filled chocolates and 6 caramel-filled chocolates. What is the ratio of nougat-filled chocolates to caramel-filled chocolates?

As you can see, the recessive trait showed up again, but not as often as the dominant trait showed up. Mendel decided to calculate the *ratio* of dominant traits to recessive traits for each characteristic. Follow in Mendel's footsteps by calculating the dominant-to-recessive ratio for each characteristic. (If you need help, check out the MathBreak at left.) Can you find a pattern among the ratios?

A Brilliant Idea

Mendel realized that his results could be explained only if each plant had two sets of instructions for each characteristic. Each parent donates one set of instructions, now known as **genes,** to the offspring. The fertilized egg would then have two forms of the same gene for every characteristic—one from each parent. The two forms of a gene are known as **alleles.**

The Proof Is in the Punnett Square To understand Mendel's conclusions, we'll use a diagram called a Punnett square. A *Punnett square* is used to visualize all the possible combinations of alleles from the parents. Dominant alleles are symbolized with capital letters, and recessive alleles are symbolized with lowercase letters. Therefore, the alleles for a true-breeding purple-flowered plant are written as *PP.* The alleles for a true-breeding white-flowered plant are written as *pp.* The cross between these two parent plants, as shown in **Figure 7,** is then written as *PP × pp.* The squares contain the allele combinations that could occur in the offspring. The inherited combination of alleles is known as the offspring's **genotype.**

Figure 7 shows that all of the offspring will have the same genotype: *Pp.* The dominant allele, *P,* in each genotype ensures that all of the offspring will be purple-flowered plants. An organism's appearance is known as its **phenotype.** The recessive allele, *p,* may be passed on to the next generation.

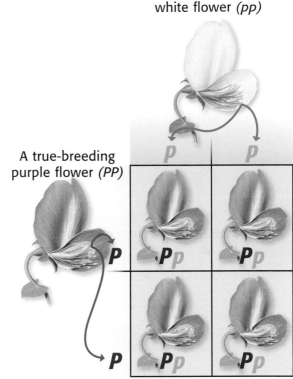

Figure 7 *The possible allele combinations in the offspring for this cross are all the same:* **Pp.**

A true-breeding white flower *(pp)*

A true-breeding purple flower *(PP)*

How to Make a Punnett Square

Draw a square, and divide it into four sections. Next, write the letters that represent alleles from one parent along the top of the box. Write the letters that represent alleles from the other parent along the side of the box.

The cross shown at right is between a plant that produces only round seeds, **RR,** and a plant that produces only wrinkled seeds, **rr.** Follow the arrows to see how the inside of the box was filled. The resulting alleles inside the box show all the possible genotypes for the offspring from this cross. What would the phenotypes for these offspring be?

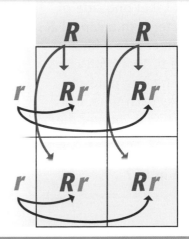

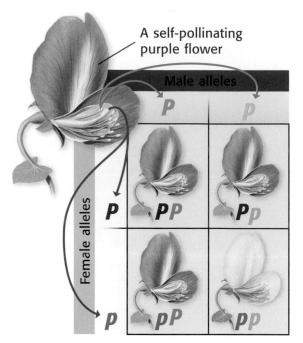

A self-pollinating purple flower

Male alleles

Female alleles

	P	**p**
P	**PP**	**Pp**
p	**pP**	**pp**

Figure 8 *This Punnett square shows the possible results from the cross* **Pp** × **Pp.**

More Evidence In Mendel's second experiment, he allowed the first-generation plants to self-pollinate. **Figure 8** shows a self-pollination cross of a first-generation plant with the genotype **Pp.** The parental alleles in the cross indicate that the egg and sperm can contain either a **P** allele or a **p** allele.

What might the genotypes of the offspring be? Notice that one square shows the **Pp** combination, while another shows the **pP** combination. These are exactly the same genotype, even though the letters are written in a different order. The other possible genotypes in the offspring are **PP** and **pp.** The combinations **PP, Pp,** and **pP** have the same phenotype—purple flowers—because they each contain at least one dominant allele (**P**). Only one combination, **pp,** produces plants with white flowers. The ratio of dominant to recessive is 3:1, just as Mendel calculated from his data.

What Are the Chances?

It's important to understand that offspring are equally likely to inherit either allele from either parent. Think of a coin toss. There's a 50 percent chance you'll get heads and a 50 percent chance you'll get tails. Like the toss of a coin, the chance of inheriting one allele or another is completely random.

Probability The mathematical chance that an event will occur is known as **probability.** Probability is usually expressed as a fraction or percentage. If you toss a coin, the probability of tossing tails is $\frac{1}{2}$. This means that half the number of times you toss a coin, you will get tails. To express probability as a percentage, divide the numerator of the fraction by the denominator, and then multiply the answer by 100.

$$\frac{1}{2} \times 100 = 50\%$$

To find the probability that you will toss two heads in a row, multiply the probability of the two events.

$$\frac{1}{2} \times \frac{1}{2} = \frac{1}{4}$$

The percentage would be $1 \div 4 \times 100$, which equals 25 percent.

Take Your Chances

You have two guinea pigs you would like to breed. Each has brown fur and the genotype **Bb.** What are the chances that their offspring will have white fur with the genotype **bb?** Try this to find out. Stick a piece of **masking tape** on both sides of **two quarters.** Label one side of each quarter with a capital **B** and the other side with a lowercase **b.** Toss both coins 50 times, making note of your results each time. How many times did you get the **bb** combination? What is the probability that the next toss will result in **bb?**

TRY at HOME

APPLY

Curly Eared Cats

A curly eared cat, like the one at right, mated with a cat that had normal ears. If half the kittens had the genotype **Cc** and curly ears, and the other half had the genotype **cc** and normal ears, which was the allele for curly ears?

What was the genotype of each parent? (**Hint:** Use a Punnett square to fill in the genotypes of the offspring, and then work backward.)

Genotype Probability The same method is used to calculate the probability that an offspring will inherit a certain genotype. For a pea plant to inherit the white flower trait, it must receive a **p** allele from each parent. There is a 50 percent chance of inheriting either allele from either parent. So the probability of inheriting two **p** alleles from a **Pp** × **Pp** cross is $\frac{1}{2} \times \frac{1}{2}$. This equals $\frac{1}{4}$ or 25 percent.

Gregor Mendel—Gone but Not Forgotten Good ideas are often overlooked or misunderstood when they first appear. This was the fate of Gregor Mendel's ideas. In 1865, he published his findings for the scientific community. Unfortunately, his work didn't get much attention. It wasn't until after his death, more than 30 years later, that Mendel finally got the recognition he deserved. Once Mendel's ideas were rediscovered and understood, the door was opened to modern genetics.

internet connect

SC*LINKS*
NSTA

TOPIC: Heredity, Dominant and Recessive Traits
GO TO: www.scilinks.org
*sci*LINKS NUMBER: HSTL110, HSTL115

SECTION REVIEW

1. The allele for a cleft chin, *C*, is dominant among humans. What would be the results from a cross between a woman with the genotype *Cc* and a man with the genotype *cc*? Create a Punnett square showing this cross.

2. Of the possible combinations you found in question 1, what is the ratio of offspring with a cleft chin to offspring without a cleft chin?

3. **Applying Concepts** The Punnett square at right shows the possible combinations of alleles for fur color in rabbits. Black fur, *B*, is dominant over white fur, *b*. Given the combinations shown, what are the genotypes of the parents?

	?	**?**
?	*Bb*	*Bb*
?	*Bb*	*Bb*

Meiosis

Terms to Learn

sex cells
homologous chromosomes
meiosis
sex chromosomes

What You'll Do

◆ Explain the difference between mitosis and meiosis.
◆ Describe how Mendel's ideas are supported by the process of meiosis.
◆ Explain the difference between male and female sex chromosomes.

In the early 1900s, scientists began doing experiments similar to those done by Gregor Mendel. Excited by their findings, they searched for similar results obtained by others. They came across Mendel's forgotten paper and realized that their discoveries were not new; Mendel had made the same observation 35 years earlier. However, genes were still a mystery. Where were they located, and how did they pass information from one cell to another? Understanding reproduction was the first step in finding the answers to these questions.

Two Kinds of Reproduction

You know that there are two types of reproduction: asexual reproduction and sexual reproduction.

One Makes Two In *asexual reproduction,* only one parent cell is needed for reproduction. First, the internal structures of the cell are copied by a process known as mitosis. The parent cell then divides, producing new cells that are exact copies of the parent cell. Most single-celled organisms reproduce in this way. Most of the cells in your body also divide this way.

Two Make One A different type of reproduction is used to make a new human being or a new pea plant. In *sexual reproduction,* two parent cells join together to form a new individual. The parent cells, known as **sex cells,** are different from ordinary body cells. Human body cells, for example, have 46 chromosomes (or 23 pairs), as shown in **Figure 9.** The chromosomes in each pair are called **homologous** (hoh MAHL uh guhs) **chromosomes.** But human sex cells have only 23 chromosomes—half the usual number. Male sex cells are called *sperm.* Female sex cells are called *eggs,* or ova. Each sperm and each egg has only one of the chromosomes from each homologous pair.

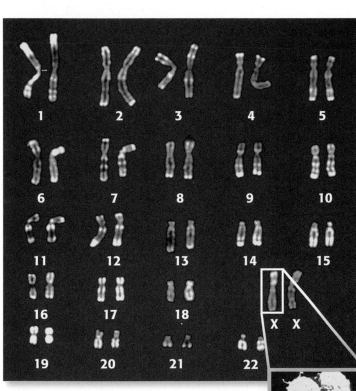

Figure 9 *Human body cells have 46 chromosomes, or 23 pairs of chromosomes. One member of a pair of homologous chromosomes is shown at right.*

Less Is More Why is it important that sex cells have half the usual number of chromosomes? When an egg and a sperm join to form a new individual, each parent donates one half of a homologous pair of chromosomes. This ensures that the offspring will receive a normal number of chromosomes in each body cell. Each body cell must have an entire set of 46 chromosomes in order to grow and function properly.

Meiosis to the Rescue Sex cells are made during meiosis, a copying process that is different from mitosis. **Meiosis** (mie OH sis) produces new cells with half the usual number of chromosomes. When the sex cells are made, the chromosomes are copied once, and then the nucleus divides twice. The resulting sperm and eggs have half the number of chromosomes found in a normal body cell.

Meanwhile, Back at the Lab

What does all of this have to do with the location of genes? Not long after Mendel's paper was rediscovered, a young graduate student named Walter Sutton made an important observation. Sutton was studying sperm cells in grasshoppers. Sutton knew of Mendel's studies, which showed that the egg and sperm must each contribute the same amount of information to the offspring. That was the only way the 3:1 ratio found in the second generation could be explained. Sutton also knew from his own studies that although eggs and sperm were different, they did have something in common: their chromosomes were located inside a nucleus. Using his observations of meiosis, his understanding of Mendel's work, and some creative thinking, Sutton proposed something very important:

Genes are located on chromosomes!

And Sutton was correct, as it turned out. The steps of meiosis are outlined on the next two pages. But first, let's review mitosis so that you can compare the two processes.

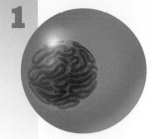

1 Inside a typical cell: each of the long strands (chromosomes) makes a copy of itself.

2 Each chromosome consists of two identical copies called chromatids. The chromosomes thicken and shorten.

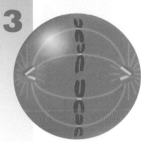

3 The nuclear membrane dissolves. The chromosomes line up along the equator (center) of the cell.

4 The chromatids pull apart.

5 The nuclear membrane forms around the separated chromatids. The chromosomes unwind, and the cell divides.

6 The result: two identical copies of the original cell.

Meiosis in Eight Easy Steps

The diagram on these two pages shows each stage of meiosis. Read about each step as you look at the diagram. Different types of living things have different numbers of chromosomes. In this diagram, only four chromosomes are shown.

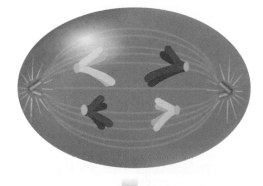

One pair of homologous chromosomes

Two chromatids

1 Before meiosis begins, the chromosomes are in a threadlike form. Each chromosome makes an identical copy of itself, forming two exact halves called *chromatids.* The chromosomes then thicken and shorten into a form that is visible under a microscope. The nuclear membrane disappears.

2 Each chromosome is now made up of two chromatids, the original and an exact copy. Similar chromosomes pair with one another, forming *homologous chromosome pairs.* The paired homologous chromosomes line up at the equator of the cell.

3 The chromosomes separate from their homologous partners and move to opposite ends of the cell.

4 The nuclear membrane re-forms, and the cell divides. The paired chromatids are still joined.

Each cell contains one member of each homologous chromosome pair. The chromosomes are not copied again between the two cell divisions.

The chromosomes line up at the equator of each cell.

The chromatids pull apart and move to opposite ends of the cell. The nuclear membrane forms around the separated chromosomes, and the cells divide.

The result: Four new cells have formed from the original single cell. Each new cell has half the number of chromosomes present in the original cell.

✓ Self-Check

1. How many chromosomes are in the original single cell in the diagram on page 66?

2. How many homologous pairs are shown in the original cell?

3. How many times do the chromosomes make copies of themselves during meiosis? How many times do cells divide during meiosis?

4. How many chromosomes are present in each cell at the end of meiosis? at the end of mitosis?

(See page 216 to check your answers.)

📶 internet**connect**

SC*i*LINKS.
NSTA

TOPIC: Cell Division
GO TO: www.scilinks.org
*sci***LINKS NUMBER:** HSTL120

Meiosis and Mendel

As Walter Sutton realized, the steps in meiosis explain Mendel's findings. **Figure 10** illustrates what happens to a pair of homologous chromosomes during meiosis and fertilization. The cross is between a plant that is true breeding for round seeds and a plant that is true breeding for wrinkled seeds.

Figure 10 *Meiosis helps explain Mendel's findings.*

Male Parent In the plant cell nucleus below, each homologous chromosome has an allele for seed shape and each allele carries the same instructions: to make wrinkled seeds.

Female Parent In the plant cell nucleus below, each homologous chromosome has an allele for seed shape and each allele carries the same instruction: to make round seeds.

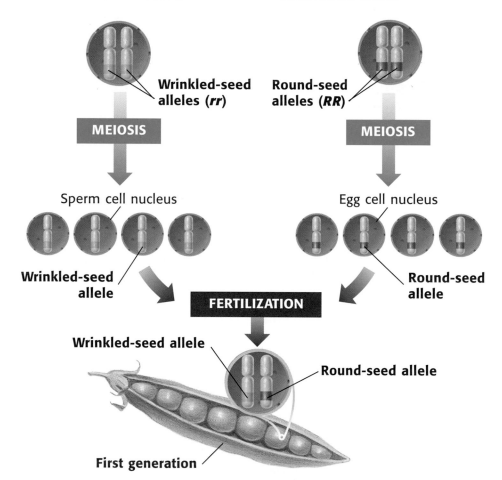

Following **meiosis**, each sperm cell contains a recessive allele for wrinkled seeds and each egg cell contains a dominant allele for round seeds.

Fertilization of any egg by any sperm results in the same genotype (*Rr*) and the same phenotype (round). This is exactly what Mendel found in his studies.

Each fertilized egg in the first generation contained one dominant allele and one recessive allele for seed type. Only one genotype was possible because all sperm formed during meiosis contained the wrinkled-seed allele and all eggs contained the round-seed allele. When the first generation was allowed to self-pollinate, the possible genotypes changed. There are three genotype possibilities for this cross: *RR*, *Rr*, and *rr.*

Male or Female?

There are many ways that different organisms become male or female. To see how this happens in humans, examine **Figure 11.** Then look back at Figure 9, on page 64. Each figure shows the chromosomes in human body cells. Which chromosome photograph is from a female, and which is from a male? Here's a hint: Females have 23 matched pairs, while males have 22 matched pairs and one unmatched pair.

Sex Chromosomes The chromosomes in Figure 11 are from a male, and the chromosomes in Figure 9 are from a female. **Sex chromosomes** carry genes that determine whether the offspring is male or female. In humans, females have two X chromosomes (the matching pair), and males have one X chromosome and one Y chromosome (the unmatched pair).

During meiosis, one of each of the chromosome pairs ends up in a sex cell. This is also true of the sex chromosomes. Females have two X chromosomes in each body cell. When meiosis produces the egg cells, each egg contains one X chromosome. Males have both an X chromosome and a Y chromosome in each body cell. During meiosis, these chromosomes separate, so each sperm cell contains either an X or a Y chromosome. An egg fertilized by a sperm with an X chromosome will produce a female. If the sperm contains a Y chromosome, the offspring will be male. This is illustrated in **Figure 12.**

Figure 11 *Are these chromosomes from a male or female? How can you tell?*

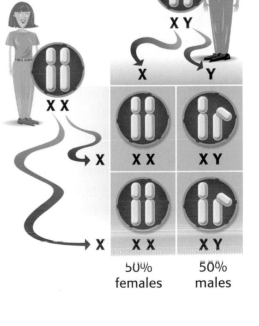

Figure 12 *Egg and sperm combine to form either the XX or XY combination.*

SECTION REVIEW

1. Explain the difference between sex cells and sex chromosomes.

2. If there are 14 chromosomes in pea plant cells, how many chromosomes are present in a sex cell of a pea?

3. **Interpreting Illustrations** Examine the illustration at right. Does it show a stage of mitosis or meiosis? How can you tell?

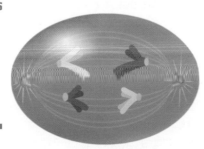

Bug Builders, Inc.

Imagine that you are a designer for a toy company that makes toy bugs. The president of Bug Builders, Inc., wants new kinds of the wildly popular Space Bugs, but he wants to use the bug parts that the company already has. It's your job to come up with new bugs. You have studied how traits are passed from one generation to the next. You will use this knowledge to come up with new combinations of traits and to build the bug parts in new ways. Model A and Model B, shown on this page, will act as the "parent" bugs.

MATERIALS

- 14 allele sacks (supplied by your teacher)
- large marshmallows (head and body segments)
- red and green toothpicks (antennae)
- green and blue pushpins (noses)
- pipe cleaners (tails)
- green and black gumdrops (feet)
- map pins (eyes)
- scissors

Ask a Question

1 What are the possible genotypes and phenotypes for the offspring of a cross between Model A and Model B?

Collect Data

2 Your teacher will have fourteen allele sacks for the class—two for each characteristic. The sacks will hold slips of paper with capital or lowercase letters printed on them. Take one piece of paper from each sack. (Remember: Capital letters are dominant alleles, and lowercase letters are recessive alleles.) For each characteristic, one allele sack carries the alleles from "Mom" and one allele sack carries the alleles from "Dad." After you have recorded the alleles you have drawn, place the slips of paper back into the sacks.

Model A ("Mom")
- red antennae
- 3 body segments
- curly tail
- 2 pairs of legs
- green nose
- black feet
- 3 eyes

Model B ("Dad")
- green antennae
- 2 body segments
- straight tail
- 3 pairs of legs
- blue nose
- green feet
- 2 eyes

3 Make a table like the one below in your ScienceLog or on a computer. Fill in the first two columns with the alleles you picked in step 2. Next, fill in the third column with the genotype of the new model ("Baby").

Bug Family Traits				
Trait	Model A "Mom" allele	Model B "Dad" allele	New model "Baby" genotype	New model "Baby" phenotype
Antennae color				
Number of body segments				
Tail shape				
Number of leg pairs				
Nose color				
Foot color				
Number of eyes				

4 Use the data at right to fill in the last column of the table.

5 Now that you have your table filled out, you are ready to pick the parts that you need to build your bug.

Analyze the Results

6 Take a class poll of the traits of the offspring. What are the ratios for each trait?

Genotypes and Phenotypes	
RR or *Rr* = red antennae	*rr* = green antennae
SS or *Ss* = 3 body segments	*ss* = 2 body segments
CC or *Cc* = curly tail	*cc* = straight tail
LL or *Ll* = 3 pairs of legs	*ll* = 2 pairs of legs
BB or *Bb* = blue nose	*bb* = green nose
GG or *Gg* = green feet	*gg* = black feet
EE or *Ee* = 2 eyes	*ee* = 3 eyes

Draw Conclusions

7 What are the possible genotypes of the parents? How many different genotypes are possible in the offspring?

Going Further

Find a mate for your "Baby" bug. What are the possible genotypes and phenotypes of the offspring from this match?

Chapter Highlights

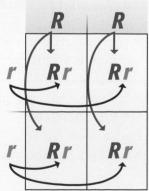

Vocabulary

heredity *(p. 56)*
dominant trait *(p. 59)*
recessive trait *(p. 59)*
genes *(p. 61)*
alleles *(p. 61)*
genotype *(p. 61)*
phenotype *(p. 61)*
probability *(p. 62)*

Section Notes

- Heredity is the passing of traits from parents to offspring.

- Traits are inherited forms of characteristics.

- Gregor Mendel used pea plants to study heredity.

- Mendel's pea plants were self-pollinating. They contained both male and female reproductive structures. They were also true breeding, always producing offspring with the same traits as the parents.

- Offspring inherit two sets of instructions for each characteristic, one set from each parent.

- The sets of instructions are known as genes.

- Different versions of the same gene are known as alleles.

- If both the dominant allele and the recessive allele are inherited for a characteristic, only the dominant allele is expressed.

- Recessive traits are apparent only when two recessive alleles for the characteristic are inherited.

- A genotype is the combination of alleles for a particular trait.

- A phenotype is the physical expression of the genotype.

- Probability is the mathematical chance that an event will occur. It is usually expressed as a fraction or as a percentage.

Labs

Tracing Traits *(p. 188)*

☑ Skills Check

Math Concepts

RATIOS A jar contains 24 green marbles and 96 red marbles. There are 4 red marbles for every 1 green marble.

$$\frac{96}{24} = \frac{4}{1}$$

This can also be written as follows:

$$4:1$$

Visual Understanding

PUNNETT SQUARES
A Punnett square can help you visualize all the possible combinations of alleles passed from parents to offspring. See page 61 to review how Punnett squares are made.

	R	R
r	Rr	Rr
r	Rr	Rr

Vocabulary

sex cells *(p. 64)*

homologous chromosomes
(p. 64)

meiosis *(p. 65)*

sex chromosomes *(p. 69)*

Section Notes

- Genes are located on chromosomes.

- Most human cells contain 46 chromosomes, or 23 pairs.

- Each pair contains one chromosome donated by the mother and one donated by the father. These pairs are known as homologous chromosomes.

- Meiosis produces sex cells, eggs and sperm.

- Sex cells have half the usual number of chromosomes.

- Sex chromosomes contain genes that determine an offspring's sex.

- Human females have two X chromosomes, and males have one X chromosome and one Y chromosome.

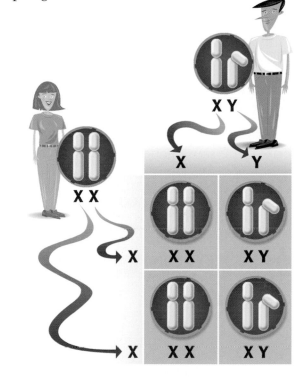

Chapter Review

To complete the following sentences, choose the correct term from each pair of terms listed below:

1. Sperm and eggs are known as __?__. (*sex cells* or *sex chromosomes*)

2. The __?__, the expression of a trait, is determined by the __?__, the combination of alleles. (*genotype* or *phenotype*)

3. __?__ produces cells with half the normal number of chromosomes. (*Meiosis* or *Mitosis*)

4. Different versions of the same genes are called __?__. (*sex cells* or *alleles*)

5. A __?__ plant can pollinate its own eggs. (*self-pollinating* or *true-breeding*)

UNDERSTANDING CONCEPTS

Multiple Choice

6. Genes are found on
   a. chromosomes.
   b. alleles.
   c. proteins.
   d. anthers.

7. The process that produces sex cells is
   a. mitosis.
   b. photosynthesis.
   c. meiosis.
   d. probability.

8. The passing of traits from parents to offspring is
   a. probability.
   b. heredity.
   c. recessive.
   d. meiosis.

9. If you cross a white flower (with the genotype *pp*) with a purple flower (with the genotype *PP*), the possible genotypes in the offspring are:
   a. *PP* and *pp*.
   b. all *Pp*.
   c. all *PP*.
   d. all *pp*.

10. For the above cross, what would the phenotypes be?
    a. all white
    b. all tall
    c. all purple
    d. $\frac{1}{2}$ white, $\frac{1}{2}$ purple

11. In meiosis,
    a. the chromosomes are copied twice.
    b. the nucleus divides once.
    c. four cells are produced from a single cell.
    d. All of the above

12. Probability is
    a. always expressed as a ratio.
    b. a 50% chance that an event will occur.
    c. the mathematical chance that an event will occur.
    d. a 3:1 chance that an event will occur.

Short Answer

13. Which sex chromosomes do females have? Which do males have?

14. In your own words, give a one- or two-sentence definition of the term *recessive trait*.

15. How are sex cells different from other body cells?

Concept Mapping

16. Use the following terms to create a concept map: meiosis, eggs, cell division, X chromosome, sex cells, sperm, mitosis, Y chromosome.

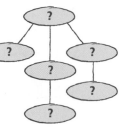

CRITICAL THINKING AND PROBLEM SOLVING

Write one or two sentences to answer the following questions:

17. If a child has blue eyes and both her parents have brown eyes, what does that tell you about the trait for blue eyes? Explain your answer.

18. Why is meiosis important for sexual reproduction?

19. Gregor Mendel used only true-breeding plants. If he had used plants that were not true breeding, do you think he would have discovered dominant and recessive traits? Why or why not?

MATH IN SCIENCE

20. Assume that **Y** is the dominant allele for yellow seeds and **y** is the recessive allele for green seeds. What is the probability that a pea plant with the genotype **Yy** crossed with a pea plant with the genotype **yy** will have offspring with the genotype **yy**?

INTERPRETING GRAPHICS

Examine the Punnett square below, and then answer the following questions:

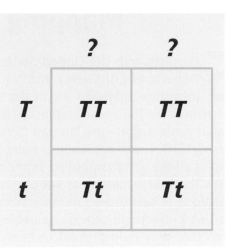

	?	?
T	**TT**	**TT**
t	**Tt**	**Tt**

21. What is the unknown genotype?

22. If **T** represents the allele for tall pea plants, and **t** represents the allele for short pea plants, what is the phenotype of each parent and of the offspring?

23. If each of the offspring were allowed to self-fertilize, what are the possible genotypes in the next generation?

24. What is the probability of each genotype in item 23?

Reading Check-up

Take a minute to review your answers to the Pre-Reading Questions found at the bottom of page 54. Have your answers changed? If necessary, revise your answers based on what you have learned since you began this chapter.

Science, Technology, and Society

Mapping the Human Genome

Scientists with the United States Department of Energy and National Institutes of Health are in the midst of what may be the most ambitious scientific research project ever—the Human Genome Project (HGP). These researchers want to create a map of all the genes found on human chromosomes. The body's complete set of genetic instructions is called the genome. Scientists hope this project will provide valuable information that may help prevent or even cure many genetic diseases.

Whose Genes Are These?

You might be wondering whose genome the scientists are decoding. Actually, it doesn't matter because each person is unique in only about 1 percent of his or her genetic material. The scientists' goal is to identify how tiny differences in that 1 percent of DNA make each of us who we are, and to understand how some changes can cause disease.

Genetic Medicine

The tiny changes that can cause disease, called mutations, are often inherited. Once scientists determine the normal order of our genes, doctors may be able to use this information to help detect mutations in patients. Then doctors would be able to warn patients of an increased risk of a disease before any symptoms appear! For example, a doctor's early warning about a genetic risk of high cholesterol would give a person a chance to eat healthier and exercise more before any serious symptoms were detectable.

Advancing Technology

Scientists organizing the HGP hope to have a complete and accurate sequence of the human

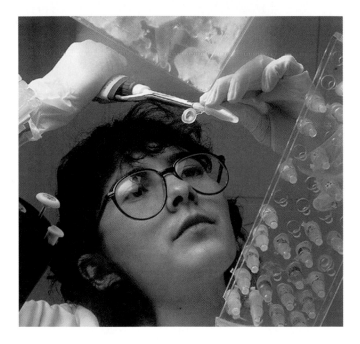

▲ *This scientist is performing one of the many steps involved in the research for the Human Genome Project.*

genome—estimated to have between 50,000 and 100,000 genes—by 2003. One day in the future, scientists may even be able to provide people with a healthy gene to replace a mutated one. This technique, called gene therapy, may eventually be the cure for many genetic diseases.

What Do You Think?

▶ Despite the medical advancements the Human Genome Project will bring, many people continue to debate ethical, social, and legal issues surrounding this controversial project. Look into these issues, and discuss them with your classmates!

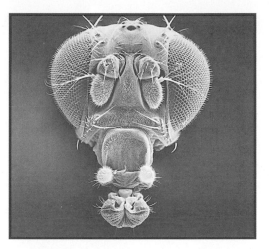

▲ *This is what a normal fruit fly looks like under a scanning electron microscope.*

Lab Rats with Wings

What's less than 1 mm in length, can be extremely annoying when buzzing around your kitchen, and sometimes grows legs out of its eyes? The answer is *Drosophila melanogaster*—better known as the fruit fly because it feeds on fruit. This tiny insect has played a big role in helping us understand many illnesses, especially those that occur at certain stages of human development. Scientists use fruit flies to find out more about diseases and disorders such as cancer, Alzheimer's disease, muscular dystrophy, and Down's syndrome.

Why a Fly?

Fruit flies are some scientists' favorite research animal. Scientists can raise several generations of fruit flies in just a few months. Because fruit flies have only a two-week life cycle, scientists can alter a fruit-fly gene as part of an experiment and then see the results very quickly.

Another advantage to using these tiny animals is their small size. Thousands of fruit flies can be raised in a relatively small space.

▲ *This fruit fly has legs growing out of its eyes!*

Researchers can afford to buy and maintain a variety of fruit fly strains to use in experiments.

Comparing Codes

Another important reason for using these "lab rats with wings" is that their genetic code is relatively simple and well understood. Fruit flies have 12,000 genes, whereas humans have more than 70,000. Nonetheless, many fruit-fly genes are similar in function to human genes, and scientists have learned to manipulate them to produce genetic mutations. Scientists who study these mutations gain valuable information about genetic mutations in humans. Without fruit flies, some human genetic problems that we now have important information about—such as basal cell carcinoma cancer—might have taken many more years and many more dollars to study.

Where Do You Draw the Line?

▶ Do you think it is acceptable for scientists to perform research on fruit flies? What about on rats, mice, and rabbits? Have a debate with your classmates about conducting scientific experiments on other species.

77

Genes and Gene Technology

Pre-Reading Questions

1. How are proteins related to the way you look?

2. What are genes? Where are they found?

3. How does knowing about DNA help scientists treat diseases?

UNLOCKING LIFE'S MASTER CODES

Did you know that each one of your cells has a 2-meter-long strand of DNA? This computer-generated DNA model hints at just how complex a DNA molecule is. Like a giant puzzle, the patterns in the spiraling DNA strands contain the codes for the growth of all cells and processes in living things. Human DNA has about 3 billion individual codes, or puzzle pieces. As of the year 2000, gene scientists mapped them all. In this chapter, you will learn about the structure of DNA and the genetic information it contains.

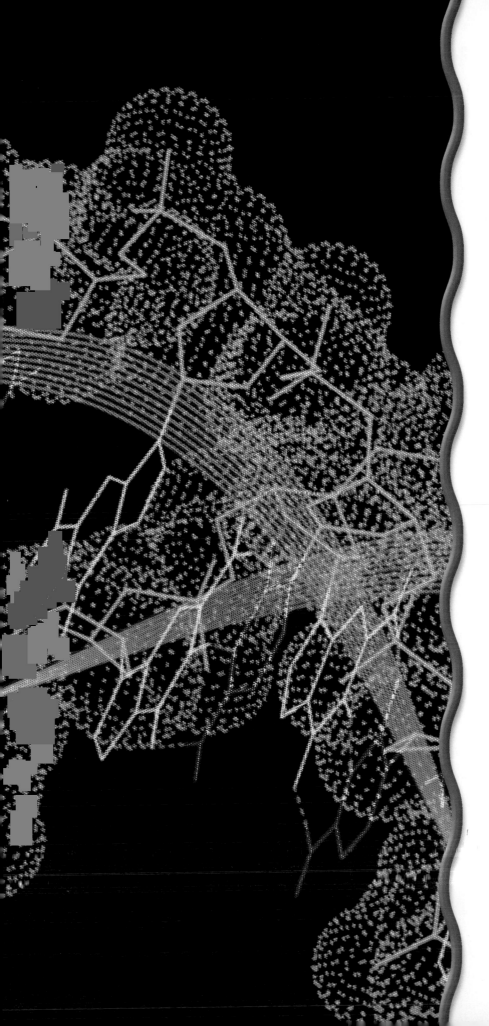

FINGERPRINT YOUR FRIENDS

One common method of identification is fingerprinting. Does it really work? Are everyone's fingerprints different? Try this activity to find out.

Procedure

1. Rub a **piece of charcoal** back and forth across a **piece of tracing paper.** Rub the tip of one of your fingers on the charcoal mark. Then place a **small piece of transparent tape** over the charcoal on your finger. Remove the tape, and stick it on a **piece of white paper.** Do the same for the rest of your fingers.

2. Observe the patterns with a **magnifying lens.** What kinds of patterns do you see? The fingerprint patterns shown below are the most common found among humans.

Analysis

3. Compare your fingerprints with those of your classmates. How many of each type do you see? Do any two people in your class have the same prints? Try to explain your findings.

Whorl   **Arch**   **Loop**

Terms to Learn

DNA   thymine
nucleotide   guanine
adenine   cytosine

What You'll Do

- Describe the basic structure of the DNA molecule.
- Explain how DNA molecules can be copied.
- Explain some of the exceptions to Mendel's heredity principles.

What Do Genes Look Like?

Scientists know that traits are determined by genes and that genes are passed from one generation to another. Scientists also know that genes are located on chromosomes, structures in the nucleus of most cells. Chromosomes are made of protein and **DNA,** short for deoxyribonucleic (dee AHKS ee RIE boh noo KLEE ik) acid. But which type of material makes the genes?

The Pieces of the Puzzle

The gene material must be able to do two things. First it must be able to supply instructions for cell processes and for building cell structures. Second it must be able to be copied each time a cell divides, so that each cell contains an identical set of genes. Early studies of DNA suggested that DNA was a very simple molecule. Because of this, most scientists thought protein probably carried hereditary information. After all, proteins are complex molecules.

In the 1940s, however, scientists discovered that genes of bacteria are made of DNA. How could something so simple hold the key to an organism's characteristics? To find the answer, let's take a closer look at the subunits of a DNA molecule.

Nucleotides—The Subunits of DNA DNA is made of only four subunits, which are known as **nucleotides.** Each nucleotide consists of three different types of material: a sugar, a phosphate, and a base. Nucleotides are identical except for the base. The four bases are **adenine, thymine, guanine,** and **cytosine,** and they each have a slightly different shape. The bases are usually referred to by the first letters in their names, A, T, G, and C. **Figure 1** shows diagrams of the four nucleotides.

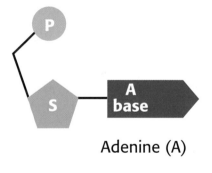

Adenine (A)

Nucleotide

Figure 1 *Can you imagine how the nucleotides might fit together?*

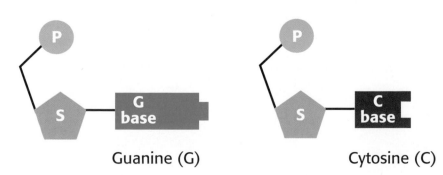

Thymine (T)   Guanine (G)   Cytosine (C)

Chargaff's Rules In the 1950s, a biochemist named Erwin Chargaff found that the amount of adenine in DNA always equals the amount of thymine, and the amount of guanine always equals the amount of cytosine. His findings are known as Chargaff's rules.

At the time, no one knew quite what to make of Chargaff's findings. How could Chargaff's rules help solve the mysteries of DNA's structure? Read on to find out.

A Picture of DNA

More clues came from the laboratory of British scientist Maurice Wilkins. There, chemist Rosalind Franklin, shown in **Figure 2,** was able to create images of DNA molecules. The process that she used to create these images is known as X-ray diffraction. In this process, X rays bombard the DNA molecule. When the X ray hits a particle within the molecule, the ray bounces off the particle. This creates a pattern that is captured on film. The images that Franklin created suggested that DNA has a spiral shape.

Figure 2 Rosalind Franklin, 1920–1958

Eureka!

Two other young scientists, James Watson and Francis Crick, shown in **Figure 3,** were also investigating the mystery of DNA's structure. Based on the work of others, Watson and Crick built models of DNA using simple materials, such as labeled pieces of cardboard. After seeing the X-ray images of DNA made by Rosalind Franklin, Watson and Crick concluded that DNA resembles a twisted ladder shape known as a *double helix.* Watson and Crick used their DNA model to predict how DNA is copied. Upon making the discovery, Crick is said to have exclaimed, "We have discovered the secret of life!"

Figure 3 *This photo shows James Watson, on the left, and Francis Crick, on the right, with their model of DNA.*

DNA Structure

The twisted ladder, or double helix, shape is represented in **Figure 4.** As you can see in **Figure 5,** the two sides of the ladder are made of alternating sugar molecules and phosphate molecules. The rungs of the ladder are composed of a pair of nucleotide bases. Adenine on one side always pairs up with thymine on the other side. Guanine always pairs up with cytosine in the same way. How might this structure explain Chargaff's findings?

Figure 4 *The structure of DNA can be compared to a twisted ladder.*

Figure 5 *In a DNA molecule, the bases must pair up in a certain way. If a mistake happens and the bases do not pair up correctly, the gene may not carry the correct information.*

Making Copies of DNA

What's so great about DNA? Because adenine always bonds with thymine and guanine always bonds with cytosine, one side of a DNA molecule is *complementary* to the other. For example, a sequence such as ACCG always binds to the sequence TGGC. This allows DNA to make a copy of itself, or *replicate*.

As illustrated in **Figure 6,** a DNA molecule replicates by splitting down the middle where the two bases meet. The bases on each side of the molecule can be used as a template, or pattern, for a new complementary side. This creates two identical molecules of DNA.

Figure 6 *The illustration shows DNA separating down the middle in order to make a copy of itself. Each half of the original molecule serves as a template along which a new complementary strand forms. The photograph shows a DNA molecule that has separated. It is magnified about 1 million times.*

✔ Self-Check

What would the complementary strand of DNA be for the following sequence of bases? ACCTAGTTG *(See page 216 to check your answer.)*

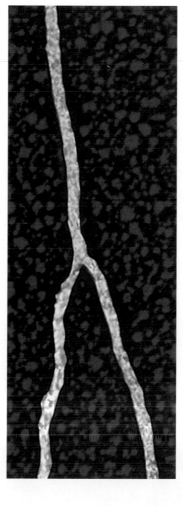

Old   New   New   Old

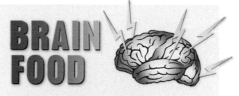

BRAIN FOOD

If you took all the DNA in your body from all of your cells and stretched it out end to end, it would extend about 610 million kilometers. That's long enough to stretch from Earth to the sun and back—twice!

From Trait to Gene

The Watson-Crick model also explains how DNA can contain so much information. The bases on one side of the molecule can be put in any order, allowing for an enormous variety of genes. Each gene consists of a string of bases. The order of the bases gives the cell information about how to make each trait.

Putting It All Together DNA functions in the same way for all organisms, from bacteria to mosquitoes to whales to humans. DNA unites us all, and at the same time, it makes each of us unique. The journey from trait to DNA base is illustrated in the diagram on these two pages.

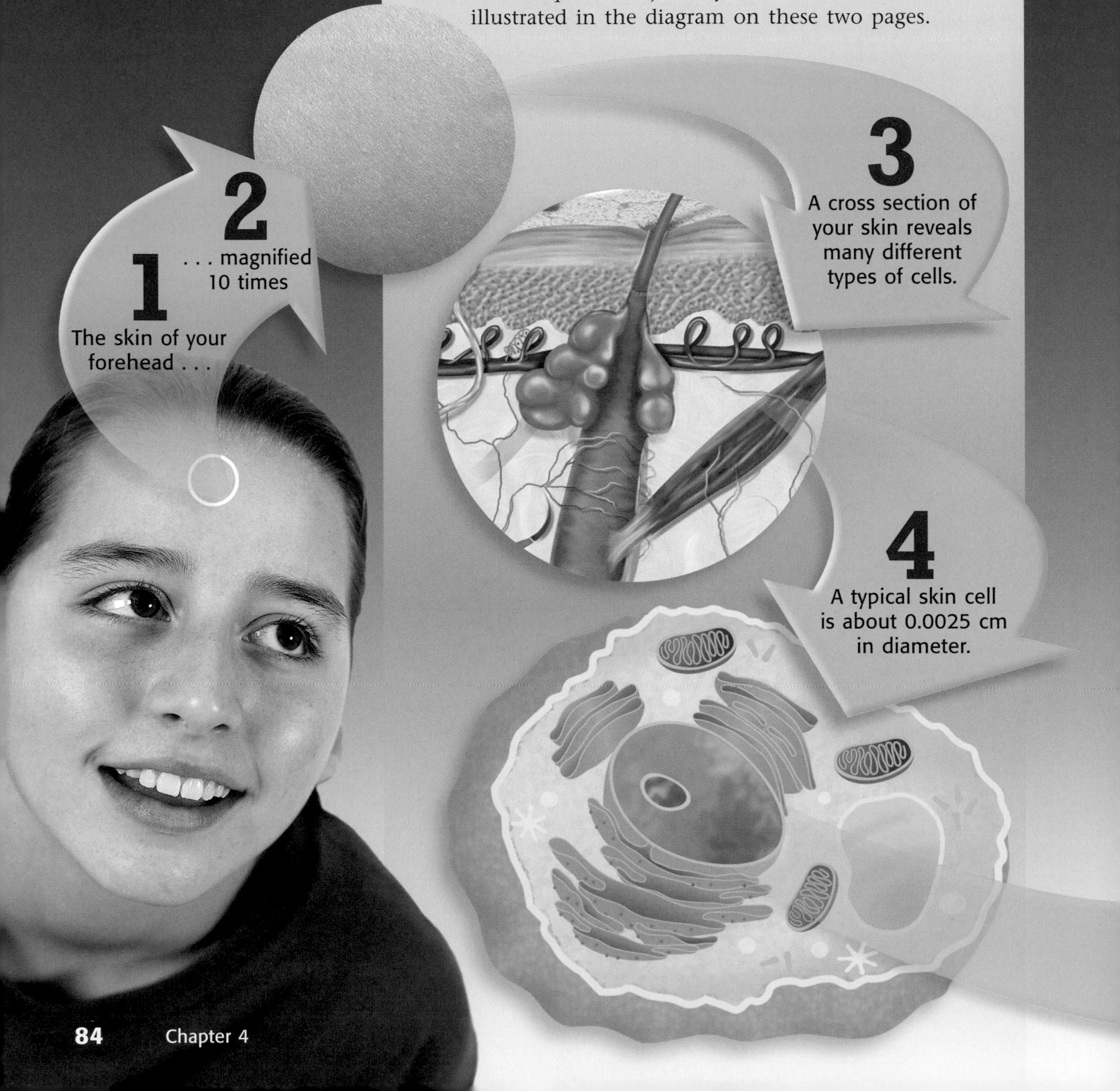

2

1 . . . magnified 10 times

The skin of your forehead . . .

3 A cross section of your skin reveals many different types of cells.

4 A typical skin cell is about 0.0025 cm in diameter.

8

A single loop of DNA . . .

7

Each chromosome contains an enormous amount of DNA.

9

. . . contains even more coils.

6

Each chromosome is made of protein and DNA.

10

Each molecule of DNA contains two halves that are connected down the center and twisted like a spiral staircase.

5

Each skin cell contains 46 chromosomes.

C . . . G

G . . . C

T . . . A

C . . . G

A . . . T

DNA on trial? Read all about it on page 100.

More News About Traits

As you may have already discovered, things are often more complicated than they first appear to be. Gregor Mendel uncovered the basic principles of how genes are passed from one generation to the next. But as scientists learned more about heredity, they began to find exceptions to Mendel's principles. A few of these exceptions are explained in the following paragraphs.

Incomplete Dominance   In his studies with peas, Mendel found that different traits did not blend together to produce an in-between form. Since then, researchers have found that sometimes one trait is not completely dominant over another. These traits do not blend together, but each allele has its own degree of influence. This is known as *incomplete dominance*. One example of this is the snapdragon flower. **Figure 7** shows a cross between a true-breeding red snapdragon (R^1R^1) and a true-breeding white snapdragon (R^2R^2). As you can see, all of the possible phenotypes for their offspring are pink because both alleles of the gene have some degree of influence.

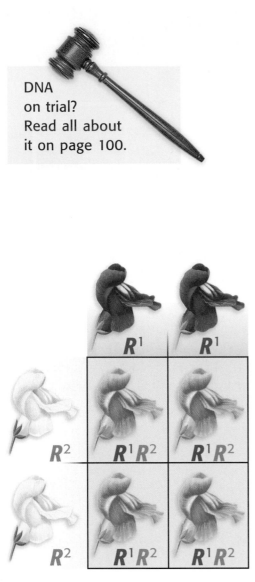

Figure 7 *The snapdragon provides a good example of incomplete dominance.*

One Gene Can Influence Many Traits Sometimes one gene influences more than one trait. An example of this phenomenon is shown by the white tiger at right. The white fur is caused by a single gene, but this gene influences more than just fur color. Do you see anything else unusual about the tiger? If you look closely, you'll see that the tiger has blue eyes. Here the gene that controls fur color also influences eye color.

Many Genes Can Influence a Single Trait Some traits, such as the color of your skin, hair, and eyes, are the result of several genes acting together. That's why it's difficult to tell if a trait is the result of a dominant or recessive gene. As shown in **Figure 8,** you may have blue eyes, but they are probably a slightly different shade of blue than the blue eyes of a classmate. Different combinations of alleles result in slight differences in the amount of pigment present.

The Importance of Environment

It's important to remember that genes aren't the only influences on your development. Many things in your environment also influence how you grow and develop. Consider the importance of a healthy diet, exercise, and examples set by family and friends. For example, your genes may determine that you can grow to be tall, but you must receive the proper nutrients as you grow in order to reach your full potential height. You may have inherited a special talent, but you need to practice.

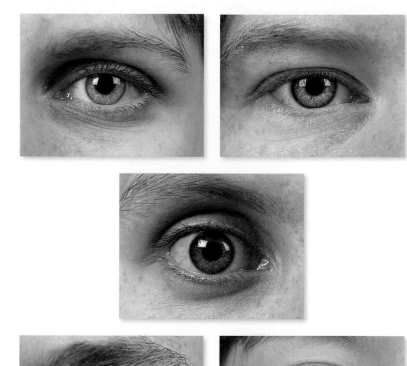
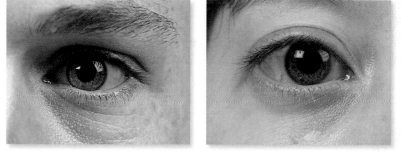

Figure 8 *At least two genes determine human eye color. That's why so many shades of a single color are possible.*

SECTION REVIEW

1. List and describe the parts of a nucleotide.

2. Which bases pair together in a DNA molecule?

3. What shape was suggested by Rosalind Franklin's X-ray images?

4. Explain what is meant by the statement, "DNA unites all organisms."

5. **Doing Calculations** If a sample of DNA were found to contain 20 percent cytosine, what percentage of guanine would be in this sample? Why?

internet connect

SCI*LINKS*
NSTA

TOPIC: DNA, Genes and Traits
GO TO: www.scilinks.org
*sci*LINKS NUMBER: HSTL130, HSTL135

How DNA Works

Scientists knew that the order of the bases formed a code that somehow told each cell what to do. The next step in understanding DNA involved breaking this code.

Terms to Learn

ribosome   mutagen
mutation   pedigree

What You'll Do

◆ Explain the relationship between genes and proteins.
◆ Outline the basic steps in making a protein.
◆ Define *mutation,* and give an example.
◆ Evaluate the information in a pedigree.

Genes and Proteins

Scientists discovered that the bases in DNA read like a book, from one end to the other and in one direction only. The bases **A**, **T**, **G**, and **C** form the alphabet of the code. Groups of three bases code for a specific amino acid. For example, the three bases **CCA** code for the amino acid proline. The bases **AGC** code for the amino acid serine. As you know, proteins are made up of long strings of amino acids. The order of the bases determines the order of amino acids in a protein. Each gene is a set of instructions for making a protein. This is illustrated in **Figure 9**.

NUCLEUS

A copy of a portion of the DNA molecule where a particular gene is located is made and transferred outside of the cell nucleus.

This single strand is a copy of one strand of the original DNA.

Base

Each group of three bases codes for one amino acid.

Figure 9 *A gene is a section of DNA that contains instructions for stringing together amino acids to make a protein.*

Why Proteins? You may be wondering, "What do proteins have to do with who I am or what I look like?" Proteins are found throughout cells. They act as chemical messengers, and they help determine how tall you will grow, what colors you can see, and whether your hair is curly or straight. Human cells contain about 100,000 genes, and each gene spells out sequences of amino acids for specific proteins. Proteins exist in an almost limitless variety. The human body contains about 50,000 different kinds of proteins. Proteins are the reason for the multitude of different shapes, sizes, colors, and textures found in living things, such as antlers, claws, hair, and skin.

The Making of a Protein

As explained in Figure 9, the first step in making a protein is to copy the section of the DNA strand containing a gene. A copy of this section is made with the help of copier enzymes. Messenger molecules take the genetic information from the sections of DNA in the nucleus out into the cytoplasm.

In the cytoplasm, the copy of DNA is fed through a kind of protein assembly line. The "factory" where this assembly line exists is known as a **ribosome.** The copy is fed through the ribosome three bases at a time. Transfer molecules act as translators of the message contained in the copy of DNA. Each transfer molecule picks up a specific amino acid from the cytoplasm. The amino acid is determined by the order of the bases the transfer molecule contains. Like pieces of a puzzle, bases on the transfer molecule then match up with bases on the copy of DNA inside the ribosome. The transfer molecules then drop off their amino acid "suitcases," which are strung together to form a protein. This process is illustrated in **Figure 10.**

✓ Self-Check

1. How many amino acids are present in a protein that requires 3,000 bases in its code?

2. Explain how proteins influence how you look.

(See page 216 to check your answers.)

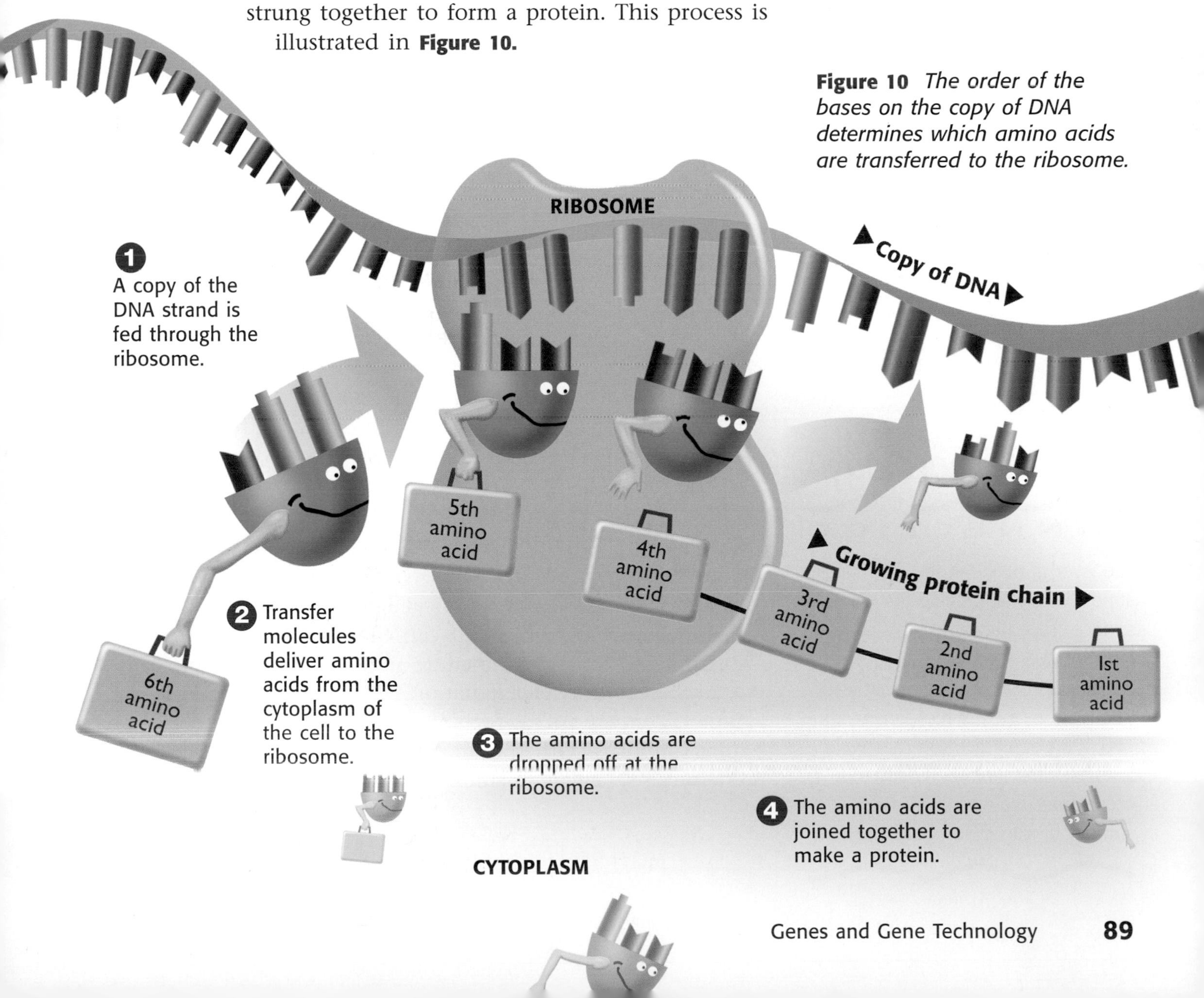

Figure 10 *The order of the bases on the copy of DNA determines which amino acids are transferred to the ribosome.*

RIBOSOME

Copy of DNA

❶ A copy of the DNA strand is fed through the ribosome.

❷ Transfer molecules deliver amino acids from the cytoplasm of the cell to the ribosome.

6th amino acid

5th amino acid

4th amino acid

3rd amino acid

2nd amino acid

1st amino acid

Growing protein chain ▶

❸ The amino acids are dropped off at the ribosome.

❹ The amino acids are joined together to make a protein.

CYTOPLASM

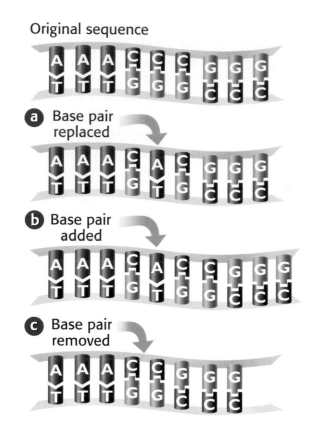

Original sequence

a Base pair replaced

b Base pair added

c Base pair removed

Figure 11 *The original base-pair sequence at the top has been changed to illustrate (a) substitution, (b) insertion, and (c) deletion.*

Meteorology

CONNECTION

The layer of ozone in the Earth's atmosphere helps shield the planet's surface from ultraviolet (UV) radiation. UV radiation can cause mutations in skin cells that can lead to cancer. Each year more than 750,000 people get skin cancer. Scientists fear that damage to the ozone layer may greatly increase the number of skin cancers each year.

Changes in Genes

Imagine that you've been invited to ride on a brand-new roller coaster at the state fair. Just before you climb into the front car, you are informed that some of the metal parts on the coaster have been replaced by parts made of a different substance. Would you still want to ride this roller coaster?

Perhaps a stronger metal was substituted. Or perhaps a material not suited to the job was used. Imagine what would happen if cardboard were used instead of metal!

Mutant Molecules Substitutions like this can occur in DNA. They are known as **mutations.** Mutations occur when there is a change in the order of bases in an organism's DNA. Sometimes a base is left out; this is known as a *deletion.* Or an extra base might be added; this is known as an *insertion.* The most common error occurs when an incorrect base replaces a correct base. This is known as a *substitution.* **Figure 11** illustrates these three types of mutations.

Mistakes Happen Fortunately, repair enzymes are continuously on the job, patrolling the DNA molecule for errors. When an error is found, it is usually repaired. But occasionally the repairs are not completely accurate, and the mistakes become part of the genetic message. There are three possible consequences to changes in DNA: an improvement, no change at all, or a harmful change. If the mutation occurs in the sex cells, it can be passed from one generation to the next.

How Can DNA Become Damaged? In addition to random errors that occur when DNA is copied, damage can be caused by physical and chemical agents known as mutagens. A **mutagen** is anything that can cause a mutation in DNA. Examples of mutagens include high-energy radiation from X rays and ultraviolet radiation. Ultraviolet radiation is the type of energy in sunlight that is responsible for suntans and sunburns. Other mutagens include asbestos and the chemicals in cigarette smoke.

An Example of a Substitution

Consider the DNA sequence containing the three bases **GAA**. **GAA** are the three letters that give the instructions: "Put the amino acid glutamic acid here." If a mistake occurs and the sequence is changed to **GTA**, a completely different message is sent: "Put valine here."

This simple change just described can cause the disease *sickle cell anemia*. Sickle cell anemia is a disease that affects red blood cells. When valine is substituted for glutamic acid in a blood protein, as shown in **Figure 12,** the red blood cells become distorted into a sickle shape.

The sickled cells are not as good as normal red blood cells at carrying oxygen. They are also more likely to get stuck in blood vessels, causing painful and dangerous clots.

Quick Lab

Mutations

The sentence below contains all three-letter words but has experienced a mutation. Can you find the mutation?

THE IGR EDC ATA TET HEB IGB ADR AT

What kind of mutation did you find? Now what does the sentence say?

TRY at HOME

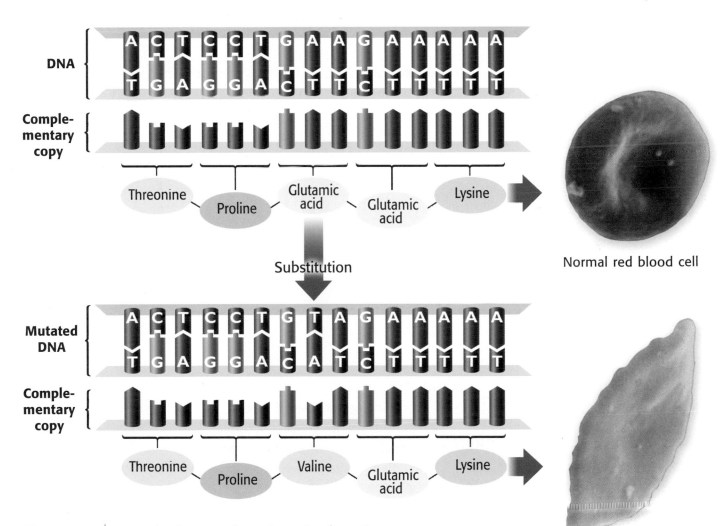

Normal red blood cell

Sickled red blood cell

Figure 12 *The simple change of one base leads to the disease called sickle cell anemia.*

Genetic Counseling

Most hereditary disorders, such as sickle cell anemia, are recessive disorders. This means that the disease occurs only when a child inherits a defective gene from both parents. Some people, called carriers, have only one allele for the disease. Carriers of the gene may pass it along to their children without knowing that they have the mutated gene.

Genetic counseling provides information and counseling to couples who wish to have children but are worried that they might pass a disease to their children. Genetic counselors often make use of a diagram known as a **pedigree,** which is a tool for tracing a trait through generations of a family. By making a pedigree, it is often possible to predict whether a person is a carrier of a hereditary disease. In **Figure 13,** the trait for the disease cystic fibrosis is tracked through four generations. Each generation is numbered with Roman numerals, and each individual is numbered with Arabic numerals.

Figure 13 *Cystic fibrosis is a recessive hereditary disease that affects the respiratory system. A pedigree for cystic fibrosis is shown below.*

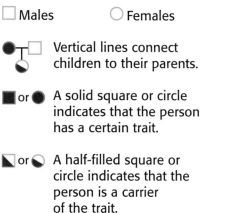

☐ Males   ◯ Females

Vertical lines connect children to their parents.

■ or ● A solid square or circle indicates that the person has a certain trait.

◩ or ◒ A half-filled square or circle indicates that the person is a carrier of the trait.

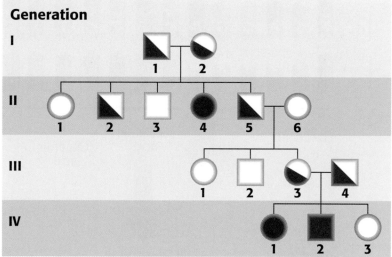

Pedigree and Punnett Squares

The pedigree at right shows the recessive trait of nearsightedness in Jane's family. Jane, her parents, and her brother all have normal vision. Which individuals in the pedigree are nearsighted? What are the possible genotypes of Jane's parents? Jane has two possible genotypes. What are they? Jane is planning to marry a person who has normal vision but carries the trait for nearsightedness. Work two Punnett squares to show the possible genotypes of Jane's future children.

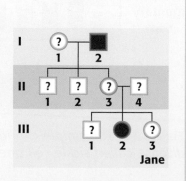

Designer Genes

For thousands of years, humans have been aware of the benefits of selective breeding. In *selective breeding*, organisms with certain desirable characteristics are mated to produce a new breed. You probably have enjoyed the benefits of selective breeding, although you may not have realized it. For example, you may have eaten an egg from a chicken that was bred to produce a large number of eggs. Your pet dog might even be a result of selective breeding. Some kinds of dogs, for example, have a thick coat so that they can retrieve game in icy waters.

Engineering Organisms Scientists now have the ability to produce desired characteristics in some organisms without breeding. They can manipulate individual genes using a technique known as genetic engineering. Like all types of engineering, genetic engineering puts scientific knowledge to practical use. Basically, *genetic engineering* allows scientists to transfer genes from one organism to another. Genetic engineering is already used to manufacture proteins, repair damaged genes, and identify individuals who may carry an allele for a disease. Some other uses are shown in **Figures 14** and **15.**

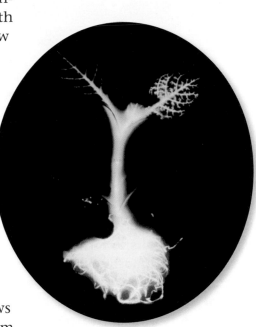

Figure 14 *Scientists added a gene found in fireflies to this tobacco plant. The plant now produces an enzyme that causes the plant to glow.*

Figure 15 *A sheep called Dolly was the first successfully cloned mammal.*

SECTION REVIEW

1. List the three types of mutations. How do they differ?

2. What type of mutation causes sickle cell anemia?

3. How is genetic engineering different from selective breeding?

4. **Applying Concepts** Mutations can occur in sex cells or in body cells. In which cell type might a mutation be passed from generation to generation? Explain.

internetconnect

SC*LINKS*
NSTA

TOPIC: Genetic Engineering
GO TO: www.scilinks.org
sci LINKS NUMBER: HSTL110

Making Models Lab

Base-Pair Basics

You have learned that DNA is shaped like a twisted ladder. The side rails of the ladder are made of sugar molecules and phosphate molecules. The sides are held together by nucleotide bases. These bases join in pairs to form the rungs of the ladder. Each nucleotide base can pair with only one other nucleotide base. Each of these pairs is called a base pair. When DNA replicates, enzymes separate the base pairs. Then each half of the DNA ladder can be used as a template to complete a new half. In this activity, you will make and replicate a model of DNA.

MATERIALS

- white paper or poster board
- colored paper or poster board
- scissors
- large paper bag

Procedure

1 Trace the bases below onto white paper or poster board. Label the pieces A (for adenine), T (for thymine), C (for cytosine), and G (for guanine). Draw the pieces again on colored paper or poster board. Use a different color for each base. Draw the pieces as large as you want, and draw as many of the white pieces and as many of the colored pieces as time will allow.

2 Carefully cut out all of the pieces.

3 Gather all of the colored pieces in the classroom into a large paper bag. Spread all of the white pieces in the classroom onto a large table.

4 Withdraw nine pieces from the bag. Arrange the colored pieces in any order in a straight column so the letters A, T, C, and G are right side up. Be sure to match the sugar and phosphate tabs and notches. Draw this arrangement in your ScienceLog.

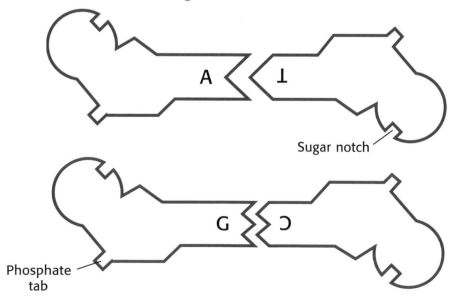

Sugar notch

Phosphate tab

5 Find the matching white nucleotide bases for the nine colored bases. Remember the base-pairing rules you have studied, and matching should be easy!

6 Fit the pieces together, matching all tabs and notches. You now have one piece of DNA containing nine base pairs. Draw your results in your ScienceLog.

7 Now separate the base pairs, keeping the sugar and phosphate notches and tabs together. Draw this arrangement in your ScienceLog.

8 Look at each string of bases you drew in step 7. Along each one, write the letters of the bases that should join the string to complete the base pairs.

9 Find all the bases you need to complete your replication. Find white pieces to match the bases on the left, and find colored pieces to match the bases on the right.

Be sure all the tabs and notches fit and the sides are straight. You have now replicated DNA. Are the two models identical? Draw your results in your ScienceLog.

Analysis

10 Name the correct base-pairing rules.

11 What happens when you attempt to pair thymine with guanine? Do they fit together? Are the sides straight? Do all of the tabs and notches fit? Explain.

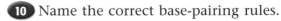

Going Further
Construct a 3-D model of the DNA molecule, showing its twisted-ladder structure. Use your imagination and creativity to select your materials. You may want to use licorice, gum balls, and toothpicks, or pipe cleaners and paper clips! Display your model in your classroom.

Chapter Highlights

Vocabulary

DNA *(p. 80)*

nucleotide *(p. 80)*

adenine *(p. 80)*

thymine *(p. 80)*

guanine *(p. 80)*

cytosine *(p. 80)*

Section Notes

- Proteins are made of long strings of amino acids.

- DNA is made of long strings of nucleotides.

- Chromosomes are made of protein and DNA.

- The DNA molecule looks like a twisted ladder. The rungs of the ladder are made of base pairs, either adenine and thymine, or cytosine and guanine.

- DNA carries genetic information in the order of the nucleotide bases.

- DNA can be copied because one strand of the molecule serves as a template for the other side.

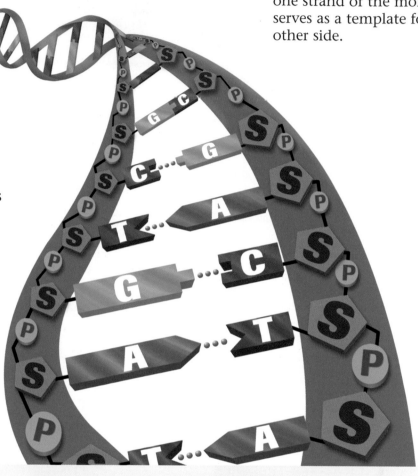

☑ Skills Check

Math Concepts

THE GENETIC CODE The MathBreak on page 83 asks you to calculate the number of bases in all of your genes. If there are about 30,000 bases in each gene and there are 100,000 genes, then multiply to find the answer.

$$30,000 \times 100,000 = 3,000,000,000$$

So, there are about 3 billion bases in all of your genes.

Visual Understanding

COPIES OF DNA Look at Figure 9 on page 88. You can see the nucleus and the pores in its membrane. The copy of DNA emerges through these pores on its way to deliver its coded message to the ribosomes. Why does DNA send a copy out of the nucleus to relay its message? The answer is that DNA is much more protected from factors that might cause a mutation if it stays inside the nucleus. The messenger copy may encounter bad luck, but the master DNA usually stays very safe!

Vocabulary

ribosome *(p. 89)*

mutation *(p. 90)*

mutagen *(p. 90)*

pedigree *(p. 92)*

Section Notes

- A gene is a set of instructions for assembling a protein.

- Each group of three bases in a gene codes for a particular amino acid.

- Genes can become mutated when the order of the bases is changed.

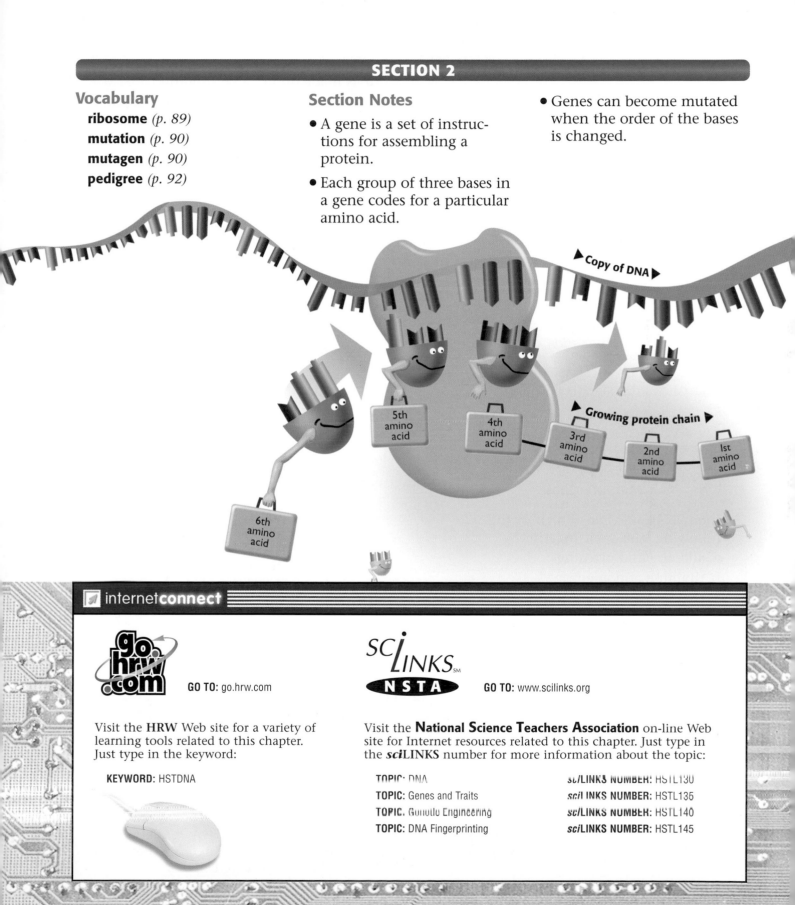

▶ Copy of DNA ▶

▶ Growing protein chain ▶

6th amino acid

5th amino acid

4th amino acid

3rd amino acid

2nd amino acid

1st amino acid

Chapter Review

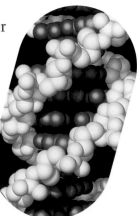

Concept Mapping

14. Use the following terms to create a concept map: bases, adenine, thymine, nucleotides, guanine, DNA, cytosine.

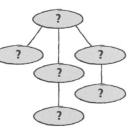

CRITICAL THINKING AND PROBLEM SOLVING

Write one or two sentences to answer the following questions:

15. If neither parent shows signs of having sickle cell anemia, does this fact guarantee that their children will not contract the disease? Explain.

16. How many amino acids does this DNA sequence code for?

    T C A G C C A C C T A T G G A

MATH IN SCIENCE

17. The goal of a project called the Human Genome Project is to discover the location and DNA sequence of all human genes. Scientists estimate that there are 100,000 human genes. In 1998, 38,000 genes had been discovered. How many more genes must the Human Genome Project discover?

18. If scientists find 6,000 genes each year, how many years will it take to finish the project?

19. Of the 38,000 genes discovered, 7,000 have been mapped to their chromosome location. What percentage of the discovered genes have been mapped?

INTERPRETING GRAPHICS

Examine the pedigree for albinism shown below, and then answer the following questions. You may need to use a Punnett square to answer some of these questions. (Albinism is a trait among individuals who produce no pigment in their skin, hair, or eyes.)

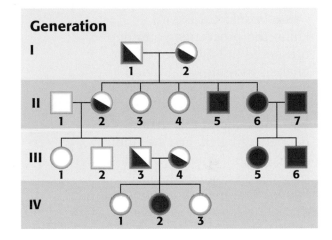

20. How many males are represented on this pedigree? How many females?

21. How many individuals in Generation II had albinism? How many were carriers of the trait?

22. Do you think albinism is a dominant trait or a recessive trait? Explain.

Reading Check-up

Take a minute to review your answers to the Pre-Reading Questions found at the bottom of page 78. Have your answers changed? If necessary, revise your answers based on what you have learned since you began this chapter.

DNA on Trial

The tension in the court-room was so thick you could cut it with a knife. The prosecuting attorney presented the evidence: "DNA analysis indicates that blood found on the defendant's shoes matches the blood of the victim. The odds of this match happening by chance are one in 20 million." The jury members were stunned by these figures. Can there be any doubt that the defendant is guilty?

Next Defendant: DNA

Court battles involving DNA fingerprinting are becoming more and more common. Traditional fingerprinting has been used for more than 100 years, and it has been an extremely important identification tool. Recently, many people have claimed that DNA fingerprinting, also called DNA profiling, will replace the traditional technique. The DNA profiling technique has been used to clear thousands of wrongly accused or convicted individuals. However, the controversy begins when the evidence is used to try to prove a suspect's guilt.

Room for Reasonable Doubt

Critics claim that the DNA fingerprinting process allows too much room for human error.

▲ *This forensic scientist is gathering dead skin cells from an article of clothing in hopes of collecting samples of DNA.*

Handling samples from a crime scene can be tricky—a sample may have been removed from a small area beneath a victim's fingernail or scraped off a dirty sidewalk. Contamination by salt, chemicals, denim, or even a lab person's sneeze can affect the accuracy of the results.

Much of the controversy about DNA fingerprinting surrounds the interpretation of the results. The question becomes, "How likely is it that someone else also has that same DNA profile?" Answers can range from one in three to one in 20 million, depending on the person doing the interpreting, the sample size, and the process used.

Critics also point out that the results may be calculated without regard for certain factors. For instance, individuals belonging to certain ethnic groups are likely to share more characteristics of their DNA with others in their group than with people outside the group.

Beyond a Reasonable Doubt

Those who support DNA evidence point out that the analysis is totally objective because the labs that do the DNA analysis receive samples labeled in code. The data either clear or incriminate a suspect. Moreover, DNA evidence alone is rarely used to convict a person. It is one of several forms of evidence, including motive and access to the crime scene, used to reach a verdict.

Supporters of DNA fingerprinting say that checks and balances in laboratories help prevent human errors. In addition, recent efforts to standardize both evidence gathering and interpretation of samples have further improved results.

What Do You Think?

▶ Should DNA fingerprinting be admitted as evidence in the courtroom? Do some additional research, and decide for yourself.

Science Fiction

"Moby James"

by Patricia A. McKillip

Rob Trask has a problem. It's his older brother, James. Rob is convinced that James is not his real brother. Rob and his family live on a space station, and he just knows that his real brother was sent back to Earth. This person who claims to be James is really either some sort of mutant, irradiated plant life or a mutant pair of dirty sweat socks.

Now Rob has another problem—his class is reading Herman Melville's novel *Moby Dick*. At first, Rob just can't get interested in the story. But as he reads more and more, Rob becomes entranced by the story of Captain Ahab and his quest for revenge against the great white whale Moby Dick. Moby Dick had taken something from Ahab—his leg—and Ahab wants to make the whale pay!

Suddenly Rob realizes that his brother is a great white mutant whale—Moby James. As Rob follows Ahab on his search for Moby Dick, Rob begins to understand what he must do to get his real brother back again. So he watches Moby James, trying to catch James in some mistake that will reveal him for the mutant he is. Once Rob catches the fake James, he will be able to get the real James back again.

To find out if Rob is successful in his quest to find his real brother, read "Moby James" in the *Hull Anthology of Science Fiction*.

The Evolution of Living Things

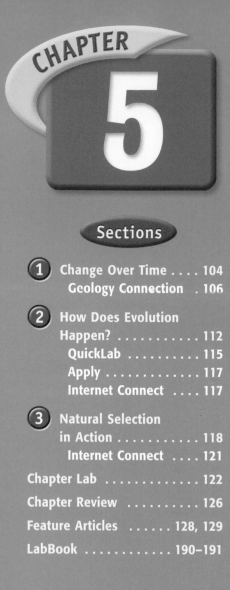

Pre-Reading
Questions

1. What is evolution?
2. What role does the
environment play in the
survival of an organism?

HIDDEN TREASURE

Can you see the fish in this picture? Look closer. The fish
are coral blennies, and they are hard to see against the
background of coral. Their coloring makes them likely to
live longer and to have more offspring than blennies that
don't blend in as well. In this chapter, you will learn how
some characteristics help organisms survive and reproduce.
You will also learn how these characteristics are passed
from parents to their offspring.

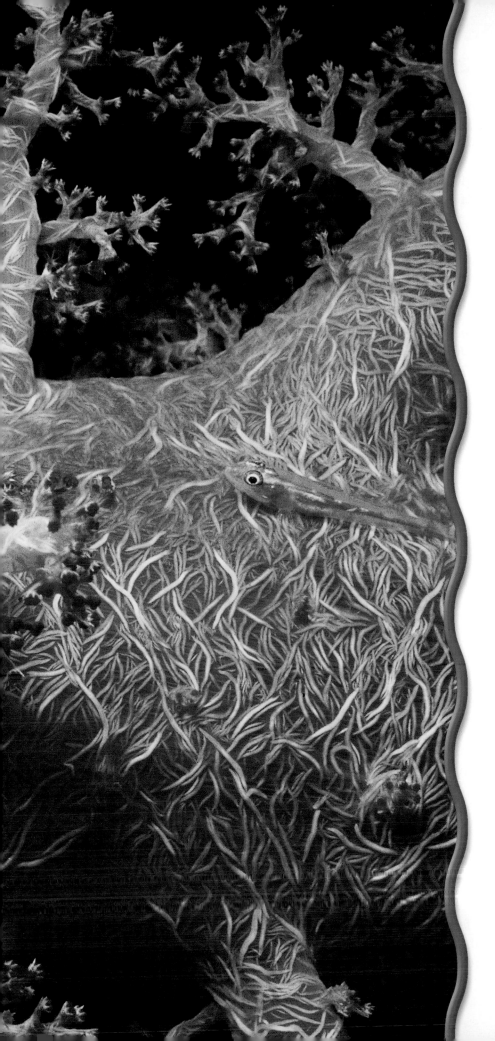

MAKING A FOSSIL

In this activity, you will make a model of a fossil.

Procedure

1. Get a **paper plate,** some **modeling clay,** and a **leaf** or a **shell** from your teacher.

2. Flatten some of the modeling clay on the paper plate. Push the leaf or shell into the clay. Be sure that your leaf or shell has made a mark in the clay. Remove the leaf or shell carefully.

3. Ask your teacher to cover the clay completely with some **plaster of Paris.** Allow the plaster to dry overnight.

4. Carefully remove the paper plate and the clay from the plaster the next day.

Analysis

5. Which of the following do you think would make good fossils—a clam, a jellyfish, a crab, or a mushroom? Explain your answer.

6. Real fossils usually are formed when a dead organism is covered in tiny bits of sand or dirt. Oxygen cannot be present when fossils are forming. What are some limitations of your fossil model?

Terms to Learn

adaptation   fossil record
species   vestigial
evolution   structure
fossil

What You'll Do

- ◆ Explain how fossils provide evidence that organisms have evolved over time.
- ◆ Identify three ways that organisms can be compared to support the theory of evolution.

Change Over Time

If someone asked you to describe a frog, you might say that a frog has long hind legs, eyes that bulge, and a habit of croaking from time to time. Then you might start to think about some of the differences among frogs—differences that set one kind of frog apart from another. Take a look at **Figures 1, 2,** and **3** on this page. These frogs look different from each other, yet they all inhabit a tropical rain forest.

Figure 1 *The red-eyed tree frog hides among a tree's leaves during the day and comes out at night.*

Figure 2 *The smoky jungle frog blends into the forest floor.*

Figure 3 *The strawberry dart-poison frog's bright coloring warns predators that it is poisonous.*

Differences Among Organisms

As you can see, these three frogs have different adaptations that enable them to survive. An **adaptation** is a characteristic that helps an organism survive and reproduce in its environment. Adaptations can include structures and behaviors for finding food, for protection, and for moving from place to place.

Living things that share the same characteristics and adaptations may be members of the same species. A **species** is a group of organisms that can mate with one another to produce fertile offspring. For example, all red-eyed tree frogs are members of the same species and can mate with one another to produce more red-eyed tree frogs.

BRAIN FOOD

Native tribes in Central America rub the poison from the strawberry dart-poison frog on their arrow tips before hunting. The poison helps to paralyze their prey.

Do Species Change over Time? These frogs are just a few of the millions of different species that share the Earth with us. The species on Earth today range from bacteria that lack cell nuclei to multicellular fungi, plants, and animals. Have these same species always existed on Earth?

Earth is a very old planet. Scientists estimate that it is 4.6 billion years old. The planet itself has changed a great deal during that long period of time. Fossil evidence shows that living things have changed as well. Since life first appeared on Earth, a great number of species have died out and have been replaced by newer species. **Figure 4** shows some of the different life-forms that have existed during Earth's history.

What causes species to change? Scientists think that newer species have descended from older species through the process of evolution. **Evolution** is the process by which populations accumulate inherited changes over time. Because of evolution, scientists think that all living things, from daisies to crocodiles to humans, share a common ancestor.

Figure 4 *This spiral diagram represents many changes in life on Earth since the formation of the planet 4.6 billion years ago.*

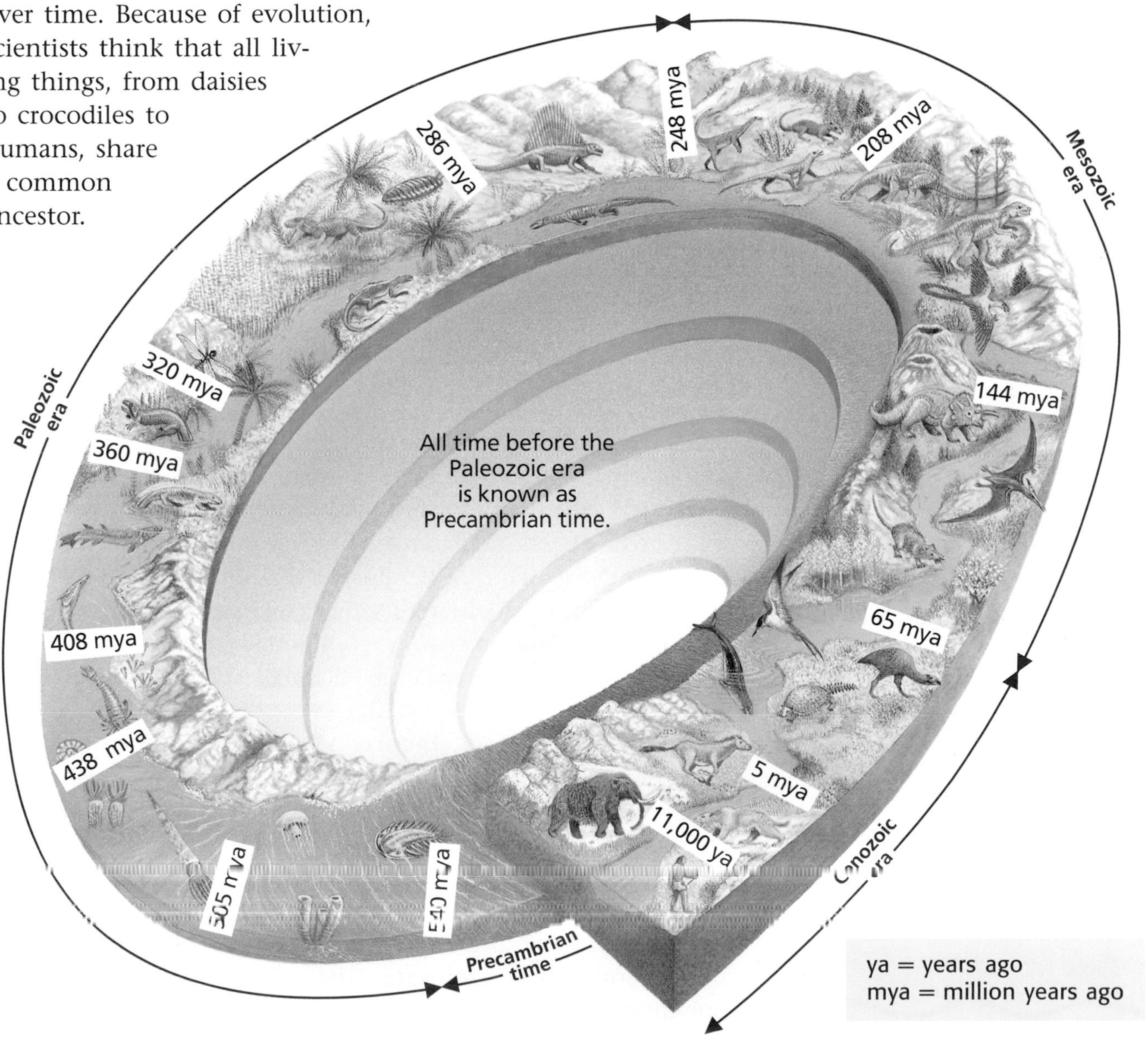

286 mya

248 mya

208 mya

Mesozoic era

320 mya

144 mya

360 mya

Paleozoic era

All time before the Paleozoic era is known as Precambrian time.

408 mya

438 mya

65 mya

505 mya

540 mya

5 mya

11,000 ya

Cenozoic era

Precambrian time

ya = years ago
mya = million years ago

The Evolution of Living Things **105**

Evidence of Evolution: The Fossil Record

Evidence that living things evolve comes from many different sources. This evidence includes fossils as well as comparisons among different groups of organisms.

Fossils The Earth's crust is arranged in layers, with different kinds of rock and soil stacked on top of one another. These layers are formed when sediments, particles of sand, dust, or soil are carried by wind and water and are deposited in an orderly fashion. Older layers are deposited before newer layers and are buried deeper within the Earth. **Fossils,** the solidified remains or imprints of once-living organisms, are found in these layers. Fossils, like those pictured in **Figure 5,** can be of complete organisms, parts of organisms, or just a set of footprints.

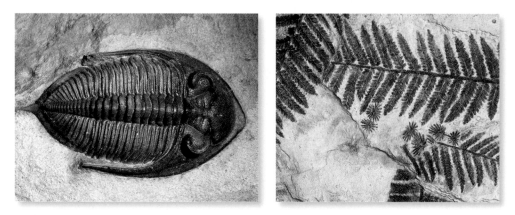

Figure 5 *The fossil on the left is of a trilobite, an ancient aquatic animal. The fossils on the right are of seed ferns.*

Fossils are usually formed when a dead organism is covered by a layer of sediment. Over time, more sediment settles on top of the organism. Minerals in the sediment may seep into the organism, gradually replacing the organism with stone. Or the organism may rot away completely after being covered, leaving a hole in the rock called a *mold.*

Reading the Fossil Record Fossils provide a historical sequence of life known as the **fossil record.** The fossil record supplies evidence about the order in which evolutionary changes have occurred. Fossils found in the upper, or newer, layers of the Earth's crust tend to resemble present-day organisms. This similarity indicates that the fossilized organisms were close relatives of present-day organisms. The deeper in the Earth's crust fossils are found, the less they tend to look like present-day organisms. These fossils are of earlier forms of life that may now be extinct.

Geology

C O N N E C T I O N

Fossils are usually found in layered rock called sedimentary rock. Sedimentary rock usually forms when rock is broken into sediment by wind, water, and other means. The wind and water move the sediment around and deposit it. Over time, layers of sediment pile up. Lower layers are compressed and changed into rock.

Gaps in the Fossil Record If every organism that lived left an imprint behind, the fossil record would resemble a very large evolutionary family tree. **Figure 6** shows a hypothetical fossil record in which all relationships between organisms are clearly mapped.

Although scientists have collected thousands of fossils, gaps remain in the current fossil record, as shown in **Figure 7.** This is because specific conditions are necessary for fossils to form. The organism must be buried in very fine sediment. Also, oxygen—which promotes decay—cannot be present. However, very few places are free of oxygen. Because the conditions needed for fossils to form are rare, fossils are often difficult to find. Nevertheless, scientists have identified some fossils that complete sections of the fossil record.

Vestigial Structures Whales are similar in shape to fish. Yet whales are *mammals*—animals that breathe air, give birth to live young, and produce milk. Although modern whales do not have hind limbs, there are remnants of hind-limb bones inside their bodies, as shown in **Figure 8.** These remnants of once-useful structures are known as **vestigial** (ves TIJ ee uhl) **structures.** Scientists think that over millions of years, whales evolved from doglike land dwellers into sea-dwelling organisms. But scientists have not had the fossil evidence to support their ideas—until now. Read the following case study to learn the story of whale evolution.

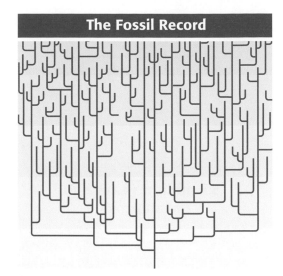

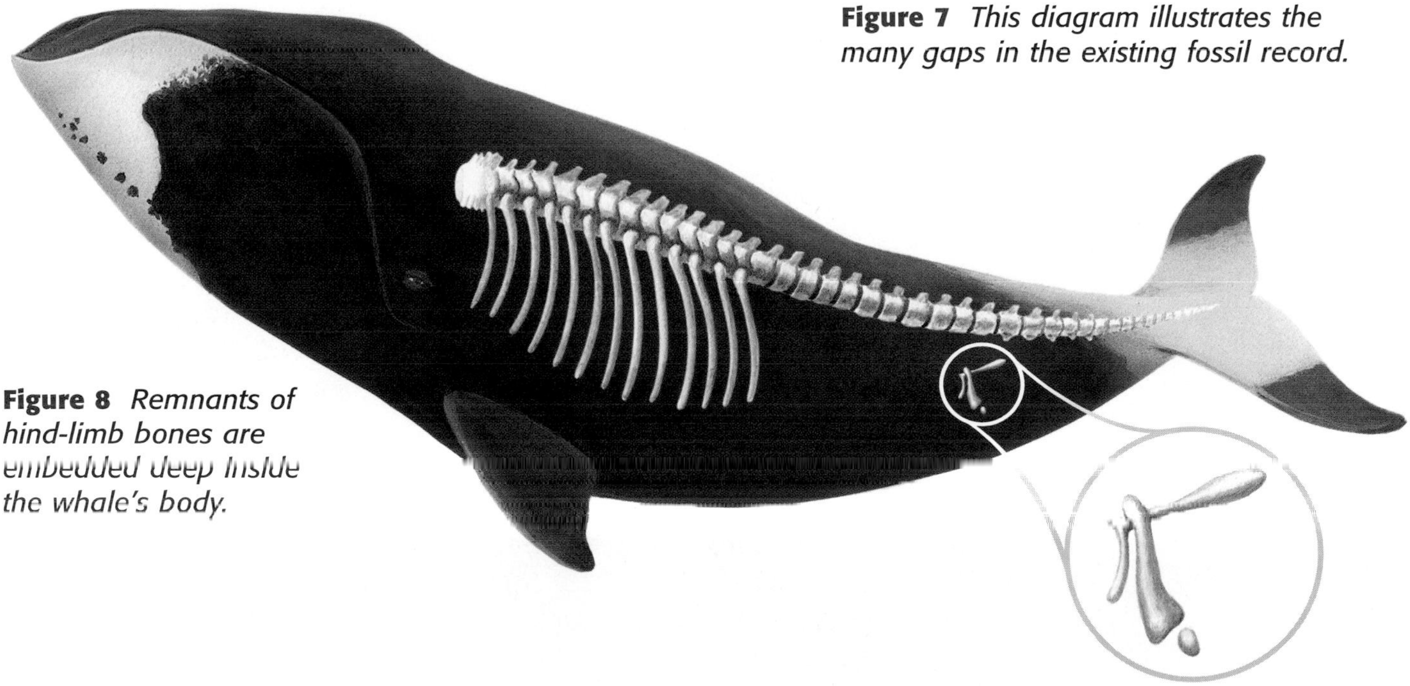

The Fossil Record

Figure 6 *This is the way the fossil record might appear if fossils from every species had been found.*

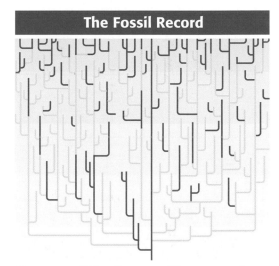

The Fossil Record

Figure 7 *This diagram illustrates the many gaps in the existing fossil record.*

Figure 8 *Remnants of hind-limb bones are embedded deep inside the whale's body.*

Case Study: Evolution of the Whale

Scientists hypothesize that whales evolved from land-dwelling mammals like *Mesonychid* (muh ZOH ni kid), shown below, which returned to the ocean about 55 million years ago. During the 1980s and 1990s, several fossils of whale ancestors were discovered. These discoveries support a theory of whale evolution.

55 million years ago
Mesonychid

Ambulocetus (AM byoo loh SEE tuhs), pictured below, lived in coastal waters. *Ambulocetus* had shorter legs than *Mesonychid*, but it still had feet and toes that could support its weight on land. Although *Ambulocetus* had a tail, scientists think it kicked its legs like an otter in order to swim and used its tail for balance.

50 million years ago
Ambulocetus

46 million years ago
Rodhocetus

Forty-six million years ago, *Rodhocetus* (roh doh SEE tuhs) appeared in the fossil record. This animal more closely resembled modern whales, but it had hind limbs and feet that it retained from its land-dwelling ancestor. Because of its short legs, *Rodhocetus* was restricted to a crocodile-like waddle while on land. Unlike the legs of *Ambulocetus*, these legs were not necessary for swimming. Instead, *Rodhocetus* depended on its massive tail to propel it through the water. While *Ambulocetus* probably pulled itself onto land every night, *Rodhocetus* probably spent most of its time in the water.

Prozeuglodon (pro ZOO gloh dahn), which appeared in the fossil record 6 million years after *Rodhocetus*, was well adapted for life at sea. Although it still had a pair of very small legs, *Prozeuglodon* lived only in the water.

BRAIN FOOD

During their early development, modern whale embryos have four limbs. The rear limbs disappear before birth, and the front limbs develop into flippers.

40 million years ago
Prozeuglodon

Evidence of Evolution: Comparing Organisms

Evidence that life has evolved also comes from comparisons of different groups of organisms. On the following pages, the different kinds of evidence that support the theory of evolution are discussed in greater detail.

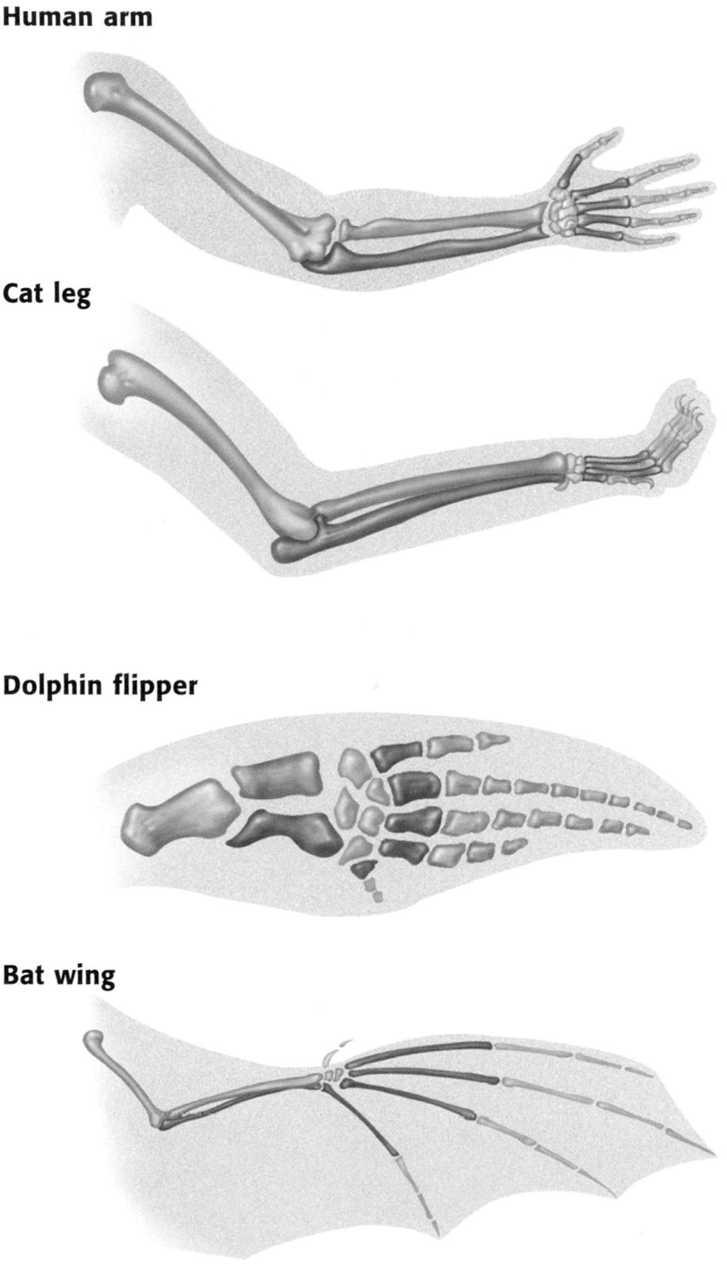

Human arm

Cat leg

Dolphin flipper

Bat wing

Figure 9 *The bones in the front limbs of these animals are similar, even though the limbs are used in different ways. Similar bones are shown in the same color.*

Comparing Skeletal Structures What does your arm have in common with the front leg of a cat, the front flipper of a dolphin, or the wing of a bat? At first glance, you might think that they have little in common. After all, these structures don't look very much alike and are not used in the same way. If you look under the surface, however, the structure and order of the bones in the front limbs of these different animals, shown in **Figure 9,** are actually similar to the structure and order of the bones found in your arm.

The similarities indicate that animals as different as a cat, a dolphin, a bat, and a human are all related by a common ancestor. The evolutionary process has modified these bones over millions of years to perform specific functions.

Comparing DNA from Different Species Scientists hypothesize that if all organisms living today evolved from a common ancestor, they should all have the same kind of genetic material. And in fact they do. From microscopic bacteria to giant polar bears, all organisms share the same genetic material—DNA.

In addition, scientists hypothesize that species appearing to be close relatives should have greater similarities in their DNA than species appearing to be distant relatives. For example, chimpanzees and gorillas appear to be close relatives. Chimpanzees and toucans appear to be distant relatives. The DNA of chimpanzees is, in fact, more similar to the DNA of gorillas than to the DNA of toucans.

Comparing Embryonic Structures Can you tell the difference between a chicken, a rabbit, and a human? It's pretty easy when you compare adults from each species. But what about comparing members of these species before they are born? Look at the left side of **Figure 10,** which depicts the very early embryos of a chicken, a rabbit, and a human.

All the organisms shown in the figure are *vertebrates*, or animals that have a backbone. Early in development, human embryos and the embryos of all other vertebrates are similar. These early similarities are evidence that all vertebrates share a common ancestor. Although the embryos look similar to each other in very early stages, none of them look like their adult forms. Embryo development has evolved over millions of years, causing the embryonic structures to grow into many different species of vertebrates. The changes in the process of embryo development therefore produce animals as different as a chicken and a human.

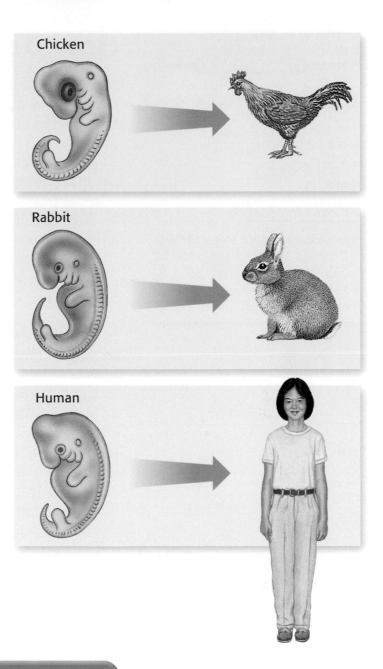

Chicken

Rabbit

Human

Figure 10 *The embryos of different vertebrates are very similar during the earliest stages of development.*

SECTION REVIEW

1. How does the fossil record suggest that species have changed over time?

2. How do the similarities in the fore-limb bones of humans, cats, dolphins, and bats support the theory of evolution?

3. **Interpreting Graphics** The photograph at right shows the layers of sedimentary rock exposed during the construction of a road. Imagine that a species which lived 200 million years ago is found in the layer designated as **b.** Its ancestor, which lived 250 million years ago, would most likely be found in which layer, **a** or **c**? Explain your answer.

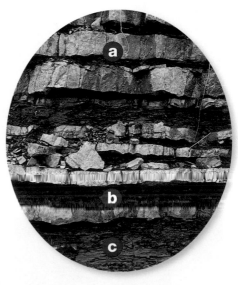

Terms to Learn

trait
selective breeding
natural selection
mutation

What You'll Do

◆ Describe the four steps of Darwin's theory of evolution by natural selection.

◆ Explain how mutations are important to evolution.

How Does Evolution Happen?

The early 1800s was a time of great scientific discovery. Geologists realized that the Earth is much older than anyone had previously thought. Evidence showed that gradual processes had shaped the Earth's surface over millions of years. Fossilized remains of bizarre organisms were found. Fossils of familiar things were also found, but some of them were in unusual places. For example, fish fossils and shells were found on the tops of mountains. The Earth suddenly seemed to be a place where great change was possible. Many people thought that evolution occurs, but no one had been able to determine *how* it happens—until Charles Darwin.

Charles Darwin

In 1831, 21-year-old Charles Darwin, shown in **Figure 11,** had just graduated from college. Like many young people just out of college, Darwin didn't know what he wanted to do with his life. His father wanted him to become a doctor. However, Darwin was sickened by watching surgery. Although he eventually earned a degree in theology, he was *really* interested in the study of plants and animals.

Darwin was able to talk his father into letting him sign on for a 5-year voyage around the world. He served as the naturalist (a scientist who studies nature) on a British naval ship, the HMS *Beagle*. During this voyage, Darwin made observations that later became the foundation for his theory of evolution by natural selection.

Figure 11 *Charles Darwin, shown at far left, sailed around the world on a ship very similar to this one.*

Darwin's Excellent Adventure

As the HMS *Beagle* made its way around the world, Darwin collected thousands of plant and animal samples and kept detailed notes of his observations. The *Beagle*'s journey is charted in **Figure 12.** During the journey, the ship visited the Galápagos Islands, shown below, which are 965 km (600 mi) west of Ecuador, a country in South America.

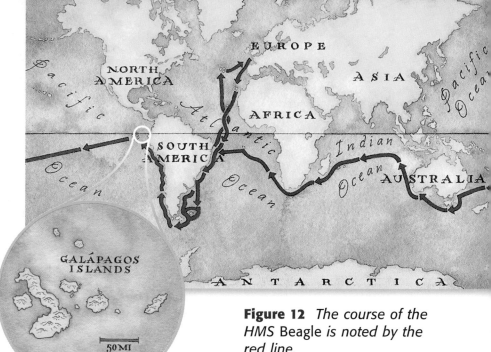

Figure 12 *The course of the HMS* Beagle *is noted by the red line.*

Darwin's Finches

Darwin observed that the animals and plants on the Galápagos Islands were very similar, yet not identical, to the animals and plants on the nearby South American mainland. For example, he noted that the finches living on the Galápagos Islands differed slightly from the finches in Ecuador. The finches on the islands were different not only from the mainland finches but also from each other. As you can see in **Figure 13,** the birds differed from each other mainly in the shape of their beaks and in the food they ate.

Figure 13 *The beaks of these three species of finches are adapted to the different ways the finches obtain food.*

The **large ground finch** has a heavy, strong beak adapted for cracking big, hard seeds. This finch's beak works like a nutcracker.

The **cactus finch** has a tough beak that is good for eating cactus and its nectar. It works like a pair of needle-nosed pliers.

The **warbler finch's** small, pointed beak is adapted for probing into cracks and crevices to obtain small insects. This beak works like a pair of tweezers.

Darwin Does Some Thinking

Darwin's observations raised questions that he couldn't easily answer, such as, "Why are the finches on the islands similar but not identical to the finches on the mainland?" and "Why do the finches from different islands differ from one another?" Darwin thought that perhaps all the finches on the Galápagos Islands descended from finches on the South American mainland. The original population of finches may have been blown from South America to the Galápagos Islands by a storm. Over many generations, the finches that survived may have adapted to various ways of living on the Galápagos Islands.

After Darwin returned to England, he spent many years working on his theory of how evolution happens. During this period, he gathered many ideas from a variety of sources.

Have you ever heard of a bank that has no money, only seeds? Read about it on page 128.

Figure 14 *Dogs are a good example of how selective breeding works. Over the past 12,000 years, dogs have been selectively bred to produce more than 150 different breeds.*

Darwin Learned from Farmers and Animal and Plant Breeders

In Darwin's time, many varieties of farm animals and plants had been selectively produced. Farmers chose certain **traits,** distinguishing qualities such as plump corn kernels, and bred only the individuals that had the desired traits. This procedure is called **selective breeding** because humans, not nature, select which traits will be passed along to the next generation. Selective breeding in dogs, shown in **Figure 14,** has exaggerated certain traits to produce more than 150 different breeds.

In your studies of genetics and heredity, you learned that a great variety of traits exists among individuals in a species. Darwin was impressed that farmers and breeders could direct and shape these traits and make such dramatic changes in animals and plants in just a few short generations. He thought that wild animals and plants could change in a similar way but that the process would take much longer because variations would be due to chance.

Darwin Learned from Geologists

Geologists told Darwin that they had evidence that the Earth was much older than anyone had imagined. He learned from reading *Principles of Geology*, by Charles Lyell, that Earth had been formed by natural processes over a long period of time. Lyell's data were important because Darwin thought that populations of organisms changed very slowly, requiring a lot of time.

Darwin Learned from the Work of Thomas Malthus

In his *Essay on the Principle of Population*, Malthus proposed that humans have the potential to reproduce beyond the capacity of their food supplies. However, he also recognized that death caused by starvation, disease, and war affects the size of human populations. Malthus's thoughts are represented in **Figure 15.**

Darwin realized that other animal species are also capable of producing too many offspring. For these animal species, starvation, disease, and predators affect the size of their populations. Only a limited number survive to reproduce. Thus, there must be something special about the survivors. What traits make them better equipped to survive and reproduce? Darwin reasoned that the offspring of the survivors inherit traits that help them survive in their environment.

Could We Run out of Food?

Malthus thought we could. Do the following activity to better understand Malthus's hypothesis. Get **2 empty egg cartons** and a **bag of rice.** Label one carton "Food supply" and the second carton "Population growth." In the food supply carton, place one grain of rice in the first cup. Increase the amount by one in each subsequent cup. Each grain represents a unit of food. In the population growth carton, place one grain of rice in the first cup, and double the number of grains of rice in each subsequent cup. This rice represents people.

1. How many "people" are there in the last cup?
2. How many units of food are there in the last cup?
3. What conclusion can you draw?

TRY at HOME

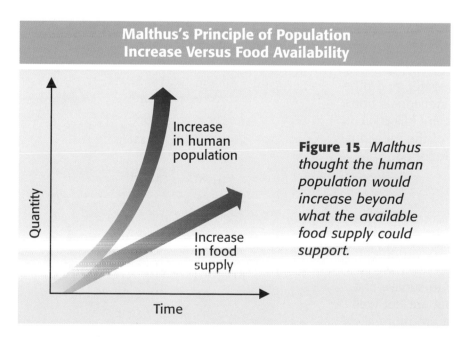

Malthus's Principle of Population Increase Versus Food Availability

Increase in human population

Increase in food supply

Quantity

Time

Figure 15 *Malthus thought the human population would increase beyond what the available food supply could support.*

Natural Selection

In 1858, about 20 years after he returned from his voyage on the HMS *Beagle*, Darwin received a letter from a naturalist named Alfred Russel Wallace. Wallace had independently arrived at the same theory of evolution that Darwin had been working on for so many years. Darwin and Wallace discussed their research and made plans to present their findings at a meeting later in the year. Then, in 1859, Darwin published his own results in his book called *On the Origin of Species by Means of Natural Selection*. Darwin theorized that evolution occurs through a process he called **natural selection.** This process, examined below, is divided into four parts.

Natural Selection in Four Steps

1 **Overproduction** Each species produces more offspring than will survive to maturity.

2 **Genetic Variation** The individuals in a population are slightly different from one another. Each individual has a unique combination of traits, such as size, color, and the ability to find food. Some traits increase the chances that the individual will survive and reproduce. Other traits decrease the chances of survival. These variations are genetic and can be inherited.

3 **Struggle to Survive** A natural environment does not have enough food, water, and other resources to support all the individuals born. In addition, many individuals are killed by other organisms. Only some of the individuals in a population survive to adulthood.

4 **Successful Reproduction** Successful reproduction is the key to natural selection. The individuals that are well adapted to their environment, that is, those that have better traits for living in their environment, are more likely to survive and reproduce. The individuals that are not well adapted to their environment are more likely to die early or produce few offspring.

A Breed All Their Own

Imagine that your grandfather has owned a kennel for more than 50 years but has never sold a dog. He cares for the dogs and keeps them in one large pen. Originally there were six labs, six terriers, and six pointers. There are now 76 dogs, and you are surprised that only a few look like pointers, labs, and terriers. The other dogs look similar to each other but not to any of the specific breeds. Your grandfather says that over the past 50 years each generation has looked less like the generation that preceded it.

By the time you visited the kennel, what may have happened to make most of the dogs look similar to each other but not to any specific original breed? Base your answer on what you've learned about selective breeding in this section.

More Evidence of Evolution

One of the observations on which Darwin based his theory of evolution by natural selection is that parents pass traits to their offspring. But Darwin did not know *how* inheritance occurs or *why* individuals vary within a population.

During the 1930s and 1940s, biologists combined the principles of genetic inheritance with Darwin's theory of evolution by natural selection. This combination of principles explained that the variations Darwin observed within a species are caused by **mutation,** or changes in a gene.

Since Darwin's time, new evidence has been collected from many fields of science. Although scientists recognize that other mechanisms may also play a part in the evolution of a species, the theory of evolution by natural selection provides the most thorough explanation for the diversity of life on Earth.

SECTION REVIEW

1. Why are some animals more likely to survive to adulthood than other animals?

2. **Summarizing Data** What did Darwin think happened to the first small population of finches that reached the Galápagos Islands from South America?

3. **Doing Calculations** A female cockroach can produce 80 offspring at a time. If half of the offspring were female, and each female produced 80 offspring, how many cockroaches would there be in 3 generations?

internet**connect**

SC*L*INKS
NSTA

TOPIC: The Galápagos Islands, Darwin and Natural Selection
GO TO: www.scilinks.org
sciLINKS NUMBER: HSTL165, HSTL170

Terms to Learn

generation time
speciation

What You'll Do

◆ Give two examples of natural selection in action.
◆ Outline the process of speciation.

Natural Selection in Action

The theory of natural selection explains how a population changes over many generations in response to its environment. In fact, members of a population tend to be well adapted to their environment because natural selection is continuously taking place.

Insecticide Resistance To keep crops safe from certain insects, some farmers use a wide variety of chemical insecticides. However, some insecticides that worked well in the past are no longer as effective. In the 50 years that insecticides have been widely used, more than 500 species of insects have developed resistance to certain insecticides.

Insects quickly develop resistance to insecticides because they produce many offspring and usually have short generation times. A **generation time** is the period between the birth of one generation and the birth of the next generation. Look at **Figure 16** to see how a common household pest, the cockroach, has adapted to become resistant to certain insecticides.

 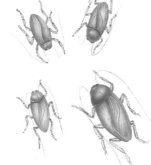 

1 An insecticide will kill most insects, but a few may survive. These survivors have genes that make them resistant to the insecticide.

2 The survivors then reproduce, passing the insecticide-resistance genes to their offspring.

3 In time, the replacement population of insects is made up mostly of individuals that have the insecticide-resistance genes.

4 When the same kind of insecticide is used on the insects, only a few are killed because most of them are resistant to that insecticide.

Figure 16 *Variety in a population's characteristics helps ensure that some individuals will be able to survive a change in the environment.*

We're off to hunt the marshmallows! Look on page 190 to find out why.

Adaptation to Pollution   There are two color variations among European peppered moths, as shown in **Figure 17.** Before 1850, the dark peppered moth was considered rare. The pale peppered moth was much more common. After the 1850s, however, dark peppered moths became more abundant in heavily industrialized areas.

Figure 17 *Against a dark tree trunk (above), the pale peppered moth stands out. Against a light tree trunk (right), the dark peppered moth stands out.*

What caused this change in the peppered moth population? Several species of birds eat peppered moths that rest on tree trunks. Before the 1850s, the trees had a gray appearance, and pale peppered moths blended into their surroundings. Dark peppered moths were easier for the birds to see and were eaten more frequently. After the 1850s, soot and smoke from newly developing industrial areas blackened nearby trees. The dark peppered moths became less visible on the dark tree trunks. The pale peppered moths stood out against the dark background and became easy prey for the birds. More dark moths survived and produced more dark offspring. Thus, the population changed from mostly light-colored moths to mostly dark colored moths.

> ✔ **Self-Check**
>
> If the air pollution in Europe were cleaned up, what do you think would happen to the population of light-colored peppered moths? *(See page 216 to check your answers.)*

Formation of New Species

The process of natural selection can explain how a species can evolve into a new species. A portion of a species' population can become separated from the original population. Over time, the two populations can become so different that they can no longer interbreed. This process is called **speciation.** One way that speciation can occur is shown in the following three steps:

1. Separation The process of speciation often begins when a portion of a population becomes isolated. **Figure 18** shows some of the ways this can happen. A newly formed canyon, mountain range, and lake are a few of the ways that populations can be divided.

Figure 18 *Populations can become separated in a variety of ways.*

2. Adaptation If a population has been divided by one of the changes illustrated above, the environment may also change. This is where natural selection comes in. As the environment changes, so may the population that lives there. Over many generations, the separated groups may adapt to better fit their environment, as shown in **Figure 19.** If the environmental conditions are different for each of the groups, the adaptations in the groups may also be different.

Figure 19 *When a single population becomes divided, the groups may evolve separately and may form separate species.*

3. Division Over many hundreds, thousands, or even millions of generations, the two groups of a population may become so different that they can no longer interbreed, even if the geographical barrier is removed. At this point, the two groups are no longer the same species. Scientists think that the finches on the Galápagos Islands evolved by these three basic steps. **Figure 20** illustrates how this might have happened.

Figure 20 *The finches on the Galápagos Islands might have evolved into different species by the process depicted below.*

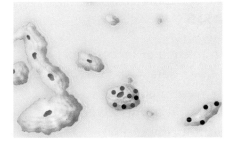

1 Some finches left the mainland and reached one of the islands (separation).

2 The finches reproduced and adapted to the environment (adaptation).

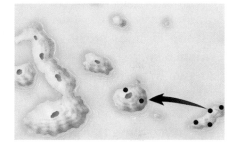

3 Some finches flew to a second island (separation).

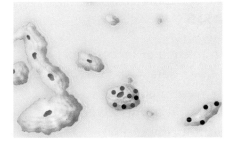

4 The finches reproduced and adapted to the different environment (adaptation).

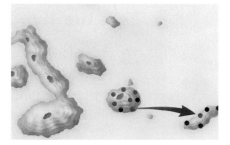

5 Some finches flew back to the first island but could no longer interbreed with the finches there (division).

6 This process may have occurred over and over again as the finches flew to the other islands.

SECTION REVIEW

1. Why did the number of dark peppered moths increase after the 1850s?

2. What factor indicates that a population has evolved into two separate species?

3. **Applying Concepts** Most cactuses have spines, which are leaves modified to protect the plant. The spines cover a juicy stem that stores water. Explain how cactus leaves and stems might have changed through the process of natural selection.

internet connect

*SCi*LINKS
NSTA

TOPIC: Species and Adaptation
GO TO: www.scilinks.org
*sci*LINKS NUMBER: HSTL155

Design Your Own Lab

USING SCIENTIFIC METHODS

Mystery Footprints

Sometimes scientists find evidence of past life in clues preserved in rocks. Evidence such as preserved footprints can give important information about an organism. Imagine that your class has been asked by a group of scientists to help study some footprints. These footprints were found in rocks just outside of town.

MATERIALS

- large box of damp sand, at least 1 m² (large enough to hold three or four footprints)
- metric ruler or meterstick

Form a Hypothesis

1 Your teacher will give you some mystery footprints in sand. Study the footprints. Brainstorm ideas about what you might learn about the people who walked on this patch of sand. As a class, formulate as many testable hypotheses as possible about the people who left the footprints.

2 Form groups of three people, and choose one hypothesis for your group to investigate.

Test the Hypothesis

3 Use a computer or graph paper to construct a table for organizing your data. If your hypothesis is that the footprints were made by two adult males who were walking in a hurry, your table might look like the one below.

Mystery Footprints		
	Footprint set 1	**Footprint set 2**
Length		
Width		
Depth of toe		
Depth of heel		
Length of stride		

DO NOT WRITE IN BOOK

4 You may first want to look at your own footprints to help you draw conclusions about the mystery footprints. For example, with the help of your group, use a meter-stick to measure your stride when you are running. How long is it when you are walking? Does your weight affect the depth of the footprint? What part of your foot touches the ground first when you are running? What part touches the ground first when you are walking? When you are running, which part of your footprint is deeper? Make a list of the kind of footprint each activity makes. For example, you might write, "When I am running, my footprints are deep near the toe. These footprints are 110 cm apart."

Analyze the Results

5 Compare the data from your footprints with the data from the mystery footprints. How are the footprints alike? How are they different?

6 Were the footprints made by one person or more than one person? Explain your interpretation.

7 Can you tell if the footprints were made by men, women, children, or a combination? Explain your interpretation.

Draw Conclusions

8 Based on your analysis of your own footprints, would you conclude that the people who made the mystery footprints were standing still, walking, or running?

9 Do your data support your hypothesis? Explain.

10 How could you improve your experiment?

Communicate Results

11 Outline your group's conclusions in a letter addressed to the scientists who asked for your help. Begin by stating your hypothesis. Then tell the scientists how you gathered information from the study of your own footprints. Include the comparisons you made between your footprints and the mystery footprints. Before stating your conclusions, offer some suggestions about how you could improve your investigation.

12 Make a poster or chart, or use a computer if one is available, to present your findings to the class.

Chapter Highlights

SECTION 1

Vocabulary

adaptation *(p. 104)*

species *(p. 104)*

evolution *(p. 105)*

fossil *(p. 106)*

fossil record *(p. 106)*

vestigial structure *(p. 107)*

Section Notes

- Evolution is the process by which populations change over time. Those changes are inherited.

- Evidence of a common ancestor for all organisms is provided by the following: the fossil record, comparisons of skeletal structures found in related species, comparisons of the embryos of distantly related vertebrates, and the presence of DNA in all living organisms.

- Species that are closely related have DNA that is more alike than DNA of distantly related species.

SECTION 2

Vocabulary

trait *(p. 114)*

selective breeding *(p. 114)*

natural selection *(p. 116)*

mutation *(p. 117)*

Section Notes

- Charles Darwin developed an explanation for evolution after years of studying the organisms he observed on the voyage of the *Beagle*.

- Darwin's study was influenced by the concepts of selective breeding, the age of the Earth, and the idea that some organisms are better equipped to survive than others.

☑ Skills Check

Math Concepts

MALTHUS'S PRINCIPLE The graph on page 115 shows two types of growth. The straight line represents an increase in which the same number is added to the previous number, as in 3, 4, 5, 6, . . . , where 1 is added to each number.

The curved line represents an increase in which each number is multiplied by the same factor, as in 2, 4, 8, 16, . . . , where each number is multiplied by 2. As you can see on the graph, the curved line increases at a much faster rate than the straight line.

Visual Understanding

SKELETAL STRUCTURE Figure 9 on page 110 illustrates skeletal evidence for evolution. By looking at the same-colored bones, you can see how the early mammalian skeletal structure has evolved in certain species to help with specialized tasks such as flying and swimming.

- Darwin explained that evolution occurs through natural selection. Natural selection can be divided into four parts:

  (1) Each species produces more offspring than will survive to reproduce.

  (2) Individuals within a population are slightly different from one another.

  (3) Individuals within a population compete with one another for limited resources.

  (4) Individuals that are better equipped to live in an environment are more likely to survive and reproduce.

- Evolution is explained today by combining the principles of natural selection with the principles of genetic inheritance.

Labs

Survival of the Chocolates
(p. 191)

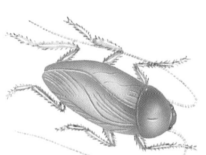

Vocabulary

generation time *(p. 118)*

speciation *(p. 120)*

Section Notes

- Natural selection allows a population to adapt to changes in environmental conditions.

- Evidence of natural selection can be seen by studying generations of organisms that have developed resistance to an insecticide or antibiotic.

- Natural selection also explains how one species may evolve into another through the process of speciation.

Labs

Out-of-Sight Marshmallows
(p. 190)

---

internet**connect**

GO TO: go.hrw.com

Visit the **HRW** Web site for a variety of learning tools related to this chapter. Just type in the keyword:

KEYWORD: HSTEVO

GO TO: www.scilinks.org

Visit the **National Science Teachers Association** on-line Web site for Internet resources related to this chapter. Just type in the *sci*LINKS number for more information about the topic:

TOPIC: Species and Adaptation — *sci*LINKS NUMBER: HSTL155

TOPIC: The Fossil Record — *sci*LINKS NUMBER: HSTL160

TOPIC: The Galápagos Islands — *sci*LINKS NUMBER: HSTL165

TOPIC: Darwin and Natural Selection — *sci*LINKS NUMBER: HSTL170

Chapter Review

UNDERSTANDING CONCEPTS

Multiple Choice

7. Although Darwin did not realize it, the variations he observed among the individuals of a population of finches were caused by
   a. genetic resistance.   c. fossils.
   b. mutations.   d. selective breeding.

8. The theory of evolution combines the principles of
   a. natural selection and artificial selection.
   b. natural selection and genetic resistance.
   c. selective breeding and genetic inheritance.
   d. natural selection and genetic inheritance.

9. Fossils are commonly found in
   a. sedimentary rock.
   b. igneous rock.
   c. granite.
   d. loose sand or granite.

10. A human's arm, a cat's front leg, a dolphin's front flipper, and a bat's wing
   a. have similar kinds of bones.
   b. are used in similar ways.
   c. share many similarities with insect wings and jellyfish tentacles.
   d. have nothing in common.

11. The fact that all organisms have DNA as their genetic material is evidence that
   a. natural selection occurred.
   b. all organisms descended from a common ancestor.
   c. selective breeding takes place every day.
   d. genetic resistance rarely occurs.

12. What body part of the Galápagos finches appears to have been most modified by natural selection?
   a. their webbed feet
   b. their beaks
   c. the bone structure of their wings
   d. the color of their eyes

Short Answer

13. Describe the four parts of Darwin's theory of evolution by natural selection.

14. How do the fossils of whales provide evidence that whales have evolved over millions of years?

15. What might account for gaps in the fossil record?

Concept Mapping

16. Use the following terms to create a concept map: struggle to survive, genetic variation, Darwin, overpopulation, natural selection, successful reproduction.

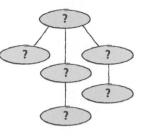

CRITICAL THINKING AND PROBLEM SOLVING

Write one or two sentences to answer the following questions:

17. In selective breeding, humans influence the course of evolution. What determines the course of evolution in natural selection?

18. Many forms of bacteria evolve resistance to antibiotics, drugs that kill bacteria. Based on what you know about how insects evolve to resist insecticides, suggest how bacteria might evolve to resist antibiotics.

19. The two species of squirrels shown below live on opposite sides of the Grand Canyon, in Arizona. The two squirrels look very similar, but they cannot interbreed to produce fertile offspring. Explain how a single species of squirrel might have become two species.

INTERPRETING GRAPHICS

Use the following graphs to answer questions 20, 21, and 22:

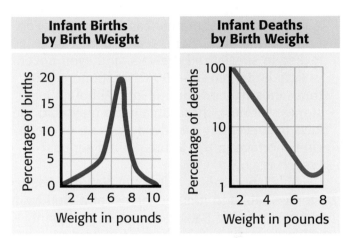

20. What is the most common birth weight?

21. What birth weight has the highest survival rate?

22. How do the principles of natural selection help explain why there are more deaths among babies with low birth weights than among babies of average birth weights?

Reading Check-up

Take a minute to review your answers to the Pre-Reading Questions found at the bottom of page 102. Have your answers changed? If necessary, revise your answers based on what you have learned since you began this chapter.

EYE ON THE ENVIRONMENT

Saving at the Seed Bank

A very unusual laboratory can be found in Fort Collins, Colorado. There, sealed in test tubes, locked in specialized drawers, and even frozen in liquid nitrogen at −196°C, are hundreds of thousands of seeds and plants. Although in storage for now, these organisms may hold the keys to preventing worldwide famine or medicine shortage in the future. Sound serious? Well, it is.

This laboratory is called the National Seed Storage Lab, and it is the largest of a worldwide network of seed banks. The seeds and plant cuttings stored within these seed banks represent almost every plant grown for food, clothing, and medicine.

▲ *To protect tomorrow's wheat fields, we need the genetic diversity of crops stored in seed banks.*

No More Pizza!

Imagine heading out for pizza only to discover a sign on the door that says, "Closed today due to flour shortage." Flour shortage? How can that be? What about burritos? When you get to the burrito stand, the sign is the same, "Closed due to flour shortage." Think this sounds far-fetched? Well, it really isn't.

If wheat crops around the world are ruined by a disease, we could have a flour shortage. And the best way to fight such devastation, and even prevent it, is by breeding new varieties. Through the process of selective breeding, many plants have been improved to increase their yields and their resistance to disease and insects. But to breed new crops, plant breeders need lots of different genetic material. Where do they get this genetic material? At the seed bank, of course!

Why We'll Never Know

But what if some plants never make it to the seed bank? We have the new and improved varieties, so why does it matter if we keep the old ones? It matters because these lost varieties often have important traits, like resistance to disease and drought, that might come in handy in the future. Once a variety of plant is improved, demand for the old variety can dwindle to nothing. If an old variety is no longer grown, it may become extinct if it is not placed in the seed bank. In fact, many varieties of plants have already been lost forever. We'll never know if one of those lost varieties was capable of resisting a severe drought.

It's All in the Bank

Fortunately, seed banks have collected seeds and plants for more than a century. They preserve the genetic diversity of crop plants while allowing farmers to grow the most productive varieties in their fields. As long as there are seed banks across the globe, it is unlikely that there will be a flour shortage. Let's go out for pizza!

Going Further

▶ Many seed banks are in jeopardy. Why? Find out by doing research to learn more about the complicated and costly process of operating a seed bank.

Science Fiction

Once up...
in a faraba...
land
there
lived a
space

who had a
...tic ship
...of silver
...great
haircut that
...was the gala...

"The Anatomy Lesson"

by Scott Sanders

You know what it's like. You have an important test tomorrow, or your semester project is due, and you've forgotten your book or just run out of clay. Suddenly things seem very serious.

That's the situation a certain medical student faces in Scott Sanders's "The Anatomy Lesson." The student needs to learn the bones of the human body for an anatomy exam the next day. After arriving at the anatomy library to check out a skeleton-in-a-box, the student finds that all the skeletons have been checked out. Without bones to assemble as practice, the student knows passing the exam will be impossible. So the student asks the librarian to look again. Sure enough, the librarian finds one last box. And that's when things start to get strange.

There are too many bones. They are the wrong shape. They don't fit together just right. Somebody must be playing a joke! The bones fit together, sort of—but not in any way that helps the medical student get ready for the exam. When the student complains to the librarian, the librarian isn't very sympathetic. It seems she has other things on her mind. Now the student is really worried.

Find out what this medical student and a quiet librarian have in common. And find out how they will never be the same after "The Anatomy Lesson." You can read it in the *Holt Anthology of Science Fiction*.

The History of Life on Earth

Pre-Reading
Questions

1. How can you tell how old
   a fossil is?

2. How long did dinosaurs
   roam the Earth?

MAMMOTH DISCOVERY

What is 23,000 years old, nine feet tall, and nicknamed
"Zharkov"? Give up? It is the partial remains of a woolly
mammoth—including huge tusks, bones, skin, and hair—
dug up from the frozen ground in Siberia in late 1999. Its
gigantic tusks appear in the photo. Scientists have determined that woolly mammoths roamed the frozen arctic
until about 3,000 years ago. In this chapter, you will learn
how scientists determine the age of fossils and about the
history of life on Earth.

EARTH'S TIMELINE

To help you understand Earth's history, make a timeline.

Procedure

1. Mark off 10 cm sections on a **strip of adding machine paper** that is 46 cm long. Divide each 10 cm section into ten 1 cm sections. (Each 1 cm represents 100 million years.)

2. Label each 10 cm section in order from top to bottom as follows: 1 bya (billion years ago), 2 bya, 3 bya, and 4 bya. The timeline begins at 4.6 bya.

3. At the appropriate place on your timeline, mark these important events of Earth's history:

   a. Earth began about 4.6 billion years ago.

   b. The earliest cells appeared about 3.5 billion years ago.

   c. Dinosaurs first appeared on Earth about 215 million years ago. Then about 65 million years ago, they became extinct.

   d. About 100,000 years ago, humans with modern features appeared.

4. Continue to mark events on your timeline as you learn about them in this chapter.

Analysis

5. Compare the length of time dinosaurs roamed the Earth with the length of time humans have existed.

The History of Life on Earth **131**

Terms to Learn

fossil   extinct
relative dating   plate tectonics
absolute dating
geologic time
  scale

What You'll Do

◆ Explain how fossils are dated.

◆ Describe the geologic time scale and the information it provides scientists.

◆ Describe the possible causes of mass extinctions.

◆ Explain the theory of plate tectonics.

Evidence of the Past

Some scientists look for clues to help them reconstruct what happened in the past. These scientists are called paleontologists. *Paleontologists,* like the man in **Figure 1,** use fossils to reconstruct the history of life millions of years before humans existed. Fossils show us that life on Earth has changed a great deal. They also provide us with clues to how those changes occurred.

Figure 1 *In 1995, Paul Sereno found this dinosaur fossil in the Sahara Desert. The dinosaur may have been the largest land predator that has ever existed!*

Fossils

Fossils are traces or imprints of living things—such as animals, plants, bacteria, and fungi—that are preserved in rock. Fossils are usually formed when a dead organism is covered by a layer of sediment. These sediments may later be pressed together to form sedimentary rock. **Figure 2** shows one way fossils can be formed in this type of rock.

Figure 2 *The pictures below show one way fossils can form.*

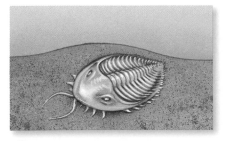

❶ An organism dies and becomes buried in sediment.

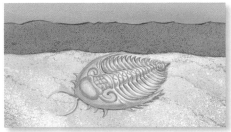

❷ The organism gradually dissolves, leaving a hollow impression, or mold, in the sediment.

❸ Over time, the mold fills with sediment that forms a cast of the original organism.

The Age of Fossils

When paleontologists find a fossil, how do they determine its age? They can use one of two methods: relative dating or absolute dating.

Relative Dating A cross section of sedimentary rock shows many layers. The oldest layers are on the bottom, and the newer layers are on the top. If fossils are found in the rock, a scientist could start at the bottom and work upward to examine a sequence of fossils in the order that the organisms existed. This method of ordering fossils to estimate their age is known as **relative dating.**

Absolute Dating How can scientists determine the age of a fossil? The answer lies in particles called *atoms* that make up all matter. Atoms, in turn, are made of smaller particles. These particles are held together by strong forces. If there isn't enough force to hold them together, the atom is said to be unstable. Unstable atoms decay by releasing either energy or particles or both. That way, the atom becomes stable, but it also becomes a different kind of atom.

Each kind of unstable atom decays at its own rate. As shown in **Figure 3,** the time it takes for half of the unstable atoms in a sample to decay is its *half-life*. Half-lives range from fractions of a second to billions of years. By measuring the ratio of unstable atoms to stable atoms, scientists can determine the approximate age of a rock sample and the fossil it contains. This method is called **absolute dating.**

Figure 3 *Sometimes volcanic rock will cover a dead organism. By finding the age of the rock, scientists can get a good idea about the age of the fossil.*

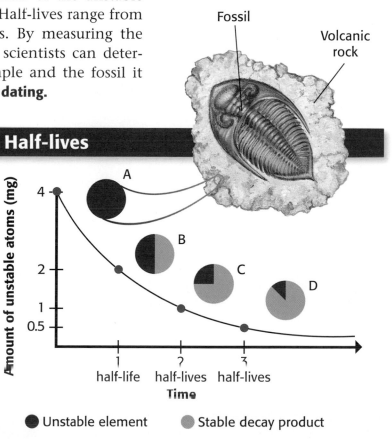

Half-lives

A. The unstable atoms in the sample of volcanic rock have a half-life of 1.3 billion years. The sample contained 4 mg of unstable atoms when the rock formed.

B. After 1.3 billion years, or one half-life, only 2 mg of the unstable atoms will be left in the rock, and 2 mg of its stable decay product will have formed.

C. After another 1.3 billion years (two half-lives), there will only be 1 mg of the unstable atoms and 3 mg of the decay atoms.

D. How many milligrams of unstable atoms are left after 3 half-lives?

● Unstable element   ● Stable decay product

The Geologic Time Scale

When you consider important events that have happened during your lifetime, you usually recall each event in terms of the day, month, or year in which it occurred. These divisions of time make it easier to recall when you were born, when you kicked the winning soccer goal, or when you started the fifth grade. Because the span of time is so great from the formation of the Earth to now, scientists also use a type of calendar to divide the Earth's long history into very long units of time.

The calendar scientists use to outline the history of life on Earth is called the **geologic time scale,** shown in the table at left. After a fossil is dated using relative and absolute dating techniques, a paleontologist can place the fossil in chronological order with other fossils. This forms a picture of the past that shows how organisms have changed over time.

Divisions in the Geologic Time Scale Paleontologists have divided the time scale into large blocks of time called *eras.* Each era has been subdivided into smaller blocks of time as paleontologists have continued to find more fossil information.

Eras are characterized by the type of animal that dominated the Earth at the time. For instance, the Mesozoic era—dominated by dinosaurs and other reptiles—is referred to as the Age of Reptiles. The end of each era is marked by the extinction of certain organisms. The next section analyzes the different eras of the geologic time scale in greater detail.

The Geologic Time Scale

Era	Period	MYA	Representative Organisms
CENOZOIC	Quaternary	1.8	
CENOZOIC	Tertiary	65	
MESOZOIC	Cretaceous	144	
MESOZOIC	Jurassic	206	
MESOZOIC	Triassic	248	
PALEOZOIC	Permian	290	
PALEOZOIC	Carboniferous	354	
PALEOZOIC	Devonian	417	
PALEOZOIC	Silurian	443	
PALEOZOIC	Ordovician	490	
PALEOZOIC	Cambrian	540	
PRECAMBRIAN		4,600	

Figure 4 *A meteorite hit Earth about 65 million years ago, perhaps leading to major climatic changes.*

Mass Extinctions   Some of the important divisions in the geologic time scale are marked by events that caused many animal and plant species to die out completely, or become **extinct.** Once a species is extinct, it does not reappear. There have been several periods in the Earth's history when a large number of species died out at the same time. These periods of large-scale extinction are called *mass extinctions.*

Scientists are not sure what causes mass extinctions. Mass extinctions may result from major changes in the Earth's climate or atmosphere. Some scientists think the mass extinction of the dinosaurs occurred when a meteorite collided with Earth and caused catastrophic climate changes. An artist's depiction of this event is shown in **Figure 4.** Changes in the climate may have also been caused by the movement of continents. Read on to find out how this is possible.

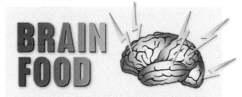

Scientists estimate that only a small fraction ($1/20$ of 1 percent) of all the species that have ever existed on Earth are living today. All the other species existed in the past and then became extinct.

✔ Self-Check

Ten grams of an unstable atom were present in a rock when the rock solidified. In grams, how much of these atoms will be present after one half-life? What amount of the unstable atoms will be present after two half-lives? *(See page 216 to check your answers.)*

The Changing Earth

Do you know that dinosaur fossils have been found on Antarctica? Antarctica, now frozen, must have once had a warm climate to support these large reptiles. How could this be? Antarctica and the other continents have not always been in their present position. Antarctica was once located nearer the equator!

Pangaea If you take a look at a map of the world, you might notice that the shapes of the continents seem to resemble pieces of a puzzle. If you could move the pieces around, you might find that some of them almost fit together. A similar thought occurred to the German scientist Alfred Wegener in the early 1900s. He proposed that long ago the continents were part of one great landmass surrounded by a single gigantic ocean. Wegener called that single landmass *Pangaea* (pan JEE uh), meaning "all Earth."

Wegener thought our present continents were once part of one great supercontinent for three reasons. First, the shapes of the continents seemed to "fit" together. Second, fossils of plants and animals discovered on either side of the Atlantic Ocean were very similar. Third, Wegener noticed that glaciers had existed in places that now have very warm climates. **Figure 5** shows how the continents may have formed from Pangaea.

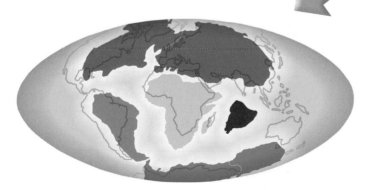

About **245 million years ago,** the continents were one giant landmass called Pangaea. The grey outlines indicate where the continents are today.

About **180 million years ago,** Pangaea began to divide into two pieces: Laurasia and Gondwanaland.

Even as recently as **65 million years ago,** the location of Earth's continents was very different from their current location.

Figure 5 *Because the continents are moving 1–10 cm per year, the continents will be arranged very differently in 150 million years.*

Do the Continents Move? In the mid-1960s, J. Tuzo Wilson of Canada came up with the idea that it wasn't the continents that were moving. Wilson thought that huge pieces of the Earth's crust are driven back and forth by forces within the planet. Each huge piece of crust is called a *tectonic plate*. Wilson's theory of how these huge pieces of crust move around the globe is called **plate tectonics.**

According to Wilson, the outer crust of the Earth is broken into seven large, rigid plates and several smaller ones, shown in **Figure 6.** The continents and oceans ride on top of these plates. It is the motion of the plates that causes continents to move.

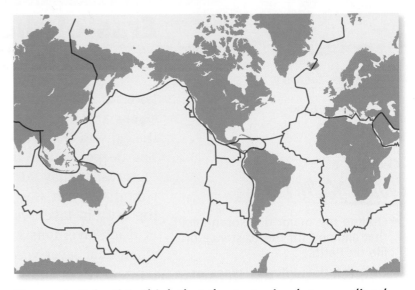

Figure 6 *Scientists think that the tectonic plates, outlined above, have been slowly rearranging the continents since the crust cooled billions of years ago.*

Adaptation in Slow Motion Although tectonic plates move very slowly, the motion of continents affects living organisms. Living things usually have time to adapt, through evolution, to the changes brought about by moving continents. That is why you are able to see living things that are well adapted to the environment they live in. In the same location, however, you may find fossil evidence of very different organisms that could not survive the changes.

SECTION REVIEW

1. What information does the geologic time scale provide, and what are the major divisions of time?

2. What is one possible cause of mass extinctions?

3. Explain one way that geological changes in the Earth can cause plants and animals to change.

4. What is the difference between relative dating and absolute dating of fossils?

5. **Understanding Concepts** Fossils of *Mesosaurus,* a small aquatic lizard, shown at right, have been found only in Africa and South America. Using what you know about plate tectonics, how would you explain this finding?

Terms to Learn

Precambrian time
Paleozoic era
Mesozoic era
Cenozoic era

What You'll Do

◆ Outline the major developments that allowed for the existence of life on Earth.

◆ Describe the different types of organisms that arose during the four eras of the geologic time scale.

Eras of the Geologic Time Scale

Look at the photograph of the Grand Canyon shown in **Figure 7.** If you look closely, you will notice that the walls of the canyon are layered with different kinds and colors of rocks. The deeper you go down into the canyon, the older the layer of rocks. It may surprise you to learn that each layer of the Grand Canyon was once the top layer. Billions of years ago the bottom layer was on top!

Each layer tells a story about what was happening on Earth when that layer was on top. The story is told mainly by the types of rocks and fossils found in the layer. In studying these different rocks and fossils, scientists have divided geologic history into four eras: Precambrian time, the Paleozoic era, the Mesozoic era, and the Cenozoic era.

Precambrian Time

If you journey to the bottom of the Grand Canyon, you can see layers of Earth that are over 1 billion years old. These layers are from Precambrian time. **Precambrian time** began when the Earth originated 4.6 billion years ago, and continued until about 540 million years ago. During this time life began and transformed the planet.

Figure 7 *Each rock layer of the Grand Canyon is like a page in the "history book of the Earth."*

The Early Earth Scientists hypothesize that life began when conditions were quite different from Earth's current environment. These conditions included an atmosphere that lacked oxygen but was rich in other gases, such as carbon monoxide, carbon dioxide, hydrogen, and nitrogen. Also, the early Earth, as illustrated in **Figure 8,** was a place of great turmoil. Meteorites crashed into the Earth's surface. Violent thunderstorms and volcanic eruptions were constant on the young planet. Intense radiation, including ultraviolet radiation from the sun, bombarded Earth's surface.

Figure 8 *The early Earth was a violent place.*

How Did Life Begin? Scientists hypothesize that under these conditions, life developed from nonliving matter. In other words, life started from the chemicals that already existed in the environment. These chemicals included water, clay, dissolved minerals in the oceans, and the gases present in the atmosphere. The energy present in the early Earth caused these chemicals to react with one another, forming the complex molecules that made life possible.

Some scientists further hypothesize that for millions of years these small, complex molecules floated in the ancient oceans and joined together to form larger molecules. These larger molecules combined into more-complicated structures. As time passed, complicated structures developed into cell-like structures that eventually became the first true cells, called prokaryotes. *Prokaryotes* are cells that lack a nucleus. Early prokaryotic cells, like the one shown in **Figure 9,** were *anaerobic,* which means they did not require oxygen to survive. Many varieties of anaerobic organisms still live on Earth today. Organisms that need oxygen could not have survived on early Earth because there was no free oxygen in the atmosphere.

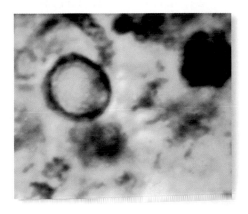

Figure 9 *Fossilized prokaryotes (such as the circular structure in the photograph) suggest that life first appeared on Earth more than 3.5 billion years ago.*

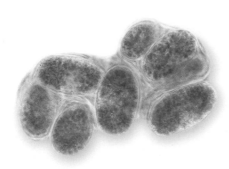

Figure 10 *Cyanobacteria are the simplest living organisms that photosynthesize.*

The Earth's First Pollution—Oxygen! As indicated by the fossil record, prokaryotic organisms called cyanobacteria appeared more than 3 billion years ago. Cyanobacteria, pictured in **Figure 10,** are photosynthetic organisms, which means that they use sunlight to produce food. One of the byproducts of this process is oxygen. As cyanobacteria carried out photosynthesis, they released oxygen gas into the oceans. The oxygen then escaped out into the air, changing Earth's atmosphere forever. Over the next several million years, more and more oxygen was added to the atmosphere.

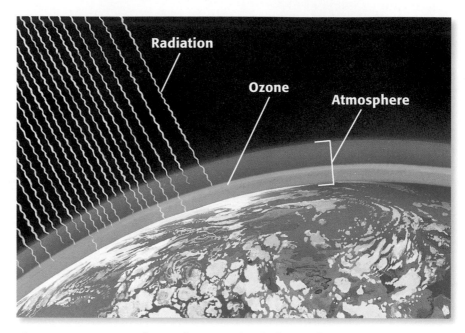

Figure 11 *Oxygen from photosynthesis formed ozone, which helps to absorb ultraviolet radiation.*

Environment

C O N N E C T I O N

Ozone depletion in the upper atmosphere is a serious problem. Chemicals, such as those used in refrigerators and air conditioners, are slowly destroying the ozone layer in the Earth's atmosphere. Because of ozone depletion, all living things are exposed to higher levels of radiation, which can cause skin cancer. Some countries have outlawed ozone-depleting chemicals.

Radiation Shield As the atmosphere filled with oxygen, some of the oxygen formed a layer of ozone in the upper atmosphere, as shown in **Figure 11.** *Ozone* is a gas that absorbs ultraviolet (UV) radiation from the sun. UV radiation damages DNA but is absorbed by water. Before ozone formed, therefore, life was restricted to the oceans and underground. But the new ozone blocked out most of the UV radiation. This brought radiation on Earth's surface down to a level that allowed life to move onto dry land.

Life's So Complex The fossil record tells us that after a long period of time, about 1 billion years, more-complex life-forms appeared. These organisms, known as *eukaryotes,* are much larger than prokaryotes. They contain a central nucleus and a complicated internal structure. Scientists think that over the past 2.5 billion years, eukaryotic cells have evolved together to form organisms that are composed of many cells.

The Paleozoic Era

The **Paleozoic era** began about 540 million years ago and ended about 248 million years ago. *Paleozoic* comes from the Greek words meaning "ancient life." Considering how long Precambrian time lasted, the Paleozoic era was relatively recent. Rocks from the Paleozoic era are rich in fossils of animals such as sponges, corals, snails, clams, squids, and trilobites. Fishes, the earliest animals with backbones, also appeared during this era, and ancient sharks became abundant. Some Paleozoic organisms are shown in **Figure 12**.

The Greening of the Earth During the Paleozoic era, plants, fungi, and air-breathing animals colonized dry land over a period of 30 million years. Plants provided the first land animals with food and shelter. By the end of the Paleozoic era, forests of giant ferns, club mosses, horsetails, and conifers covered much of the Earth. All major plant groups except for flowering plants appeared during this era.

Creepers Crawl onto Land Fossils indicate that crawling insects were some of the first animals to appear on land. They were followed by large salamanderlike animals. Near the end of the Paleozoic era, reptiles, winged insects, cockroaches, and dragonflies appeared.

The largest mass extinction known occurred at the end of the Paleozoic era, about 248 million years ago. As many as 90 percent of all marine species died out.

Figure 12 *Organisms that appeared in the Paleozoic era include the first reptiles, amphibians, fishes, worms, and ferns.*

✔ Self-Check

Place the following events in chronological order:

a. The ozone layer formed, and living things moved onto dry land.

b. Gases in the atmosphere and minerals in the oceans combined to form small molecules.

c. The first prokaryotic, anaerobic cells appeared.

d. Cyanobacteria appeared.

(See page 216 to check your answer.)

Figure 13 *The Mesozoic era ended with the mass extinction of most of the large animals. Survivors included small mammals and* Archaeopteryx.

The Mesozoic Era

The **Mesozoic era** began about 248 million years ago and lasted about 183 million years. *Mesozoic* comes from the Greek words meaning "middle life." Scientists think that, after the extinctions of the Paleozoic era, a burst of evolution occurred among the surviving reptiles, resulting in many different species. Therefore, the Mesozoic era is commonly referred to as the Age of Reptiles.

Life in the Mesozoic Era Dinosaurs are the most well known of the reptiles that evolved during the Mesozoic era. Dinosaurs dominated the Earth for about 150 million years. (Consider that humans and their ancestors have been around for only about 4 million years.) Dinosaurs had a great variety of physical characteristics, such as duck bills and projecting spines. In addition to dinosaurs, there were giant marine lizards that swam in the ocean. The first birds also appeared during the Mesozoic era. The most important plants during the early part of the Mesozoic era were cone-bearing seed plants, which formed large forests. Flowering plants appeared later in the Mesozoic era. Some of the organisms that appeared during the Mesozoic era are shown in **Figure 13.**

A Bad Time for Dinosaurs At the end of the Mesozoic era, 65 million years ago, dinosaurs and many other animal and plant species became extinct. What happened to the dinosaurs? According to one hypothesis, a large meteorite hit the Earth and generated giant dust clouds and enough heat to cause worldwide fires. The dust and smoke from these fires blocked out much of the sunlight, causing many plants to die out. Without enough plants to eat, the plant-eating dinosaurs died out. As a result, the meat-eating dinosaurs that fed on the plant-eating dinosaurs died. Global temperatures may have dropped for many years. Only a few organisms, including some small mammals, were able to survive.

The Cenozoic Era

The **Cenozoic era** began about 65 million years ago and continues today. *Cenozoic* comes from the Greek words meaning "recent life." Scientists have more information about the Cenozoic era than about any of the previous eras because fossils from the Cenozoic era are embedded in rock layers that are close to the Earth's surface. This makes them easier to find. During the Cenozoic era, many kinds of mammals, birds, insects, and flowering plants appeared. Some organisms that appeared in the Cenozoic era are shown in **Figure 14.**

A Good Time for Large Mammals The Cenozoic era is sometimes referred to as the Age of Mammals. Mammals came to dominate the Cenozoic era much as reptiles dominated the Mesozoic era. Early Cenozoic mammals were small forest dwellers. Larger mammals appeared later. Some of these larger mammals had long legs for running, teeth that were specialized for eating different kinds of food, and large brains. Cenozoic mammals include mastodons, saber-toothed cats, camels, giant ground sloths, and small horses.

Figure 14 *Many types of mammals evolved during the Cenozoic era.*

SECTION REVIEW

1. What is the main difference between the atmosphere 3.5 billion years ago and the atmosphere today?

2. How do prokaryotic cells and eukaryotic cells differ?

3. Explain why cyanobacteria are so important to the development of new life-forms.

4. **Identifying Relationships** Match the organisms to the time period in which they first appeared.

   1. eukaryotes
   2. dinosaurs
   3. fishes
   4. flowering plants
   5. birds

   a. Precambrian time
   b. Paleozoic era
   c. Mesozoic era
   d. Cenozoic era

Terms to Learn

primate   australopithecine
hominid   Neanderthal

What You'll Do

- ◆ Discuss the shared characteristics of primates.
- ◆ Describe what is known about the differences between hominids.

Human Evolution

After studying thousands of fossilized skeletons and other evidence, scientists theorize that humans evolved over millions of years from a distant ancestor that is also common to apes and monkeys. This common ancestor is thought to have lived more than 30 million years ago. How did we get from that distant ancestor to who we are today? This section presents some of the evidence that has been gathered so far.

Primates

To understand human evolution, we must first understand the characteristics that make us human beings. Humans are classified as primates. **Primates** are a group of mammals that includes humans, apes, monkeys, and prosimians. Primates have the characteristics illustrated below and in **Figure 15.**

Figure 15 *The gorilla (left) and these orangutans (right) have characteristics that make them nonhuman primates, including opposable big toes!*

Characteristics of Primates

Most primates have five flexible fingers—four fingers plus an opposable thumb.

This opposable thumb enables primates to grip objects.

Both eyes are located at the front of the head, providing **binocular,** or three-dimensional, vision. Each eye sees a slightly different image of the same scene. The brain merges these two images to create one three-dimensional image.

Based on physical and genetic similarities, the closest living relative of humans is thought to be the chimpanzee. This conclusion does not mean that humans descended from chimpanzees. Rather, it means that humans and chimpanzees share a common ancestor. The ancestor of humans is thought to have diverged from the ancestor of the chimpanzee about 7 million years ago. Since then, humans and chimpanzees have evolved along different paths.

Hominids Humans are assigned to a family separate from other primates, called **hominids.** The word *hominid* refers specifically to humans and their human-like ancestors. The main characteristic that distinguishes hominids from other primates is walking upright on two legs as their main way of moving around. Walking on two legs is called *bipedalism*. Examine **Figure 16** to see some skeletal similarities and differences between a hominid and an ape. Except for present-day humans, all hominid species are now extinct.

Figure 16 *The bones of a gorilla and a human are basically the same in form, but the human pelvis is suited for walking upright.*

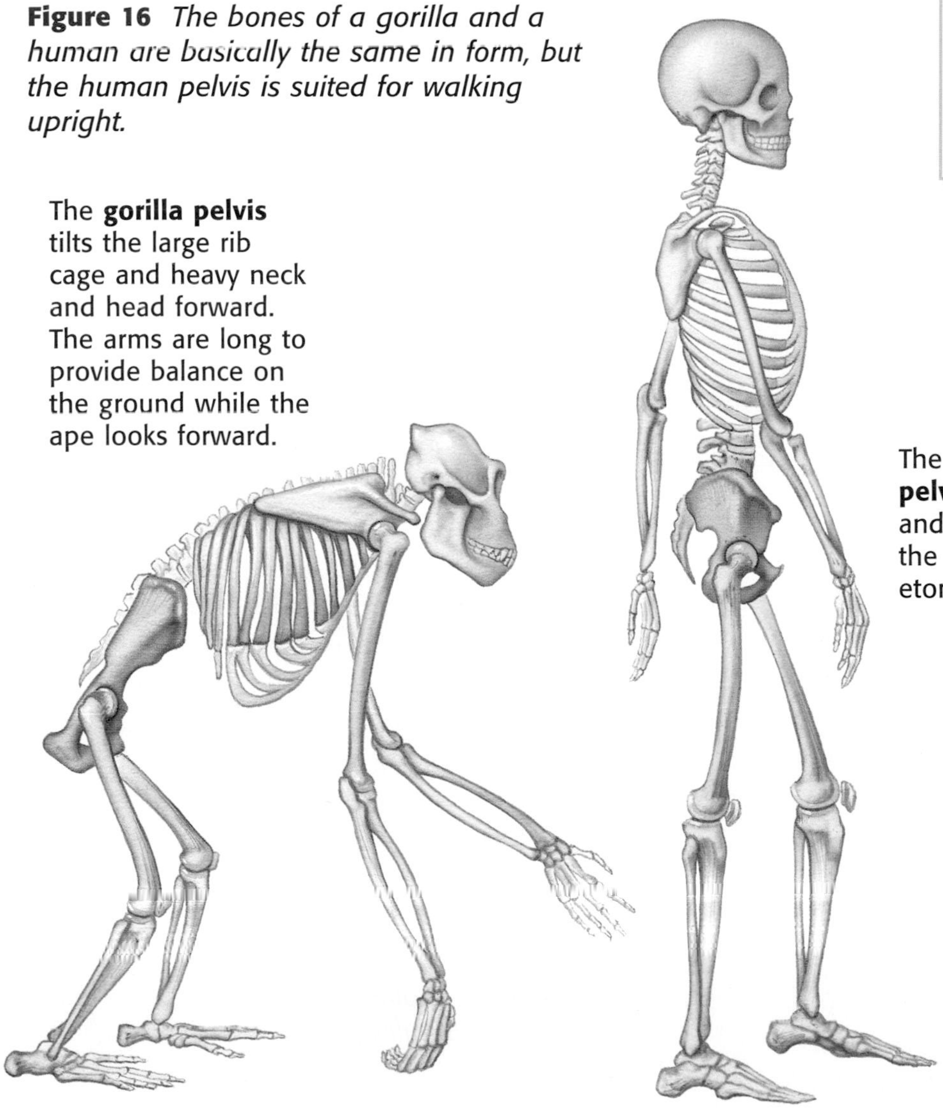

The **gorilla pelvis** tilts the large rib cage and heavy neck and head forward. The arms are long to provide balance on the ground while the ape looks forward.

The **human pelvis** is vertical and helps hold the entire skeleton upright.

QuickLab

Thumb Through This

Tape your thumbs to the side of your hands so they cannot be used. Attempt each of the tasks listed below.

- Sharpen a pencil.
- Cut a circle out of a piece of paper using scissors.
- Tie your shoelaces.
- Button several buttons.

After each attempt, answer the following questions:

1. Is the task more difficult with or without an opposable thumb?

2. Without an opposable thumb, do you think you would carry out this task on a regular basis?

TRY at HOME

Hominid Evolution

The first primate ancestors appeared during the Cenozoic era, 55 million years ago, and evolved in several directions. These ancestors are thought to have been mouse-like mammals that were active during the night, lived in trees, and ate insects. When the dinosaurs died out, these mammals survived and gave rise to the first primates called *prosimians,* which means "before monkeys." Only a few species, such as the one pictured in **Figure 17,** survive today. How long after prosimians appeared did the first hominid appear? No one has been able to answer that question, but scientists have discovered fossil bones of hominids that date back to 4.4 million years ago.

Figure 17 *Prosimians, such as this lemur, hunt in trees for insects and small animals.*

Australopithecines Scientists think hominid evolution began in Africa. Among the oldest hominids are **australopithecines** (ah STRA loh PITH uh seens). The word *Australopithecus* means "southern man ape." These early hominids had long arms, short legs, and small brains. Fossil evidence shows that the australopithecines differed from apes in several important ways. For example, they were bipedal. Also, australopithecine brains were generally larger than ape brains, although they were still much smaller than the brains of present-day humans.

In 1976, paleoanthropologist Mary Leakey discovered a series of footprints in Tanzania. Mary Leakey and the footprints are pictured in **Figure 18.** By determining the age of the rock containing the prints, she learned that the footprints were more than 3.6 million years old. The footprints indicated that a group of three hominids had walked in an upright position across the wet volcanic ash-covered plain.

Figure 18 *Mary Leakey is shown here with the 3.6-million-year-old footprints.*

Lucy In 1979, a group of fossils was discovered in Ethiopia. Included in this group was the most complete skeleton of an australopithecine ever found. Nicknamed Lucy, this australopithecine lived about 2 million years ago. Lucy had a sturdy body and stood upright, but her brain was about the size of a chimpanzee's. Fossil discoveries like this one demonstrate that upright posture evolved long before the brain enlarged.

A Face Like Ours Hominids with more humanlike facial features appeared approximately 2.3 million years ago, probably evolving from australopithecine ancestors. This species is known as *Homo habilis*. Its skull is shown in **Figure 19.** Fossils of *Homo habilis* have been found along with crude stone tools. About 2 million years ago, *Homo habilis* was replaced by its larger-brained descendant, *Homo erectus,* pictured in **Figure 20.** *Homo erectus* was larger than *Homo habilis* and had a smaller jaw.

Figure 19 Homo habilis *is called handy man because this group of hominids made stone tools.*

Hominids Go Global Fossil evidence shows that *Homo erectus* may have lived in caves, built fires, and wore clothing. They successfully hunted large animals and butchered them using tools made of flint and bone. The appearance of *Homo erectus* marks the beginning of the expansion of human populations across the globe. *Homo erectus* survived for more than 1 million years, which is longer than any other species of hominid has lived. *Homo erectus* disappeared about 200,000 years ago. This is about the time present-day humans, called *Homo sapiens,* first appear in the fossil record.

Although *Homo erectus* migrated across the globe, it is thought that *Homo sapiens* evolved in Africa and then migrated to Asia and Europe.

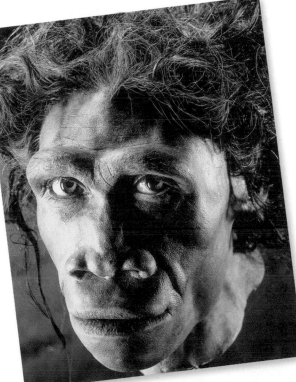

Figure 20 Homo erectus *lived about 2 million years ago and may have looked like the sculpture above.*

Figure 21 *Neanderthals had heavy brow ridges, like* Homo erectus, *but a larger brain than modern humans.*

Neanderthals In the Neander Valley, in Germany, fossils were discovered that belonged to a group of hominids referred to as **Neanderthals** (nee AN duhr TAHLS). They lived in Europe and western Asia beginning about 230,000 years ago.

Neanderthals hunted large animals, made fires, and wore clothing. There is evidence that they also cared for the sick and elderly and buried their dead, sometimes placing food, weapons, and even flowers with the dead bodies. Pictured in **Figure 21** is an artist's idea of how a Neanderthal might have looked. About 30,000 years ago, Neanderthals disappeared; nobody knows what caused their extinction.

Some scientists think the Neanderthals are a separate species, *Homo neanderthalensis*, from present-day humans, *Homo sapiens*. Other scientists think Neanderthals are a race of *Homo sapiens*. There is not yet enough evidence to fully answer this question.

Cro-Magnons In 1868, fossil skulls were found in caves in southwestern France. The skulls were about 35,000 years old, and they belonged to a group of *Homo sapiens* with modern features, called *Cro-Magnons*. Cro-Magnons may have existed in Africa 100,000 years ago and migrated from Africa about 40,000 years ago, coexisting with Neanderthals. Compared with Neanderthals, Cro-Magnons had a smaller and flatter face, and their skulls were higher and more rounded, like an artist has modeled in **Figure 22.** The only significant physical difference between Cro-Magnons and present-day humans is that Cro-Magnons had thicker and heavier bones.

Activity

Neanderthals made sophisticated spear points and other stone tools. Examine the Neanderthal tools below. Each of these tools was specialized for a particular task. Can you suggest what each stone tool was used for?

TRY at HOME

Figure 22 *This is an artist's idea of how a Cro-Magnon woman may have looked.*

Some Cro-Magnon people made beautiful cave paintings. These paintings are the earliest known examples of human art. In fact, Cro-Magnon culture is marked by an amazing diversity of artistic efforts, including cave paintings, sculptures, and carvings, like the one shown in **Figure 23.** The preserved villages and burial grounds of Cro-Magnon groups also show that they had a complex social organization.

Figure 23 *Cro-Magnons left many kinds of paintings, sculptures, and carvings, such as this carving of a bull.*

New Evidence of Human Evolution Although we know a great deal about our hominid ancestors, much remains to be understood. Each fossil discovery causes great excitement and raises new questions, such as, "Where did *Homo sapiens* evolve?" Current evidence suggests that *Homo sapiens* evolved in Africa. "Which australopithecine gave rise to humans?" Some scientists think *Australopithecus afarensis* is the ancestor of all hominids, including present-day humans. But recent fossil discoveries indicate another australopithecine species gave rise to human ancestors. There is still much to be learned about the evolution of humans.

SECTION REVIEW

1. Identify three characteristics of primates.

2. Compare *Homo habilis* with *Homo erectus*. What made the two species different from one another?

3. What evidence suggests Neanderthals were like present-day humans?

4. **Inferring Conclusions** Imagine you are a scientist excavating an ancient campsite. What might you conclude about the people who used the site if you found the charred bones of large animals and various stone blades among human fossils?

internet**connect**

SCI*LINKS*
NSTA

TOPIC: Human Evolution
GO TO: www.scilinks.org
*sci*LINKS NUMBER: HSTL106

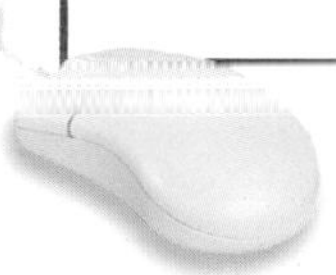

The Half-life of Pennies

Carbon-14 is an unstable element that is used in the absolute dating of material that was once alive, such as fossil bones. Every 5,730 years, half of the carbon-14 in a fossil specimen decays or breaks down into a more stable element. In the following activity, you will see how pennies can show the same kind of "decay."

MATERIALS

- 100 pennies
- large container with a cover

Procedure

1 Place 100 pennies in a large, covered container. Shake the container several times.

2 Remove the cover from the container. Carefully empty the contents of the container on a flat surface, making sure the pennies don't roll away.

3 Remove all the pennies that have the "head" side turned upward. In a data table similar to the one below, record the number of pennies removed and the number of pennies remaining.

4 Repeat the process until no pennies are left in the container. Remember to remove only the coins showing "heads."

Shake number	Number of coins remaining	Number of coins removed
1		
2		
3		
4		
5		

DO NOT WRITE IN BOOK

5 In your ScienceLog, draw a graph similar to the one at right. Label the x-axis "Number of shakes," and label the y-axis "Pennies remaining." Use data from your data table to plot on your graph the number of coins remaining at each shake.

Analysis

6 Examine the "Half-life of Carbon-14" graph at right. Compare the graph you have made for the pennies with the one for carbon-14. Explain any similarities that you see.

7 The probability of landing "heads" in a coin toss is $\frac{1}{2}$. Use this information to explain why the remaining number of pennies is reduced by about half each time they are shaken and tossed.

8 Assume that each flip equals 5,000 years. How long did it take to remove all the pennies from the container?

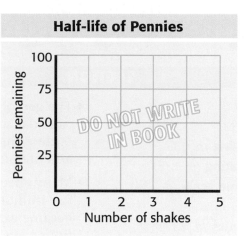

Half-life of Pennies

DO NOT WRITE IN BOOK

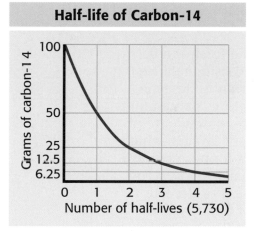

Half-life of Carbon-14

Chapter Highlights

Vocabulary

fossil (*p. 132*)

relative dating (*p. 133*)

absolute dating (*p. 133*)

geologic time scale (*p. 134*)

extinct (*p. 135*)

plate tectonics (*p. 137*)

Section Notes

- Paleontologists are scientists who study fossils.

- The age of a fossil can be determined using relative dating and absolute dating. Relative dating is an estimate based on the known age of the sediment layer in which the fossil is found. Absolute dating usually involves the measurement of the rate of decay of the unstable atoms found in the rock surrounding the fossil.

- The geologic time scale is a calendar scientists use to outline the history of Earth and life on Earth.

- Many species existed for a few million years and then became extinct. Mass extinctions have occurred several times in Earth's history.

Vocabulary

Precambrian time (*p. 138*)

Paleozoic era (*p. 141*)

Mesozoic era (*p. 142*)

Cenozoic era (*p. 143*)

Section Notes

- Precambrian time includes the formation of the Earth, the beginning of life, and the evolution of simple multi-cellular organisms.

☑ Skills Check

Math Concepts

HALF-LIFE To understand half-life better, imagine that you have $10.00 in your pocket. You determine that you are going to spend half of all the money you have in your possession every 30 minutes. How much will you have after 30 minutes? ($5.00) How much will you have after another 30 minutes? ($2.50) How much will you have after 3 hours? (a little more than 15¢)

Visual Understanding

THE GEOLOGIC TIME SCALE You have probably seen old movies or cartoons that show humans and dinosaurs inhabiting the same environment. Can this be possible? Dinosaurs and humans did not exist at the same time. Dinosaurs became extinct 65 million years ago. Humans and their ancestors have been around for less than 4 million years. Review the Geologic Time Scale on page 134.

SECTION 2

- The Earth is about 4.6 billion years old. Life formed from nonliving matter on the turbulent early Earth.

- The first cells, prokaryotes, were anaerobic. Later, photosynthetic cyanobacteria evolved and caused oxygen to enter the atmosphere.

- During the Paleozoic era, animals appeared in the oceans, and plants and animals colonized the land.

- Dinosaurs and other reptiles roamed the Earth during the Mesozoic era. Flowering plants, birds, and primitive mammals also appeared.

- Primates evolved during the Cenozoic era, which extends to the present day.

SECTION 3

Vocabulary

primate *(p. 144)*

hominid *(p. 145)*

australopithecine *(p. 146)*

Neanderthal *(p. 148)*

Section Notes

- Humans, apes, and monkeys are primates. Primates are distinguished from other mammals by their opposable thumbs and binocular vision.

- Hominids, a subgroup of primates, include humans and their human-like ancestors. The oldest known hominids are australopithecines.

- Neanderthals were a species of humans that disappeared about 30,000 years ago.

- Cro-Magnons did not differ very much from present-day humans.

Chapter Review

USING VOCABULARY

To complete the following sentences, choose the correct term from each pair of terms listed below:

1. During the ___?___ of the Earth's history, life is thought to have originated from nonliving matter. *(Precambrian time period or Paleozoic era)*

2. The Age of Mammals refers to the ___?___. *(Mesozoic era or Cenozoic era)*

3. The Age of Reptiles refers to the ___?___. *(Paleozoic era or Mesozoic era)*

4. Plants colonized dry land during the ___?___. *(Precambrian time or Paleozoic era)*

5. The most ancient hominids are called ___?___. *(Neanderthals or australopithecines)*

UNDERSTANDING CONCEPTS

Multiple Choice

6. Scientists estimate the age of the Earth to be about
   a. 10 billion years.
   b. 4.6 billion years.
   c. 3.8 billion years.
   d. 4.4 million years.

7. The first cells probably appeared about
   a. 10 billion years ago.
   b. 4.6 billion years ago.
   c. 3.5 billion years ago.
   d. 4.4 million years ago.

8. How is the age of a fossil estimated?
   a. by using the geologic time scale
   b. by measuring unstable elements in the rock that holds the fossil
   c. by studying the relative position of continents
   d. by measuring the amount of oxygen in the fossil rock

9. Plants and air-breathing animals appeared during this time period.
   a. Precambrian time
   b. Paleozoic era
   c. Mesozoic era
   d. Cenozoic era

10. These hominids made sophisticated tools, hunted large animals, wore clothing, and cared for the sick and elderly. Their extinction is a mystery.
    a. australopithecines
    b. hominids in the genus *Homo*
    c. Neanderthals
    d. Cro-Magnons

Short Answer

11. What kinds of information do fossils provide about the evolutionary history of life?

12. Name at least one important biological event that occurred during each of the following geologic eras: Precambrian time, Paleozoic era, Mesozoic era, and Cenozoic era.

13. Why are there usually more fossils from the Cenozoic era than from other geologic eras?

Concept Mapping

14. Use the following terms to create a concept map: Earth's history, humans, Paleozoic era, dinosaurs, Precambrian time, cyanobacteria, Mesozoic era, land plants, Cenozoic era.

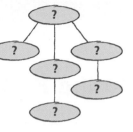

CRITICAL THINKING AND PROBLEM SOLVING

Write one or two sentences to answer the following questions:

15. Why do scientists think the first cells were anaerobic?

16. List three evolutionary changes in early hominids that led to the rise of modern humans.

MATH IN SCIENCE

17. A rock containing a newly discovered fossil is found to contain 5 mg of an unstable form of potassium and 5 mg of the stable element formed from its decay. If the half-life of the unstable form of potassium is 1.3 billion years, how old is the rock? What can you infer about the age of the fossil?

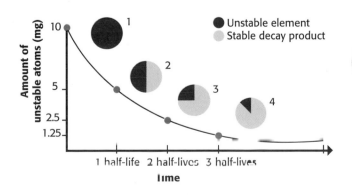

INTERPRETING GRAPHICS

The figure below illustrates the evolutionary relationships between some primates. Examine the figure, and answer the questions.

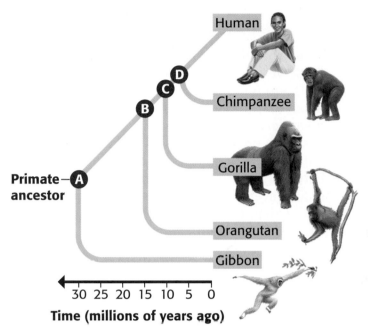

18. Which letter represents when gorillas took a different evolutionary path?

19. About how long ago did orangutan diverge from the human evolutionary line?

20. Which group has been separated from the human line of evolution the longest?

Reading Check-up

Take a minute to review your answers to the Pre-Reading Questions found at the bottom of page 130. Have your answers changed? If necessary, revise your answers based on what you have learned since you began this chapter.

Windows into the Past

When you think about the history of life on Earth, you may not think of rocks. After all, rocks are nonliving! What can they tell you about life? It may surprise you to learn that a great deal of what we know about life on Earth has been provided by rocks. How? It just so happens that life-forms have been fossilized between layers of rock for million of years—maybe even since life first appeared on Earth. And finding these fossils is like finding an old snapshot of ancient life-forms.

Layers of Rock

Fossils are most likely to be found in sedimentary rock. This is a type of rock that forms as exposed rock surfaces are worn away by wind, rain, and ice. The particles from these rock surfaces then collect in low-lying areas. As these layers build up, their combined weight compacts the particles, and chemical reactions cement them together. After thousands of years, the layers of particles become solid rock— and so do parts of any organism that has been trapped in the layers.

The Rock Cycle

The illustration at right shows how sedimentary rock forms. It also shows how igneous rock and metamorphic rock form. Notice that sedimentary and metamorphic rock can melt and become igneous rock; this happens deep underground. Can you see why fossils would not normally be found in igneous rock?

The rock cycle is a continuous process. All three kinds of rock eventually become another type of rock. Fortunately for life scientists, this process can take millions of years. If this process happened more quickly—and sedimentary rock became either metamorphic or igneous rock at a faster pace—our fossil record would be much shorter. We may not have found out about the dinosaurs!

Cycle This!

▶ Suppose you found several fossils of the same organism. You found some fossils in very deep layers of sedimentary rock and some fossils in very shallow layers of sedimentary rock. What does this say about the organism?

▼ *The Rock Cycle*

CAREERS

PALEOBOTANIST

In school **Bonnie Jacobs** was fascinated by fossils, ancient cultures, and geology. "I have always had an interest in ancient things," she says. To pursue her interests, Jacobs became a paleobotanist. "A paleobotanist is someone who studies fossil plants," she explains. "That means you study fossilized leaves, wood, pollen, flower parts, or anything else that comes from a plant."

Bonnie Jacobs teaches and does research at Southern Methodist University, in Dallas, Texas. As a paleobotanist, she uses special "snapshots" that let her "see" back in time. If you look at these snapshots, you might see an ancient grassland, desert, or rain forest. Jacobs's snapshots might even give you a glimpse of the place where our human family may have started.

Fossil Plants and Ancient Climates

Jacobs and other paleobotanists study present-day plant species and how they grow in different climates. Plants that grow in warm, wet climates today probably grew in the same kind of climate millions of years ago. So when Jacobs finds ancient plant fossils that are similar to plants that exist today, she can determine what the ancient climate was like. But her fossils give more than just a climate report.

Plants and . . . Ancient Bones

Because some of these same plant fossils are found in rocks that also contain bits of bone—some from human ancestors—they may hold clues to human history. "Ideas about the causes of human evolution have a lot to do with changes in the landscape," Jacobs explains. "For instance, many scientists who study human evolution assumed that there was a big change from forested to more-open environments just before the origin of the human family. That assumption needs to be tested. The best way to do that is to go back to the plants themselves."

It's an Adventure!

In doing her research, Jacobs has traveled to many different places and worked with a wide variety of people. "Kiptalam Chepboi, a colleague we worked with in Kenya, grew up in the area where we do fieldwork. He took me to a sweat-bee hive. Sweat bees don't sting. You can take a honeycomb out from under a rock ledge, pop the whole thing in your mouth, and suck out the honey without worrying about getting stung. That was one of the neatest things I did out there."

Making a Modern Record

▶ Make your own plant fossil. Press a leaf part into a piece of clay. Fill the depression with plaster of Paris. Then write a report describing what the fossil tells you about the environment it came from.

▲ *Fossilized leaves*

Classification

Pre-Reading
Questions

1. What is classification?
2. How do people use classification in their everyday lives?
3. Why do scientists classify living things?

ALL SORTS OF INSECTS!

Look at the katydids, grasshoppers, and other insects on this page. Every insect has a label that bears the insect's name and other information. Suppose you discovered a new insect. How would you name, sort, and identify— or classify—the new insect? Where would you start? In this chapter, you will learn how scientists classify living things. You will also learn about the six kingdoms into which all living things are classified.

CLASSIFYING SHOES

In this activity, you will develop a system of classification for shoes.

Procedure

1. Gather **10 different shoes.** Use **masking tape** to label each sole with a number (1–10).

2. Make a list of shoe features, such as left or right, color, size, and laces or no laces. In your ScienceLog, make a table with a column for each feature. Complete the table by describing each shoe.

3. Use the data in the table to make a shoe identification key. The key should be a list of steps. Each step should have two statements about the shoes. The statements will lead you to two more statements. For example, step 1 might be:
   1a. This is a red sandal.
       Shoe 4
   1b. This isn't a red sandal.
       Go to step 2.

4. Each step should eliminate more shoes until only one shoe fits the description, such as in 1a, above. Check the number on the sole of the shoe to see if you are correct.

5. Trade keys with another group. How did their key help you to identify the shoes?

Analysis

6. How helpful was it to list the shoe features before making the key?

7. Could you identify the shoes using another group's key? Explain.

Terms to Learn

classification   family
kingdom   genus
phylum   species
class   taxonomy
order   dichotomous key

What You'll Do

◆ List the seven levels of classification.

◆ Explain the importance of having scientific names for species.

◆ Explain how scientific names are written.

◆ Describe how dichotomous keys help in identifying organisms.

Classification: Sorting It All Out

Imagine that you live in a tropical rain forest and are responsible for getting your own food, shelter, and clothing from the forest. If you are going to survive, you will need to know which plants you can eat and which are poisonous. You will need to know which animals to eat and which may eat you. You will need to organize the living things around you into categories, or classify them. **Classification** is the arrangement of organisms into orderly groups based on their similarities.

Why Classify?

For thousands of years, humans have classified different kinds of organisms based on their usefulness. For example, the Chácabo people of Bolivia, like the family shown in **Figure 1,** know of 360 species of plants in the forest where they live, and they have uses for 305 of those plants. How many plants can you name that are useful in your life?

Biologists also classify organisms—both living and extinct. Why? There are millions of different living things in the world. Making sense of the sheer number and diversity of living things requires classification. Classifying living things makes it easier for biologists to find the answers to many important questions, including the following:

■ How many known species are there?

■ What are the characteristics of each?

■ What are the relationships between these species?

In order to classify an organism, a biologist must use a system that groups organisms according to shared characteristics and their relationships between one another. There are seven levels of classification used by biologists—kingdom, phylum, class, order, family, genus, and species.

Figure 1 *The Chácabo people have a great amount of knowledge about their environment.*

Levels of Classification

Each organism is classified into one of several **kingdoms,** which are the largest, most general groups. All the organisms in a kingdom are then sorted into several *phyla* (singular, **phylum**). The members of one phylum are more like each other than they are like members of another phylum. Then all the organisms in a given phylum are further sorted into **classes.** Each class is subdivided into one or more **orders,** orders are separated into **families,** families are sorted into *genera* (singular, **genus**), and genera are sorted into **species.**

Examine **Figure 2** to follow the classification of the ordinary house cat from kingdom Animalia to species *Felis domesticus*.

Kingdom Animalia contains all the different phyla of animals.
Phylum Chordata contains animals with a hollow nerve cord.

Class Mammalia contains only animals that have a backbone and nurse their young.

Order Carnivora contains animals with a backbone that nurse their young and whose ancestors had special teeth for tearing meat.
Family Felidae contains animals with a backbone that nurse their young, have well-developed claws and special teeth for tearing meat, and are cats.
Genus *Felis* contains animals that have characteristics of the previous classifications, but they can't roar; they can only purr.
Species *Felis domesticus* contains only one kind of animal, the common house cat. It has characteristics of all the levels above it, but it has other unique characteristics.

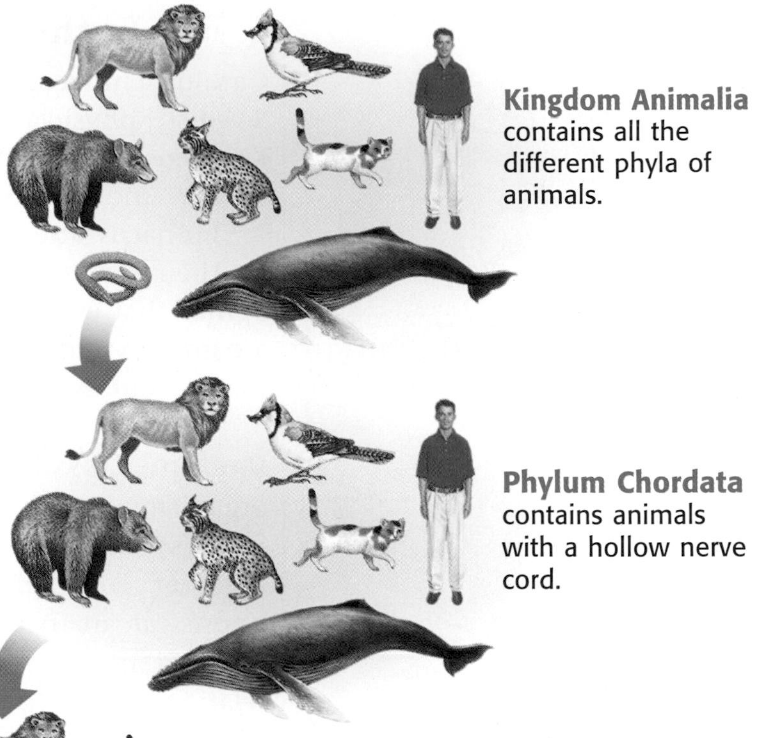

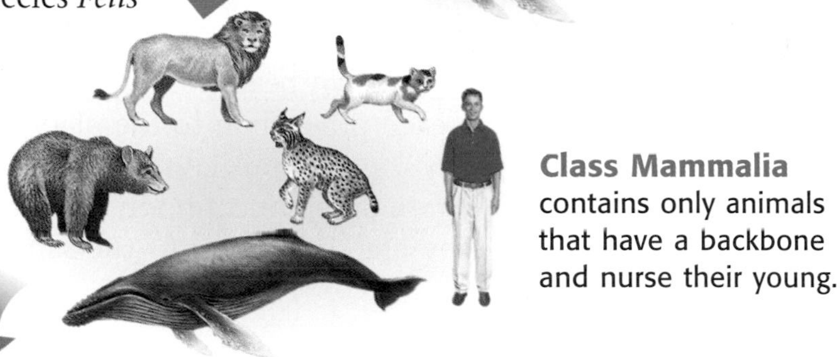

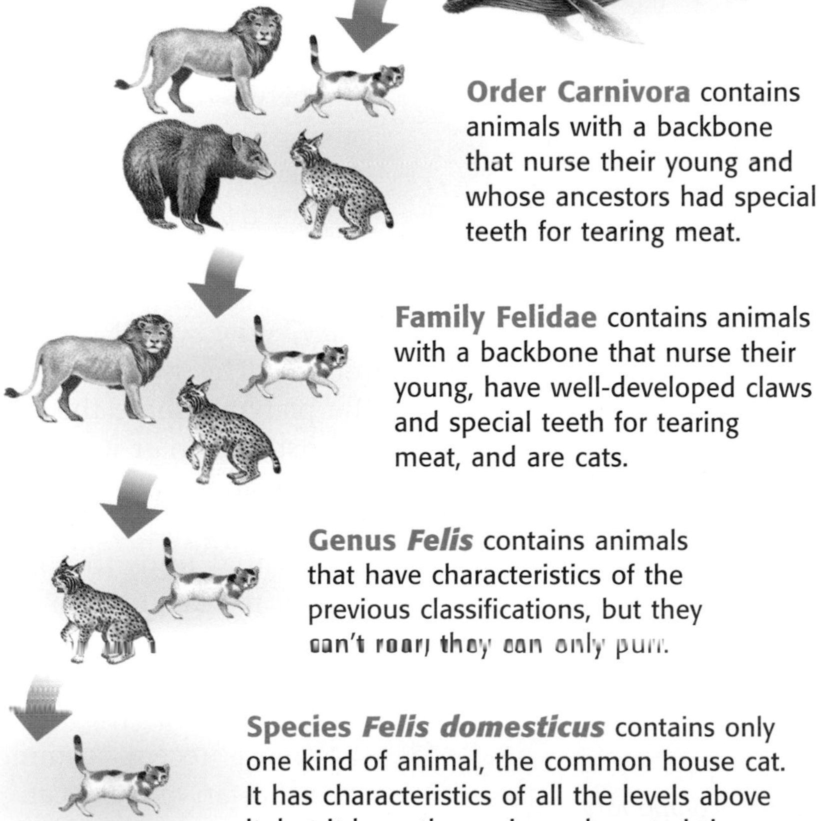

Figure 2 *Kingdom Animalia contains all species of animals, while species* Felis domesticus *contains only one.*

Activity

A mnemonic device is a tool to help you remember something. One way to remember the levels of classification is to use a mnemonic device like this sentence:

King **P**hillip **C**ame **O**ver
For **G**rape **S**oda.

Invent your own mnemonic device for the levels of classification using words that are meaningful to you.

TRY at HOME

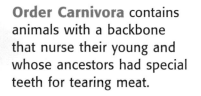

What Is the Basis for Classification?

Carolus Linnaeus (lin AY uhs), pictured in **Figure 3,** was a Swedish physician and botanist who lived in the 1700s. Linnaeus founded **taxonomy,** the science of identifying, classifying, and naming living things.

Linnaeus attempted to classify all known organisms only by their shared characteristics. Later, scientists began to recognize that evolutionary changes form a line of descent from a common ancestor. Taxonomy changed to include these new ideas about evolutionary relationships.

Figure 3 *Carolus Linnaeus classified more than 7,000 species of plants.*

Modern Classification Today's taxonomists still classify organisms based on presumed evolutionary relationships. Species with a recent common ancestor can be classified together. For example, the platypus, brown bear, lion, and house cat are related because they are thought to have an ancestor in common—an ancient mammal. Because of this relationship, all four animals are grouped into the same class—Mammalia.

A brown bear, lion, and house cat are more closely related to each other than to the platypus. They are all mammals, but only the platypus lays eggs. Brown bears, lions, and house cats share a different common ancestor—an ancient carnivore. Thus, they are classified into the same order—Carnivora.

Branching Diagrams The close evolutionary relationship between lions and house cats is shown by the branching diagram in **Figure 4.** The characteristics listed on the arrow pointing to the right are the characteristics that make the next animal unique. The house cat and the platypus share the characteristics of hair and mammary glands. But they are different in many ways. The branch that leads to lions is closest to the branch that leads to house cats. The lion and the house cat are closely related because they share the most recent common ancestor—an ancient cat.

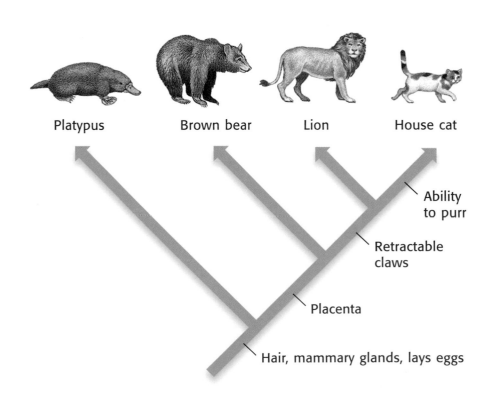

Platypus   Brown bear   Lion   House cat

Ability to purr

Retractable claws

Placenta

Hair, mammary glands, lays eggs

Figure 4 *This branching diagram shows the evolutionary relationships between four mammals.*

Naming Names

By classifying organisms, biologists are also able to give them scientific names. A scientific name is always the same for a specific organism no matter how many common names it might have.

Before Linnaeus's time, scholars used Latin names up to 12 words long to identify species. Linnaeus simplified the naming of organisms by giving each species a two-part scientific name. The first part of the name identifies the genus, and the second part identifies the species. The scientific name for the Indian elephant, for example, is *Elephas maximus*. No other species has this name, and all scientists know that *Elephas maximus* refers to the Indian elephant.

It's All Greek (or Latin) to Me Scientific names might seem difficult to understand because they are in Latin or Greek. Most scientific names, however, are actually full of meaning. Take a look at **Figure 5.** You probably already know this animal's scientific name. It's *Tyrannosaurus rex*! The first word is a combination of two Greek words meaning "tyrant lizard," and the second word is Latin for "king." The genus name always begins with a capital letter, and the species name begins with a lowercase letter. Both words are underlined or italicized. You may have heard *Tyrannosaurus rex* called *T. rex*. This is acceptable in science as long as the genus name is spelled out the first time it is used. The species name is incomplete without the genus name or its abbreviation.

Come aboard the starship USS *Adventure*! Turn to page 192 in your LabBook.

QuickLab

Evolutionary Diagrams

A branching evolutionary diagram can be used to show evolutionary relationships between different organisms.

Construct a diagram similar to the one on page 162. Use a frog, a snake, a kangaroo, and a rabbit. What do you think is one major evolutionary change between one organism and the next? Write them on your diagram.

TRY at HOME

Figure 5
You would never call Tyrannosaurus rex *just* rex!

Why Are Scientific Names So Important? Examine the cartoon in **Figure 6.** What name do you have for the small black and white and sometimes smelly animal pictured? The skunk is called by several common names in English and has even more names—at least one name in every language! All of these common names can cause quite a bit of confusion for biologists who want to discuss the skunk. Biologists from different parts of the world who are interested in skunks need to know that they are all talking about the same animal, so they use its scientific name, *Mephitis mephitis.* All known living things have a two-part scientific name.

Figure 6 *Using an organism's two-part scientific name is a sure way for scientists to know they are discussing the same organism.*

When and where did the first bird live? Find out about the debate on page 178.

Dichotomous Keys

Taxonomists have developed special guides known as **dichotomous keys** to aid in identifying unknown organisms. A dichotomous key consists of several pairs of descriptive statements that have only two alternative responses. From each pair of statements, the person trying to identify the unknown organism chooses the appropriate statement. From there, the person is directed to another pair of statements. By working through the statements in the key, the person can eventually identify the organism. Using the simple dichotomous key on the next page, try to identify the two animals shown.

Dichotomous Key to 10 Common Mammals in the Eastern United States

1. a. This mammal flies. Its hand is formed into a wing.   **Little brown bat**
   b. This mammal does not fly.   **Go to step 2**

2. a. This mammal has a naked (no fur) tail.   **Go to step 3**
   b. This mammal doesn't have a naked tail.   **Go to step 4**

3. a. This mammal has a short, naked tail.   **Eastern mole**
   b. This mammal has a long, naked tail.   **Go to step 5**

4. a. This mammal has a black mask across its face.   **Raccoon**
   b. This mammal does not have a black mask across its face.   **Go to step 6**

5. a. This mammal has a tail that is flattened and shaped like a paddle.   **Beaver**
   b. This mammal has a tail that is not flattened or shaped like a paddle.   **Opossum**

6. a. This mammal is brown with a white underbelly.   **Go to step 7**
   b. This mammal is not brown with a white underbelly.   **Go to step 8**

7. a. This mammal has a long, furry tail that is black on the tip.   **Longtail weasel**
   b. This mammal has a long tail without much fur.   **White-footed mouse**

8. a. This mammal is black with a narrow white stripe on its forehead and broad white stripes on its back.   **Striped skunk**
   b. This mammal is not black with white stripes.   **Go to step 9**

9. a. This mammal has long ears and a short, cottony tail.   **Eastern cottontail**
   b. This mammal has short ears and a medium-length tail.   **Woodchuck**

SECTION REVIEW

1. Why do scientists use scientific names for organisms?

2. Explain the two parts of a scientific name.

3. List the seven levels of classification.

4. Describe how a dichotomous key helps to identify unknown organisms.

5. **Interpreting Illustrations** Study the figure at right. Which plant is the closest relative of the hibiscus? Which plant is most distantly related to the hibiscus? Which plants have seeds?

Moss   Fern   Pine tree   Hibiscus

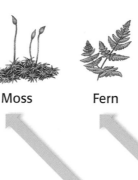

Flowers

Seeds

Vascular tissue

Ability to live on land

Terms to Learn

Archaebacteria   Plantae
Eubacteria   Fungi
Protista   Animalia

What You'll Do

◆ Explain how classification schemes for kingdoms developed as greater numbers of different organisms became known.

◆ List the six kingdoms, and provide two characteristics of each.

Figure 7 *How would you classify this organism? Euglena, shown here magnified 1,000 times, has characteristics of both plants and animals.*

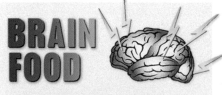

BRAIN FOOD

If *Euglena*'s chloroplasts are shaded from light or removed, it will begin to hunt for food like an animal. If the chloroplasts are shaded long enough, the chloroplasts degenerate and never come back.

The Six Kingdoms

For hundreds of years, all living things were classified as either plants or animals. These two kingdoms, Plantae and Animalia, worked just fine until organisms like the species *Euglena,* shown in **Figure 7,** were discovered. If you were a taxonomist, how would you classify such an organism?

What Is It?

As you know, organisms are classified by their characteristics. Being the excellent taxonomist that you are, you decide to list the characteristics of *Euglena*:

■ *Euglena* are a species of single-celled organisms that live in pond water.

■ *Euglena* are green and, like most plants, can make their own food through photosynthesis.

"This is easy!" you think to yourself. "*Euglena* are plants." Not so fast! There are other important characteristics to consider:

■ *Euglena* can move about from place to place by whipping their "tails," called flagella.

■ Sometimes *Euglena* use food obtained from other organisms.

Plants don't move around and usually do not eat other organisms. Does this mean that *Euglena* are animals? As you can see, neither category seems to fit. Scientists ran into the same problem, so they decided to add another kingdom for classifying organisms such as *Euglena*. This kingdom is known as Protista.

More Kingdoms As scientists continued to learn more about living things, they added kingdoms in order to account for the differences and similarities between organisms. Currently, most scientists agree that the six-kingdom classification system works best. There is still some disagreement, however, and still more to be learned. In the following pages, you will learn more about each of the kingdoms.

The Two Kingdoms of Bacteria

Bacteria are extremely small single-celled organisms. Bacteria are different from all other living things in that they are *prokaryotes*, organisms that do not have nuclei. Many biologists divide bacteria into two kingdoms, **Archaebacteria** (AHR kee bak TEER ee uh) and **Eubacteria** (YOO bak TEER ee uh).

Archaebacteria have been on Earth at least 3 billion years. The prefix *archae* comes from a Greek word meaning "ancient." Today you can find archaebacteria living in places where most organisms could not survive. **Figure 8** shows a hot spring in Yellowstone National Park. The yellow and orange rings around the edge of the hot spring are formed by the billions of archaebacteria that live there.

Most of the other thousands of kinds of bacteria are eubacteria. These microscopic organisms live in the soil, in water, and even on and inside the human body! For example, the eubacterium *Escherichia coli*, pictured in **Figure 9,** is present in great numbers in human intestines, where it produces vitamin K. Another kind of eubacterium converts milk to yogurt, and yet another species causes ear and sinus infections and pneumonia.

Figure 8 *The Grand Prismatic Spring, in Yellowstone National Park, contains water that is about 90°C (194°F). The spring is home to archaebacteria that thrive in its hot water.*

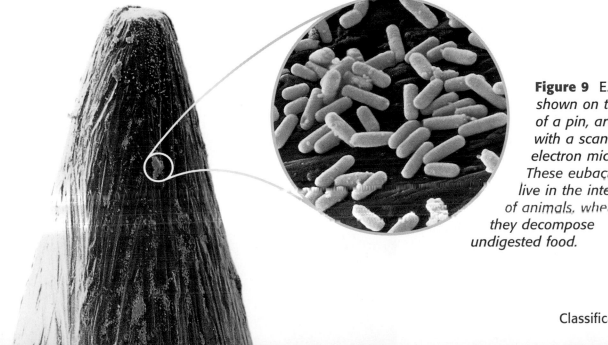

Figure 9 E. coli, *shown on the point of a pin, are seen with a scanning electron microscope. These eubacteria live in the intestines of animals, where they decompose undigested food.*

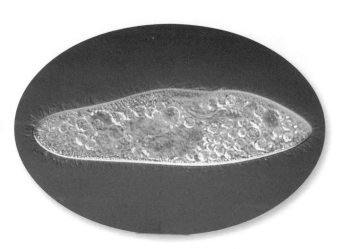

Figure 10 Paramecium *usually moves about rapidly.*

Kingdom Protista

Members of the kingdom **Protista,** commonly called protists, are single-celled or simple multicellular organisms. Unlike bacteria, protists are *eukaryotes,* organisms that have cells with a nucleus and membrane-bound organelles. Kingdom Protista contains all eukaryotes that are not plants, animals, or fungi. Scientists think the first protists evolved from ancient bacteria about 2 billion years ago. Much later, protists gave rise to plants, fungi, and animals as well as to modern protists.

As you can see, kingdom Protista contains many different kinds of organisms. Protists include protozoa, which are animal-like protists; algae, which are plantlike protists; and slime molds and water molds, which are funguslike protists. *Euglena,* which were discussed earlier, are also members of kingdom Protista, as are the *Paramecium* and the slime mold pictured in **Figures 10** and **11.** Most protists are single-celled organisms, but some are multicellular, such as the giant kelp shown in **Figure 12.**

> ## ✔ Self-Check
>
> 1. How are the two kingdoms of bacteria different from all other kingdoms?
> 2. How would you distinguish Protista from the two kingdoms of bacteria?
>
> *(See page 216 to check your answers.)*

Figure 11 *A slime mold spreads over a fallen log on the forest floor.*

Figure 12
This giant kelp is a multicellular protist.

Kingdom Plantae

Although plants vary remarkably in size and form, most people easily recognize the members of kingdom **Plantae.** Plants are complex multicellular organisms that are usually green and use the sun's energy to make sugar by a process called *photosynthesis.* The giant sequoias and flowering plants shown in **Figures 13** and **14** are examples of the different organisms classified in the kingdom Plantae.

MATH BREAK

Building a Human Chain Around a Giant Sequoia

How many students would it take to join hands and form a human chain around a giant sequoia that is 30 m in circumference? Assume for this calculation that the average student can extend his or her arms about 1.3 m. NOTE: You can't have a fraction of a student, so be sure to round up your answer to the nearest whole number.

Environment
CONNECTION

Giant sequoia trees are very rare. They grow only in California and are a protected species. Some of them are over 3,000 years old.

Figure 13 *A giant sequoia can measure 30 m around its base and can grow to more than 91.5 m tall.*

Figure 14 *Plants such as these are common in the rain forest.*

Kingdom Fungi

Molds and mushrooms are examples of the complex multi-cellular members of the kingdom **Fungi.** Fungi (singular, *fungus*) were originally classified as plants, but fungi do not obtain nutrients by photosynthesis. Moreover, fungi do not have many animal characteristics. Because of their unusual combination of characteristics, fungi are classified in a separate kingdom.

Fungi do not perform photosynthesis, as plants do, and they do not eat food, as animals do. Instead, fungi absorb nutrients from their surroundings after breaking them down with digestive juices. **Figure 15** shows a pretty but deadly mushroom, and **Figure 16** shows black bread mold (a fungus) growing on a piece of bread. Have you ever seen this type of mold on bread?

Figure 15 *This beautiful mushroom of the genus* Amanita *is poisonous.*

Figure 16 *This black bread mold can be dangerous if you inhale the spores. Some molds are dangerous, and others produce life-saving antibiotics.*

Classify This!

You and a friend are walking through the forest and you come upon the organism shown at right. You think it is a plant, but you are not sure. It has a flower and seeds, very small leaves, and roots that are growing into a rotting log. But this organism is white from its roots to its petals. To which kingdom do you think this organism belongs? What characteristic is your answer based on? What additional information would you need in order to give a more accurate answer?

Kingdom Animalia

Animals are complex multicellular organisms that belong to the kingdom **Animalia.** Most animals can move about from place to place and have nervous systems that help them sense and react to their surroundings. At the microscopic level, animal cells differ from those of fungi, plants, most protists, and bacteria because animal cells lack cell walls. **Figure 17** shows some members of the kingdom Animalia.

Figure 17 *The kingdom Animalia contains many different organisms, such as eagles, tortoises, beetles, and dolphins.*

SECTION REVIEW

1. Name the six kingdoms.

2. Which of the six kingdoms include prokaryotes, and which include eukaryotes?

3. Explain the different ways plants, fungi, and animals obtain nutrients.

4. Why are protists placed in their own kingdom?

5. **Applying Concepts** To which kingdom do humans belong? What characteristics place humans in this kingdom?

■ internet**connect**

SC*L*INKS.
NSTA

TOPIC: The Basis for Classification,
The Six Kingdoms
GO TO: www.scilinks.org
SciLINKS NUMBER: HSTL205, HSTL220

Skill Builder Lab

Shape Island

You are a biologist looking for new animal species. You sailed for days across the ocean and finally found an uncharted island hundreds of miles south of Hawaii. You decided to call it "Shape Island." This island has some very unusual organisms. Each of them has some variation of a geometric shape. You have spent over a year collecting specimens and classifying them according to Linnaeus's system. You have given a scientific name to most species you have collected. You must give names to the last 12 specimens before you sail for home.

Procedure

1. In your ScienceLog, draw each of the organisms shown below. Beside each organism, draw a line for its name, as shown on the following page. The first organism has been named for you, but you have 12 more to name. Use the glossary of Greek and Latin prefixes, suffixes, and root words on page 173 to help you name the organisms.

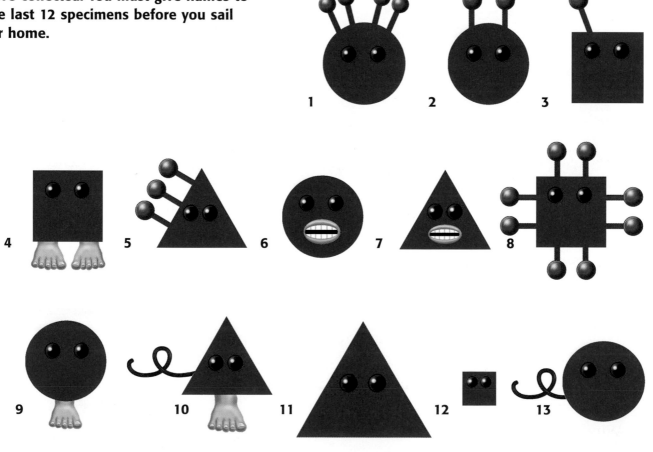

1. *Cycloplast quadantennae*
(cyclo + plast quad + antennae)

2. _____

3. _____

DO NOT WRITE IN BOOK

Glossary	
Greek and Latin roots, prefixes and suffixes	**Meaning**
ankylos	angle
antennae	external sense organs
tri-	three
bi-	two
cyclo-	circle
macro-	large
micro-	small
mono-	one
peri-	all around
-plast	body
-pod	foot
quad-	four
stoma	mouth
uro-	tail

2 One more organism lives on Shape Island, but you have not been able to capture it. Unfortunately, your supplies are running out, and soon you must sail home. You have had a good look at the unusual animal and can draw it in detail. In your ScienceLog, draw an animal that is different from all the others. Then use the glossary at right to help you give the animal a two-part scientific name.

Analysis

3 If you gave Species 1 a common name, such as round-face-no-nose, would other scientists know which new organism you were referring to? Explain.

4 Describe two characteristics shared by all your specimens from Shape Island.

Going Further

Look up the scientific names listed below. You can use the library, the Internet, a taxonomy index, or field guides.
 • *Mertensia virginica*
 • *Porcellio scaber*

For each organism answer the following questions: Is it a plant or an animal? How many common names does it have? How many scientific names does it have?

Think of the name of your favorite fruit or vegetable. Find out if it has other common names, and find out its two-part scientific name.

Chapter Highlights

Vocabulary

classification *(p. 160)*

kingdom *(p. 161)*

phylum *(p. 161)*

class *(p. 161)*

order *(p. 161)*

family *(p. 161)*

genus *(p. 161)*

species *(p. 161)*

taxonomy *(p. 162)*

dichotomous key *(p. 164)*

Section Notes

- Classification refers to the arrangement of organisms into orderly groups based on their similarities and evolutionary relationships.

- Biologists classify organisms in order to organize the number and diversity of living things and to give them scientific names.

- The classification scheme used today is based on the work of Carolus Linnaeus. Linnaeus founded the science of taxonomy, in which organisms are described, named, and classified.

- Modern classification schemes include evolutionary relationships.

- Today organisms are classified using a seven-level system of organization. The seven levels are kingdom, phylum, class, order, family, genus, and species. The genus and species of an organism compose its two-part scientific name.

- A scientific name is always the same for a specific organism, no matter how many common names it has.

- Dichotomous keys help to identify organisms.

Labs

Voyage of the USS *Adventure* *(p. 192)*

☑ Skills Check

Math Concepts

LARGE ORGANISMS The rounding-off rule states: If the number you wish to round is greater than or equal to the midpoint, round the number to the next greater number.

Sometimes when you are working with objects instead of numbers, you have to use a different rule! The MathBreak on page 169 asks you to round up your answer even though the answer includes a fraction that is less than halfway to the next number. Why is that? The answer is that if you don't round up, you won't have enough students to encircle the tree.

Visual Understanding

LEVELS OF CLASSIFICATION If you are still a little unsure about how organisms are grouped into levels of classification, turn back to page 161. Review Figure 2. Notice that the broadest, most inclusive level is kingdom. For example, all animals are grouped into kingdom Animalia. From there, the groups become more and more specific until only one animal is included under the level of species. Working from species up, notice that more and more animals are included in the group as you move toward the level of kingdom.

Vocabulary

Archaebacteria *(p. 167)*

Eubacteria *(p. 167)*

Protista *(p. 168)*

Plantae *(p. 169)*

Fungi *(p. 170)*

Animalia *(p. 171)*

Section Notes

- At first, living things were classified as either plants or animals. As scientists discovered more about living things and discovered more organisms, new kingdoms were added that were more descriptive than the old two-kingdom system.

- Most biologists recognize six kingdoms—Archaebacteria, Eubacteria, Protista, Plantae, Fungi, and Animalia.

- Bacteria are prokaryotes, single-celled organisms that do not contain nuclei. The organisms of all other kingdoms are eukaryotes, organisms that have cells with nuclei.

- Archaebacteria have been on Earth for about 3 billion years and can live where most other organisms cannot survive.

- Most bacteria are eubacteria and live almost everywhere. Some are harmful, and some are beneficial.

- Plants, most fungi, and animals are complex multicellular organisms. Plants perform photosynthesis. Fungi break down material outside their body and then absorb the nutrients. Animals eat food, which is digested inside their body.

---

internetconnect

GO TO: go.hrw.com

SCiLINKS

NSTA

GO TO: www.scilinks.org

Visit the **HRW** Web site for a variety of learning tools related to this chapter. Just type in the keyword:

KEYWORD: HSTCLS

Visit the **National Science Teachers Association** on-line Web site for Internet resources related to this chapter. Just type in the **sci**LINKS number for more information about the topic:

TOPIC: The Basis for Classification

TOPIC: Levels of Classification

TOPIC: Dichotomous Keys

TOPIC: The Six Kingdoms

sciLINKS NUMBER: HSTL205

sciLINKS NUMBER: HSTL210

sciLINKS NUMBER: HSTL215

sciLINKS NUMBER: HSTL220

Chapter Review

To complete the following sentences, choose the correct term from each pair of terms listed below:

1. Linnaeus founded the science of __?__. (*DNA analysis* or *taxonomy*)

2. All of the organisms classified into a single kingdom are then divided into one of several __?__. (*phyla* or *classes*)

3. The narrowest level of classification is the __?__. (*genus* or *species*)

4. Linnaeus began naming organisms using __?__. (*two-part scientific names* or *evolutionary relationships*)

5. Archaebacteria and eubacteria are __?__. (*prokaryotes* or *eukaryotes*)

UNDERSTANDING CONCEPTS

Multiple Choice

6. When scientists classify organisms, they
   a. arrange them in orderly groups.
   b. give them many common names.
   c. decide whether they are useful.
   d. ignore evolutionary relationships.

7. When the seven levels of classification are listed from broadest to narrowest, which level is in the fifth position?
   a. class
   b. order
   c. genus
   d. family

8. The scientific name for the European white water lily is *Nymphaea alba*. What is the genus to which this plant belongs?
   a. *Nymphaea*   c. water lily
   b. *alba*   d. alba lily

9. "Kings Play Chess On Fine-Grained Sand" is a mnemonic device that helps one remember
   a. the scientific names of different organisms.
   b. the six kingdoms.
   c. the seven levels of classification.
   d. the difference between prokaryotic and eukaryotic cells.

10. Most bacteria are classified in which kingdom?
    a. Archaebacteria   c. Protista
    b. Eubacteria   d. Fungi

11. What kind of organism thrives in hot springs and other extreme environments?
    a. archaebacteria   c. protists
    b. eubacteria   d. fungi

Short Answer

12. Why is the use of scientific names so important in biology?

13. List two kinds of evidence used by modern taxonomists to classify organisms based on evolutionary relationships.

14. Is a eubacterium a type of eukaryote? Explain your answer.

Concept Map

15. Use the following terms to create a concept map: kingdom, fern, lizard, Animalia, Fungi, algae, Protista, Plantae, mushroom.

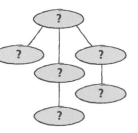

Write one or two sentences to answer the following questions:

16. How are the levels of classification related to evolutionary relationships among organisms?

17. Explain why two species that belong to the same genus, such as white oak *(Quercus alba)* and cork oak *(Quercus suber)*, also belong to the same family.

18. What characteristic do the members of all six kingdoms have in common?

MATH IN SCIENCE

19. Scientists estimate that millions of species are yet to be discovered and classified. If only 1.5 million, or 10 percent, of species have been discovered and classified, how many species do scientists think exist on Earth?

20. Sequoia trees can grow to more than 90 m in height. There are 3.28 ft per meter. How many feet are in 90 m?

INTERPRETING GRAPHICS

The diagram below illustrates the evolutionary relationships among several primates.

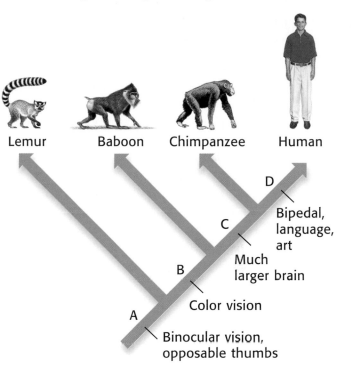

21. Which primate is the closest relative to the common ancestor of all primates?

22. Which primate shares the most traits with humans?

23. Do lemurs share the characteristics listed at point D with humans? Explain your answer.

24. What characteristic do baboons have that lemurs do not have? Explain your answer.

Reading Check-up

Take a minute to review your answers to the Pre-Reading Questions found at the bottom of page 158. Have your answers changed? If necessary, revise your answers based on what you have learned since you began this chapter.

It's a Bird, It's a Plane, It's a *Dinosaur*?

Think about birds. Parrots, pigeons, buzzards, emus . . . they're everywhere! But once there were no birds. So where did they come from? When did birds evolve? Was it 225 million years ago, just 115 million years ago, or somewhere in between? No one really knows for sure, but the topic has fueled a long-standing debate among scientists.

The debate began when the fossil remains of a 150-million-year-old dinosaur with wings and feathers—*Archaeopteryx*—were found in Germany in 1860 and 1861.

▲ Archaeopteryx *was the first true bird.*

Birds Are Dinosaurs!

Some scientists think that birds evolved from small, carnivorous dinosaurs like *Velociraptor* about 115 million to 150 million years ago. Their idea relies on similarities between modern birds and these small dinosaurs. Particularly impor-

tant are the size, shape, and number of toes and "fingers"; the location and shape of the breastbone and shoulder; the presence of a hollow bone structure; and the development of wrist bones that "flap" for flight. To many scientists, all this evidence is overwhelming. It can lead to only one conclusion: Modern birds are descendants of dinosaurs.

No They Aren't!

"Not so fast!" say a smaller but equally determined group of scientists who think that birds developed 100 million years before *Velociraptor* and its relatives. They point out that all these dinosaurs were ground dwellers and were the wrong shape and size for flying. They would never get off the ground! Further, these dinosaurs lacked at least one of the bones necessary for flight in today's birds.

This "birds came before dinosaurs" idea rests on fossils of *thecodonts,* small tree-dwelling reptiles that lived about 225 million years ago. One thecodont, a small, four-legged tree dweller called *Megalancosaurus,* had the right bones and body shape—and the right center of gravity—for flight. The evidence is clear, say these scientists, that birds flew long before dinosaurs even existed!

▲ *This small tree-dwelling reptile,* Megalancosaurus, *may have evolved into the birds we know today.*

So Who Is Right?

Both sides are debating fossils 65 million years to 225 million years old. Some species left many fossils, while some left just a few. In the last few years, new fossils discovered in China, Mongolia, and Argentina have just added fuel to the fire. So scientists will continue to study the available evidence and provide their educated guesses. Meanwhile, the debate rages on!

Compare for Yourself

▶ Find photographs of *Sinosauropteryx* and *Archaeopteryx* fossils, and compare them. How are they similar? How are they different? Do you think birds could be modern dinosaurs? Debate your idea with someone who holds the opposite view.

WEIRD SCIENCE

LOBSTER-LIP LIFE-FORM

Have you ever stopped to think about lobsters' lips? Did you even know that lobsters have lips? Oddly enough, they do. And even stranger, scientists have found a tiny animal living on lobsters' lips. Surprised? Although scientists noticed this little critter about 30 years ago, they had never studied it closely. When they finally did, they were astounded! This tiny organism is different from anything else in the world. Meet *Symbion pandora.*

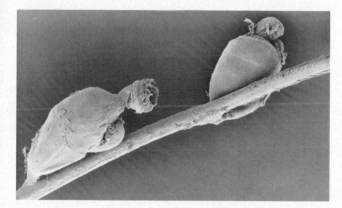

▲ *Although scientists knew of* Symbion pandora's *existence for 30 years, they did not realize how unusual it was.*

A Little Weird

What makes *Symbion pandora* so unusual? As if spending most of its life on lobster lips isn't strange enough, *S. pandora* also seems to combine the traits of very different animals. Here are some of its strange characteristics:

- **Life stages:** *S. pandora*'s life cycle involves many different *stages,* or body forms. The stages are very different from each other. For instance, at certain times in its life, *S. pandora* can swim around, while at other times, it can exist only by attaching to a lobster's mouth.
- **Dwarf males:** Male *S. pandora* are much smaller than the females. Thus, they are called *dwarf males.*

- **Feeding habits:** Dwarf males don't eat; they can only find a female, reproduce, and then die!
- **Budding:** Many individuals are neither male nor female. These animals reproduce through a process called *budding.* In budding, a new, complete animal can sprout out of the adult. In turn, the new offspring can reproduce in the same way.
- **Disappearing guts:** When an adult starts to form a new bud, its digestive and nervous systems disappear! Part of these guts help make the new bud. Then the adult forms new digestive and nervous systems to replace the old ones.

How Unusual Is It?

When scientists discover a new plant or animal, they may conclude that it represents a new species within an existing genus. In that case scientists make up a name for the new species. Usually, the person who finds the new organism gets to name it. If the new organism is *very* unusual, scientists may place it not only in a new species but also in a new genus.

S. pandora is so unusual that it was placed not only in a new species and a new genus, but also in a new family, a new order, a new class, and even a new phylum! Such a scientific discovery is extremely rare. In fact, when this discovery was made, in 1995, it was announced in newspapers all over the world!

Where Would You Look?

▶ *S. pandora* was first noticed more than 30 years ago, but no one realized how unusual it was until scientists studied it. Scientists estimate that we've identified less than 10 percent of Earth's organisms. Find out about other new animal species that have been discovered within the last 10 years. Where are some places you would look for new species?

Exploring, inventing, and investigating are essential to the study of science. However, these activities can also be dangerous. To make sure that your experiments and explorations are safe, you must be aware of a variety of safety guidelines.

You have probably heard of the saying, "It is better to be safe than sorry." This is particularly true in a science classroom where experiments and explorations are being performed. Being uninformed and careless can result in serious injuries. Don't take chances with your own safety or with anyone else's.

Following are important guidelines for staying safe in the science classroom. Your teacher may also have safety guidelines and tips that are specific to your classroom and laboratory. Take the time to be safe.

Safety Rules!

Start Out Right

Always get your teacher's permission before attempting any laboratory exploration. Read the procedures carefully, and pay particular attention to safety information and caution statements. If you are unsure about what a safety symbol means, look it up or ask your teacher. You cannot be too careful when it comes to safety. If an accident does occur, inform your teacher immediately, regardless of how minor you think the accident is.

Safety Symbols

All of the experiments and investigations in this book and their related worksheets include important safety symbols to alert you to particular safety concerns. Become familiar with these symbols so that when you see them, you will know what they mean and what to do. It is important that you read this entire safety section to learn about specific dangers in the laboratory.

If you are instructed to note the odor of a substance, wave the fumes toward your nose with your hand. Never put your nose close to the source.

Eye protection	Clothing protection	Hand safety
Heating safety	Electric safety	Chemical safety
Animal safety	Sharp object	Plant safety

Eye Safety

Wear safety goggles when working around chemicals, acids, bases, or any type of flame or heating device. Wear safety goggles any time there is even the slightest chance that harm could come to your eyes. If any substance gets into your eyes, notify your teacher immediately, and flush your eyes with running water for at least 15 minutes. Treat any unknown chemical as if it were a dangerous chemical. Never look directly into the sun. Doing so could cause permanent blindness.

Avoid wearing contact lenses in a laboratory situation. Even if you are wearing safety goggles, chemicals can get between the contact lenses and your eyes. If your doctor requires that you wear contact lenses instead of glasses, wear eye-cup safety goggles in the lab.

Safety Equipment

Know the locations of the nearest fire alarms and any other safety equipment, such as fire blankets and eyewash fountains, as identified by your teacher, and know the procedures for using them.

Be extra careful when using any glassware. When adding a heavy object to a graduated cylinder, tilt the cylinder so the object slides slowly to the bottom.

Neatness

Keep your work area free of all unnecessary books and papers. Tie back long hair, and secure loose sleeves or other loose articles of clothing, such as ties and bows. Remove dangling jewelry. Don't wear open-toed shoes or sandals in the laboratory. Never eat, drink, or apply cosmetics in a laboratory setting. Food, drink, and cosmetics can easily become contaminated with dangerous materials.

Certain hair products (such as aerosol hair spray) are flammable and should not be worn while working near an open flame. Avoid wearing hair spray or hair gel on lab days.

Sharp/Pointed Objects

Use knives and other sharp instruments with extreme care. Never cut objects while holding them in your hands. Place objects on a suitable work surface for cutting.

Heat

Wear safety goggles when using a heating device or a flame. Whenever possible, use an electric hot plate as a heat source instead of an open flame. When heating materials in a test tube, always angle the test tube away from yourself and others. In order to avoid burns, wear heat-resistant gloves whenever instructed to do so.

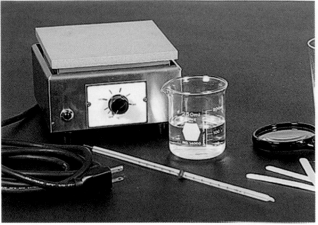

Electricity

Be careful with electrical cords. When using a microscope with a lamp, do not place the cord where it could trip someone. Do not let cords hang over a table edge in a way that could cause equipment to fall if the cord is accidentally pulled. Do not use equipment with damaged cords. Be sure your hands are dry and that the electrical equipment is in the "off" position before plugging it in. Turn off and unplug electrical equipment when you are finished.

Chemicals

Wear safety goggles when handling any potentially dangerous chemicals, acids, or bases. If a chemical is unknown, handle it as you would a dangerous chemical. Wear an apron and safety gloves when working with acids or bases or whenever you are told to do so. If a spill gets on your skin or clothing, rinse it off immediately with water for at least 5 minutes while calling to your teacher.

Never mix chemicals unless your teacher tells you to do so. Never taste, touch, or smell chemicals unless you are specifically directed to do so. Before working with a flammable liquid or gas, check for the presence of any source of flame, spark, or heat.

Animal Safety

Always obtain your teacher's permission before bringing any animal into the school building. Handle animals only as your teacher directs. Always treat animals carefully and with respect. Wash your hands thoroughly after handling any animal.

Plant Safety

Do not eat any part of a plant or plant seed used in the laboratory. Wash hands thoroughly after handling any part of a plant. When in nature, do not pick any wild plants unless your teacher instructs you to do so.

Glassware

Examine all glassware before use. Be sure that glassware is clean and free of chips and cracks. Report damaged glassware to your teacher. Glass containers used for heating should be made of heat-resistant glass.

Elephant-Sized Amoebas?

Why can't amoebas grow to be as large as elephants? An amoeba is a single-celled organism. Amoebas, like most cells, are microscopic. If an amoeba could grow to the size of a quarter, it would starve to death. To understand how this can be true, build a model of a cell and see for yourself.

Materials

- cubic cell patterns
- pieces of heavy paper or poster board
- scissors
- transparent tape
- scale or balance
- fine sand

Procedure

1. Use heavy paper to make four cube-shaped cell models from the patterns supplied by your teacher. Cut out each cell model, fold the sides to make a cube, and tape the tabs on the sides. The smallest cell model has sides that are one unit long. The next larger cell has sides of two units. The next cell has sides of three units, and the largest cell has sides of four units. These paper models represent the cell membrane, the part of a cell's exterior through which food and waste pass.

Two-unit cell model

2. In your ScienceLog, copy the data table at right. Use each formula to calculate the data about your cell models. A key to the formula symbols can be found on the next page. Record your calculations in the table. Calculations for the smallest cell have been done for you.

Data Table for Measurements				
Length of side	Area of one side $(A = S \times S)$	Total surface area of cube cell $(TA = S \times S \times 6)$	Volume of cube cell $(V = S \times S \times S)$	Mass of cube cell
1	1 unit^2	6 unit^2	1 unit^3	
2				
3				
4				

DO NOT WRITE IN BOOK

3. Carefully fill each model with fine sand until the sand is level with the top edge. Find the mass of the filled models using a scale or a balance. What does the sand in your model represent?

4. Record the mass of each cell model in the table. (Always remember to use the appropriate mass unit.)

5. In your ScienceLog, make a data table like the one below.

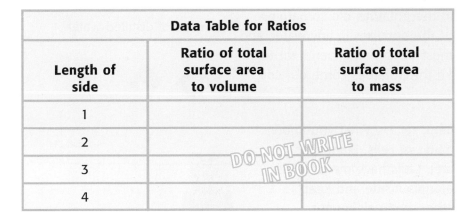

Data Table for Ratios		
Length of side	Ratio of total surface area to volume	Ratio of total surface area to mass
1		
2		
3		
4		

DO NOT WRITE IN BOOK

6. Use the data from your Data Table for Measurements to find the ratios for each of your cell models. Fill in the Data Table for Ratios for each of the cell models.

Analysis

7. As a cell grows larger, does the ratio of total surface area to volume increase, decrease, or stay the same?

8. Which is better able to supply food to all the cytoplasm of the cell—the cell membrane of a small cell or that of a large cell? Explain your answer.

9. As a cell grows larger, does the total surface area to mass ratio increase, decrease, or stay the same?

10. Is the cell membrane of a cell with high mass or the cell membrane of a cell with low mass better able to feed all the cytoplasm of the cell? You may explain your answer in a verbal presentation to the class or you may choose to write a report and illustrate it with drawings of your models.

Key to Formula Symbols
S = the length of one side
A = area
V = volume
TA = total area

DESIGN YOUR OWN

The Perfect Taters Mystery

You are the chief food detective at Perfect Taters Food Company. The boss, Mr. Fries, wants you to find a way to keep his potatoes fresh and crisp while they are waiting to be cooked. His workers have tried several methods already, but nothing has worked. Workers in Group A put the potatoes in very salty water, and the potatoes did something unexpected. Workers in Group B put the potatoes in water with no salt, and the potatoes did something else! Workers in Group C didn't put the potatoes in any water, and that didn't work either. Now you must design an experiment to find out what can be done to make the potatoes come out crisp and fresh.

Materials

- potato samples (A, B, and C)
- freshly cut potato pieces
- salt
- 6 small, clear plastic drinking cups
- 4 L of distilled water

1. Before you plan your experiment, review what you know. You know that potatoes are made of cells. Plant cells contain a large amount of water. Cells have membranes that hold water and other materials inside and keep some things out. Water and other materials must travel across cell membranes to get into and out of the cell.

2. Mr. Fries has told you that you can obtain as many samples as you need from the workers in Groups A, B, and C. Your teacher will have these samples ready for you to observe.

3. Make a data table like the one below in your ScienceLog to list your observations. Make as many observations as you can about the potatoes tested by workers in Group A, Group B, and Group C.

Observations	
Group A:	
Group B:	
Group C:	

DO NOT WRITE IN BOOK

Ask a Question

4. Now that you have made your observations, state Mr. Fries's problem in the form of a question that can be answered by your experiment.

Form a Hypothesis

5. Form a hypothesis based on your observations and your questions. The hypothesis should be a statement about what causes the potatoes to shrivel or swell. Based on your hypothesis, make a prediction about the outcome of your experiments. State your prediction in an "if-then" format.

Test the Hypothesis

6. Once you have made a prediction, design your investigation. Check your experimental design with your teacher before you begin. Mr. Fries will give you potato pieces, water, salt, and no more than six containers.

7. Keep very accurate records. Write out your plan and procedure. Make data tables. To be sure of your data, measure all materials carefully and make drawings of the potato pieces before and after the experiment.

Draw Conclusions

8. Explain what happened to the potato cells in Groups A, B, and C in your experiment. Include a discussion of the cell membrane and the process of osmosis.

Communicate Results

9. Write a letter to Mr. Fries that explains your experimental method, your results, and your conclusion. Then make a recommendation about how he should handle the potatoes so they will stay fresh and crisp.

Tracing Traits

Have you ever wondered about the traits you inherited from your parents? Do you have a trait that neither of your parents has? In this project, you will develop a family tree, or pedigree, similar to the one shown in the diagram below. You will trace an inherited trait through a family to determine how it has passed from generation to generation.

Procedure *TRY at HOME*

1. The diagram at right shows a family history. On a separate piece of paper, draw a similar diagram of the family you have chosen. Include as many family members as possible, such as grandparents, parents, children, and grandchildren. Use circles to represent females and squares to represent males. You may include other information, such as the family member's name, birthdate, or picture.

2. Draw a chart similar to the one on the next page. Survey each of the family members shown in your family tree. Ask them if they have hair on the middle segment of their fingers. Write each person's name in the appropriate square. Explain to each person that it is normal to have either trait. The presence of hair on the middle segment is the dominant form of this trait.

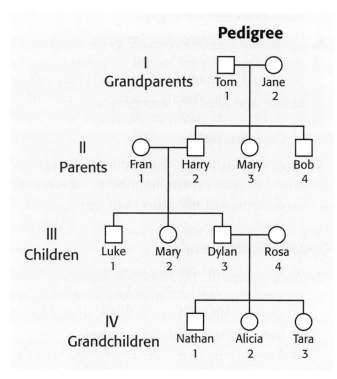

Pedigree

I Grandparents — Tom 1, Jane 2

II Parents — Fran 1, Harry 2, Mary 3, Bob 4

III Children — Luke 1, Mary 2, Dylan 3, Rosa 4

IV Grandchildren — Nathan 1, Alicia 2, Tara 3

Dominant trait	Recessive trait	Family members with the dominant trait	Family members with the recessive trait
Hair present on the middle segment of fingers (H)	Hair absent on the middle segment of fingers (h)	DO NOT WRITE IN BOOK	

3. Trace this trait throughout the family tree you diagrammed in step 1. Shade or color the symbols of the family members who demonstrate the dominant form of this trait.

Analysis

4. What percentage of the family members demonstrate the dominant form of the trait? Calculate this by counting the number of people who have the dominant trait and dividing this number by the total number of people you surveyed. Multiply your answer by 100. An example has been done at right.

5. What percentage of the family members demonstrates the recessive form of the trait? Why doesn't every family member have the dominant form of the trait?

6. Choose one of the family members who demonstrates the recessive form of the chosen trait. What is this person's genotype? What are the possible genotypes for the parents of this individual? Does this person have any brothers or sisters? Do they show the dominant or recessive trait?

7. Draw a Punnett square like the one at right. Use this to determine the genotypes of the parents of the person you chose in step 7. Write this person's genotype in the bottom right-hand corner of your Punnett square. **Hint:** There may be more than one possible genotype for the parents. Don't forget to consider the genotypes of the person's brothers and sisters.

Example: Calculating percentage

$$\frac{10 \text{ people with trait}}{20 \text{ people surveyed}} = \frac{1}{2}$$

$$\frac{1}{2} = 0.50 \times 100 = 50\%$$

Father

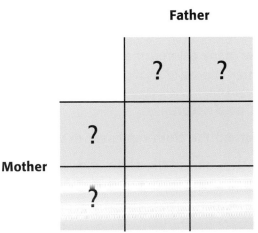

Mother

Out-of-Sight Marshmallows

An adaptation is a trait that helps an organism survive in its environment. In nature, camouflage is a form of coloration that enables an organism to blend into its immediate surroundings.

Hypothesis

Organisms that are camouflaged have a better chance of escaping from predators and therefore a better chance of survival.

Test the Hypothesis

1. Working in pairs, count out 50 white marshmallows and 50 colored marshmallows. Your marshmallows will represent the prey (food) in this experiment.

2. Place the white and colored marshmallows randomly on the piece of colored cloth.

3. One student per pair should be the hungry hunter (predator). The other student should record the results of each trial. The predator should look at the food for a few seconds, pick up the first marshmallow he or she sees, and then look away.

4. Continue this process without stopping for 2 minutes or until your teacher signals to stop.

Analyze the Results

5. How many white marshmallows did the hungry hunter choose?

6. How many colored marshmallows did the hungry hunter choose?

Draw Conclusions

7. What did the cloth represent in your investigation?

8. Did the color of the cloth affect the color of marshmallows chosen? Explain your answer.

9. Which marshmallow color represented camouflage?

10. Describe an organism that has a camouflage adaptation.

Materials

- 50 white mini-marshmallows
- 50 colored mini-marshmallows (all one color is preferable)
- 50 cm^2 of colored cloth, matching one of the marshmallow colors
- watch or clock with a second hand

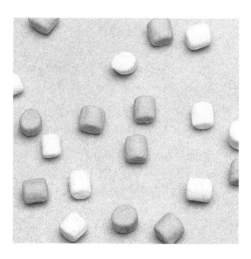

Survival of the Chocolates

Imagine a world populated with candy, and hold that delicious thought for just a moment. Try to apply the idea of natural selection to a population of candy-coated chocolates. According to the theory of natural selection, individuals who have favorable adaptations are more likely to survive. In the "species" of candy you will study in this experiment, shell strength is an adaptive advantage. Plan an experiment to find out which candy characteristics correspond to shell (candy coating) strength.

Materials

- small candy-coated chocolates in a variety of colors
- other materials as needed, according to the design of your experiment

Form a Hypothesis

1. Form a hypothesis and make a prediction. For example, if you chose to study candy color, your prediction might look like this: If the _____?_____ colored shell is the strongest, then fewer of the candies with this color of shell will _____?_____ when _____?_____.

Test Your Hypothesis

2. Design a procedure to determine which candy is best suited to survive by not "cracking under pressure." In your plan, be sure to include materials and tools you may need to complete this procedure. Check your experimental design with your teacher before you begin. Your teacher will supply the candy and assist you in gathering materials and tools.

3. Record your results in a data table you have designed in your ScienceLog. Be sure to organize your data in a clear and understandable way.

Analyze the Results

4. Write a report that describes your experiment. Explain how your data either support or do not support your hypothesis. Include possible errors and ways to improve your procedure.

Going Further

Can you think of another characteristic of these candies that can be tested to determine which candy is best adapted to survive? Explain your choice.

Voyage of the USS *Adventure*

You are a crew member on the USS *Adventure*. The *Adventure* has been on a 5-year mission to collect life-forms from outside the solar system. On the voyage back to Earth, your ship went through a meteor shower, which ruined several of the compartments containing the extraterrestrial life-forms. Now it is necessary to put more than one life-form in the same compartment.

You have only three undamaged compartments in your starship. You and your crewmates must stay in one compartment, and that compartment should be used for extraterrestrial life-forms only if absolutely necessary. You and your crewmates must decide which of the life-forms could be placed together. It is thought that similar life-forms will have similar needs. You can use only observable characteristics to group the life-forms.

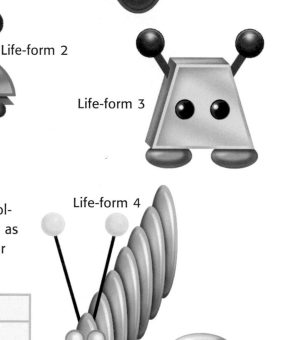

Life-form 1

Life-form 2

Life-form 3

Life-form 4

Procedure *TRY at HOME*

1. Make a data table similar to the one below. Label each column with as many characteristics of the various life-forms as possible. Leave enough space in each square to write your observations. The life-forms are pictured on this page.

Life-form Characteristics			
	Color	**Shape**	**Legs**	**Eyes**
Life-form 1				
Life-form 2				
Life-form 3				
Life-form 4				

DO NOT WRITE IN BOOK

2. Describe each characteristic as completely as you can. Based on your observations, determine which of the life-forms are most alike.

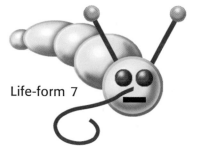

Life-form 7

Life-form 5

Life-form 6

3. Make a data table like the one below. Fill in the table according to the decisions you made in step 2. State your reasons for the way you have grouped your life-forms.

Life-form Room Assignments		
Compartment	Life-forms	Reasons
1		
2		
3		

DO NOT WRITE IN BOOK

4. The USS *Adventure* has to make one more stop before returning home. On planet X437 you discover the most interesting life-form ever found outside of Earth—the CC9, shown at right. Make a decision, based on your previous grouping of life-forms, about whether you can safely include CC9 in one of the compartments for the trip to Earth.

CC9

Analysis

5. Describe the life-forms in compartment 1. How are they similar? How are they different?

6. Describe the life-forms in compartment 2. How are they similar? How do they differ from the life-forms in compartment 1?

7. Are there any life-forms in compartment 3? If so, describe their similarities. In which compartment will you and your crewmates remain for the journey home?

8. Are you able to safely transport life-form CC9 back to Earth? Why or why not? If you are able to include CC9, in which compartment will it be placed? How did you decide?

Going Further

In 1831, Charles Darwin sailed from England on a ship called the HMS *Beagle.* You have studied the finches that Darwin observed on the Galápagos Islands. What were some of the other unusual organisms he found there? For example, find out about the Galápagos tortoise.

Concept Mapping: A Way to Bring Ideas Together

What Is a Concept Map?

Have you ever tried to tell someone about a book or a chapter you've just read and found that you can remember only a few isolated words and ideas? Or maybe you've memorized facts for a test and then weeks later discovered you're not even sure what topics those facts covered.

In both cases, you may have understood the ideas or concepts by themselves but not in relation to one another. If you could somehow link the ideas together, you would probably understand them better and remember them longer. This is something a concept map can help you do. A concept map is a way to see how ideas or concepts fit together. It can help you see the "big picture."

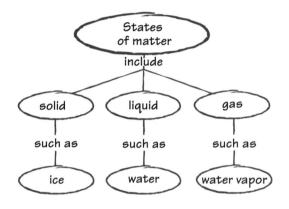

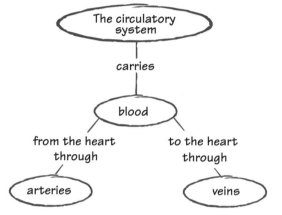

How to Make a Concept Map

❶ Make a list of the main ideas or concepts.

It might help to write each concept on its own slip of paper. This will make it easier to rearrange the concepts as many times as necessary to make sense of how the concepts are connected. After you've made a few concept maps this way, you can go directly from writing your list to actually making the map.

❷ Arrange the concepts in order from the most general to the most specific.

Put the most general concept at the top and circle it. Ask yourself, "How does this concept relate to the remaining concepts?" As you see the relationships, arrange the concepts in order from general to specific.

❸ Connect the related concepts with lines.

❹ On each line, write an action word or short phrase that shows how the concepts are related.

Look at the concept maps on this page, and then see if you can make one for the following terms:

plants, water, photosynthesis, carbon dioxide, sun's energy

One possible answer is provided at right, but don't look at it until you try the concept map yourself.

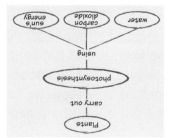

SI Measurement

The International System of Units, or SI, is the standard system of measurement used by many scientists. Using the same standards of measurement makes it easier for scientists to communicate with one another.

SI works by combining prefixes and base units. Each base unit can be used with different prefixes to define smaller and larger quantities. The table below lists common SI prefixes.

SI Prefixes			
Prefix	**Abbreviation**	**Factor**	**Example**
kilo-	k	1,000	kilogram, 1 kg = 1,000 g
hecto-	h	100	hectoliter, 1 hL = 100 L
deka-	da	10	dekameter, 1 dam = 10 m
		1	meter, liter
deci-	d	0.1	decigram, 1 dg = 0.1 g
centi-	c	0.01	centimeter, 1 cm = 0.01 m
milli-	m	0.001	milliliter, 1 mL = 0.001 L
micro-	μ	0.000 001	micrometer, 1 μm = 0.000 001 m

SI Conversion Table		
SI units	**From SI to English**	**From English to SI**
Length		
kilometer (km) = 1,000 m	1 km = 0.621 mi	1 mi = 1.609 km
meter (m) = 100 cm	1 m = 3.281 ft	1 ft = 0.305 m
centimeter (cm) = 0.01 m	1 cm = 0.394 in.	1 in. = 2.540 cm
millimeter (mm) = 0.001 m	1 mm = 0.039 in.	
micrometer (μm) = 0.000 001 m		
nanometer (nm) = 0.000 000 001 m		
Area		
square kilometer (km^2) = 100 hectares	$1\ km^2 = 0.386\ mi^2$	$1\ mi^2 = 2.590\ km^2$
hectare (ha) = 10,000 m^2	1 ha = 2.471 acres	1 acre = 0.405 ha
square meter (m^2) = 10,000 cm^2	$1\ m^2 = 10.765\ ft^2$	$1\ ft^2 = 0.093\ m^2$
square centimeter (cm^2) = 100 mm^2	$1\ cm^2 = 0.155\ in.^2$	$1\ in.^2 = 6.452\ cm^2$
Volume		
liter (L) = 1,000 mL = 1 dm^3	1 L = 1.057 fl qt	1 fl qt = 0.946 L
milliliter (mL) = 0.001 L = 1 cm^3	1 mL = 0.034 fl oz	1 fl oz = 29.575 mL
microliter (μL) = 0.000 001 L		
Mass		
kilogram (kg) = 1,000 g	1 kg = 2.205 lb	1 lb = 0.454 kg
gram (g) = 1,000 mg	1 g = 0.035 oz	1 oz = 28.349 g
milligram (mg) = 0.001 g		
microgram (μg) = 0.000 001 g		

Temperature Scales

Temperature can be expressed using three different scales: Fahrenheit, Celsius, and Kelvin. The SI unit for temperature is the kelvin (K).

Although 0 K is much colder than 0°C, a change of 1 K is equal to a change of 1°C.

Three Temperature Scales

	Fahrenheit	Celsius	Kelvin
Water boils	212°	100°	373
Body temperature	98.6°	37°	310
Room temperature	68°	20°	293
Water freezes	32°	0°	273

Temperature Conversions Table

To convert	Use this equation:	Example
Celsius to Fahrenheit °C ⟶ °F	$°F = \left(\dfrac{9}{5} \times °C\right) + 32$	Convert 45°C to °F. $°F = \left(\dfrac{9}{5} \times 45°C\right) + 32 = 113°F$
Fahrenheit to Celsius °F ⟶ °C	$°C = \dfrac{5}{9} \times (°F - 32)$	Convert 68°F to °C. $°C = \dfrac{5}{9} \times (68°F - 32) = 20°C$
Celsius to Kelvin °C ⟶ K	$K = °C + 273$	Convert 45°C to K. $K = 45°C + 273 = 318\ K$
Kelvin to Celsius K ⟶ °C	$°C = K - 273$	Convert 32 K to °C. $°C = 32\ K - 273 = -241°C$

Measuring Skills

Using a Graduated Cylinder

When using a graduated cylinder to measure volume, keep the following procedures in mind:

1 Make sure the cylinder is on a flat, level surface.

2 Move your head so that your eye is level with the surface of the liquid.

3 Read the mark closest to the liquid level. On glass graduated cylinders, read the mark closest to the center of the curve in the liquid's surface.

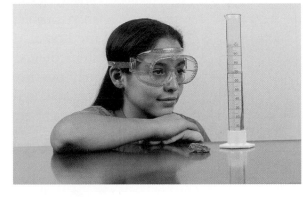

Using a Meterstick or Metric Ruler

When using a meterstick or metric ruler to measure length, keep the following procedures in mind:

1 Place the ruler firmly against the object you are measuring.

2 Align one edge of the object exactly with the zero end of the ruler.

3 Look at the other edge of the object to see which of the marks on the ruler is closest to that edge. **Note:** Each small slash between the centimeters represents a millimeter, which is one-tenth of a centimeter.

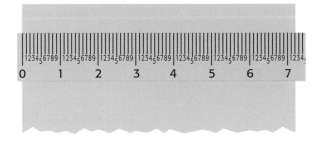

Using a Triple-Beam Balance

When using a triple-beam balance to measure mass, keep the following procedures in mind:

1 Make sure the balance is on a level surface.

2 Place all of the countermasses at zero. Adjust the balancing knob until the pointer rests at zero.

3 Place the object you wish to measure on the pan. **Caution:** Do not place hot objects or chemicals directly on the balance pan.

4 Move the largest countermass along the beam to the right until it is at the last notch that does not tip the balance. Follow the same procedure with the next-largest countermass. Then move the smallest countermass until the pointer rests at zero.

5 Add the readings from the three beams together to determine the mass of the object.

6 When determining the mass of crystals or powders, use a piece of filter paper. First find the mass of the paper. Then add the crystals or powder to the paper and re-measure. The actual mass of the crystals or powder is the total mass minus the mass of the paper. When finding the mass of liquids, first find the mass of the empty container. Then find the mass of the liquid and container together. The mass of the liquid is the total mass minus the mass of the container.

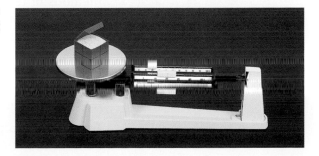

Scientific Method

The series of steps that scientists use to answer questions and solve problems is often called the **scientific method.** The scientific method is not a rigid procedure. Scientists may use all of the steps or just some of the steps of the scientific method. They may even repeat some of the steps. The goal of the scientific method is to come up with reliable answers and solutions.

Six Steps of the Scientific Method

Ask a Question

1 **Ask a Question** Good questions come from careful **observations.** You make observations by using your senses to gather information. Sometimes you may use instruments, such as microscopes and telescopes, to extend the range of your senses. As you observe the natural world, you will discover that you have many more questions than answers. These questions drive the scientific method.

Questions beginning with *what, why, how,* and *when* are very important in focusing an investigation, and they often lead to a hypothesis. (You will learn what a hypothesis is in the next step.) Here is an example of a question that could lead to further investigation.

Question: How does acid rain affect plant growth?

Form a Hypothesis

2 **Form a Hypothesis** After you come up with a question, you need to turn the question into a **hypothesis.** A hypothesis is a clear statement of what you expect the answer to your question to be. Your hypothesis will represent your best "educated guess" based on your observations and what you already know. A good hypothesis is testable. If observations and information cannot be gathered or if an experiment cannot be designed to test your hypothesis, it is untestable, and the investigation can go no further.

Here is a hypothesis that could be formed from the question, "How does acid rain affect plant growth?"

Hypothesis: Acid rain causes plants to grow more slowly.

Notice that the hypothesis provides some specifics that lead to methods of testing. The hypothesis can also lead to predictions. A **prediction** is what you think will be the outcome of your experiment or data collection. Predictions are usually stated in an "if . . . then" format. For example, **if** meat is kept at room temperature, **then** it will spoil faster than meat kept in the refrigerator. More than one prediction can be made for a single hypothesis. Here is a sample prediction for the hypothesis that acid rain causes plants to grow more slowly.

Prediction: If a plant is watered with only acid rain (which has a pH of 4), then the plant will grow at half its normal rate.

3 **Test the Hypothesis** After you have formed a hypothesis and made a prediction, you should test your hypothesis. There are different ways to do this. Perhaps the most familiar way is to conduct a **controlled experiment.** A controlled experiment tests only one factor at a time. A controlled experiment has a **control group** and one or more **experimental groups.** All the factors for the control and experimental groups are the same except for one factor, which is called the **variable.** By changing only one factor, you can see the results of just that one change.

Sometimes, the nature of an investigation makes a controlled experiment impossible. For example, dinosaurs have been extinct for millions of years, and the Earth's core is surrounded by thousands of meters of rock. It would be difficult, if not impossible, to conduct controlled experiments on such things. Under such circumstances, a hypothesis may be tested by making detailed observations. Taking measurements is one way of making observations.

Test the Hypothesis

4 **Analyze the Results** After you have completed your experiments, made your observations, and collected your data, you must analyze all the information you have gathered. Tables and graphs are often used in this step to organize the data.

Analyze the Results

5 **Draw Conclusions** Based on the analysis of your data, you should conclude whether or not your results support your hypothesis. If your hypothesis is supported, you (or others) might want to repeat the observations or experiments to verify your results. If your hypothesis is not supported by the data, you may have to check your procedure for errors. You may even have to reject your hypothesis and make a new one. If you cannot draw a conclusion from your results, you may have to try the investigation again or carry out further observations or experiments.

Draw Conclusions

Do they support your hypothesis?

No

Yes

6 **Communicate Results** After any scientific investigation, you should report your results. By doing a written or oral report, you let others know what you have learned. They may want to repeat your investigation to see if they get the same results. Your report may even lead to another question, which in turn may lead to another investigation.

Communicate Results

Scientific Method in Action

The scientific method is not a "straight line" of steps. It contains loops in which several steps may be repeated over and over again, while others may not be necessary. For example, sometimes scientists will find that testing one hypothesis raises new questions and new hypotheses to be tested. And sometimes, testing the hypothesis leads directly to a conclusion. Furthermore, the steps in the scientific method are not always used in the same order. Follow the steps in the diagram below, and see how many different directions the scientific method can take you.

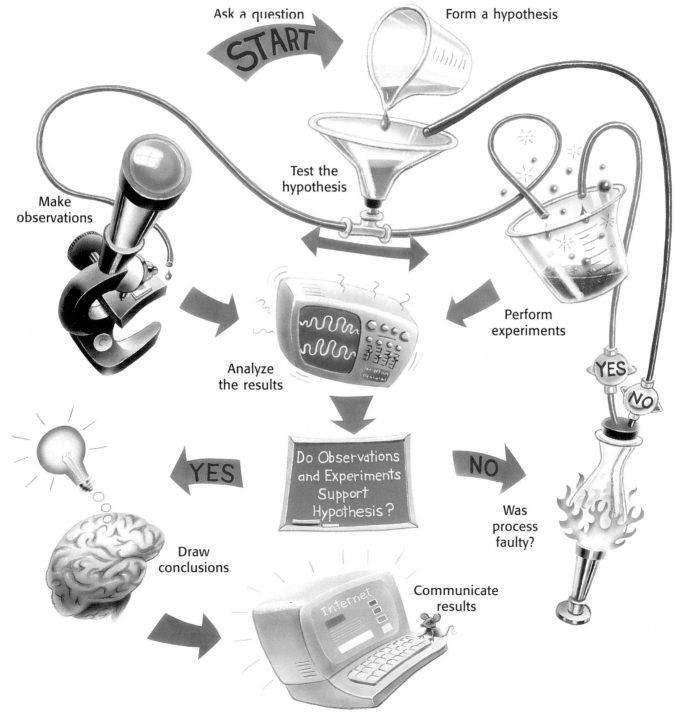

Ask a question

START

Form a hypothesis

Make observations

Test the hypothesis

Perform experiments

YES

NO

Analyze the results

Do Observations and Experiments Support Hypothesis?

YES

NO

Was process faulty?

Draw conclusions

Communicate results

Internet

Making Charts and Graphs

Circle Graphs

A circle graph, or pie chart, shows how each group of data relates to all of the data. Each part of the circle represents a category of the data. The entire circle represents all of the data. For example, a biologist studying a hardwood forest in Wisconsin found that there were five different types of trees. The data table at right summarizes the biologist's findings.

Wisconsin Hardwood Trees	
Type of tree	Number found
Oak	600
Maple	750
Beech	300
Birch	1,200
Hickory	150
Total	3,000

How to Make a Circle Graph

❶ In order to make a circle graph of this data, first find the percentage of each type of tree. To do this, divide the number of individual trees by the total number of trees and multiply by 100.

$$\frac{600 \text{ oak}}{3,000 \text{ trees}} \times 100 = 20\%$$

$$\frac{750 \text{ maple}}{3,000 \text{ trees}} \times 100 = 25\%$$

$$\frac{300 \text{ beech}}{3,000 \text{ trees}} \times 100 = 10\%$$

$$\frac{1,200 \text{ birch}}{3,000 \text{ trees}} \times 100 = 40\%$$

$$\frac{150 \text{ hickory}}{3,000 \text{ trees}} \times 100 = 5\%$$

❷ Now determine the size of the pie shapes that make up the chart. Do this by multiplying each percentage by 360°. Remember that a circle contains 360°.

$20\% \times 360° = 72°$ $25\% \times 360° = 90°$
$10\% \times 360° = 36°$ $40\% \times 360° = 144°$
$5\% \times 360° = 18°$

❸ Then check that the sum of the percentages is 100 and the sum of the degrees is 360.

$20\% + 25\% + 10\% + 40\% + 5\% = 100\%$
$72° + 90° + 36° + 144° + 18° = 360°$

❹ Use a compass to draw a circle and mark its center.

❺ Then use a protractor to draw angles of 72°, 90°, 36°, 144°, and 18° in the circle.

❻ Finally, label each part of the graph, and choose an appropriate title.

A Community of Wisconsin Hardwood Trees

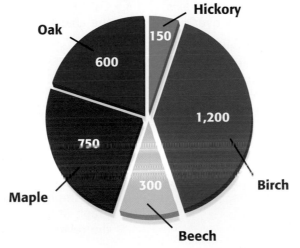

Line Graphs

Line graphs are most often used to demonstrate continuous change. For example, Mr. Smith's science class analyzed the population records for their hometown, Appleton, between 1900 and 2000. Examine the data at left.

Because the year and the population change, they are the *variables*. The population is determined by, or dependent on, the year. Therefore, the population is called the **dependent variable,** and the year is called the **independent variable.** Each set of data is called a **data pair.** To prepare a line graph, data pairs must first be organized in a table like the one at left.

Population of Appleton, 1900–2000	
Year	Population
1900	1,800
1920	2,500
1940	3,200
1960	3,900
1980	4,600
2000	5,300

How to Make a Line Graph

1 Place the independent variable along the horizontal (*x*) axis. Place the dependent variable along the vertical (*y*) axis.

2 Label the *x*-axis "Year" and the *y*-axis "Population." Look at your largest and smallest values for the population. Determine a scale for the *y*-axis that will provide enough space to show these values. You must use the same scale for the entire length of the axis. Find an appropriate scale for the *x*-axis too.

3 Choose reasonable starting points for each axis.

4 Plot the data pairs as accurately as possible.

5 Choose a title that accurately represents the data.

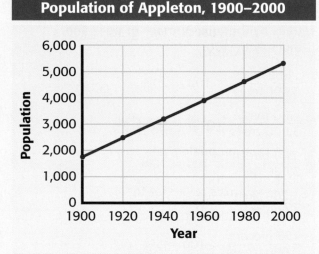

How to Determine Slope

Slope is the ratio of the change in the *y*-axis to the change in the *x*-axis, or "rise over run."

1 Choose two points on the line graph. For example, the population of Appleton in 2000 was 5,300 people. Therefore, you can define point *a* as (2000, 5,300). In 1900, the population was 1,800 people. Define point *b* as (1900, 1,800).

2 Find the change in the *y*-axis. (*y* at point *a*) − (*y* at point *b*) 5,300 people − 1,800 people = 3,500 people

3 Find the change in the *x*-axis. (*x* at point *a*) − (*x* at point *b*) 2000 − 1900 = 100 years

4 Calculate the slope of the graph by dividing the change in *y* by the change in *x*.

$$\text{slope} = \frac{\text{change in } y}{\text{change in } x}$$

$$\text{slope} = \frac{3,500 \text{ people}}{100 \text{ years}}$$

$$\text{slope} = 35 \text{ people per year}$$

In this example, the population in Appleton increased by a fixed amount each year. The graph of this data is a straight line. Therefore, the relationship is **linear.** When the graph of a set of data is not a straight line, the relationship is **nonlinear.**

Using Algebra to Determine Slope

The equation in step 4 may also be arranged to be:

$$y = kx$$

where y represents the change in the y-axis, k represents the slope, and x represents the change in the x-axis.

$$\text{slope} = \frac{\text{change in } y}{\text{change in } x}$$

$$k = \frac{y}{x}$$

$$k \times x = \frac{y \times x}{x}$$

$$kx = y$$

Bar Graphs

Bar graphs are used to demonstrate change that is not continuous. These graphs can be used to indicate trends when the data are taken over a long period of time. A meteorologist gathered the precipitation records at right for Hartford, Connecticut, for April 1–15, 1996, and used a bar graph to represent the data.

Precipitation in Hartford, Connecticut April 1–15, 1996

Date	Precipitation (cm)	Date	Precipitation (cm)
April 1	0.5	April 9	0.25
April 2	1.25	April 10	0.0
April 3	0.0	April 11	1.0
April 4	0.0	April 12	0.0
April 5	0.0	April 13	0.25
April 6	0.0	April 14	0.0
April 7	0.0	April 15	6.50
April 8	1.75		

How to Make a Bar Graph

1 Use an appropriate scale and a reasonable starting point for each axis.

2 Label the axes, and plot the data.

3 Choose a title that accurately represents the data.

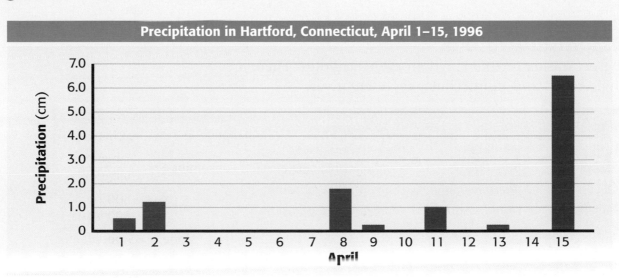

Precipitation in Hartford, Connecticut, April 1–15, 1996

The Six Kingdoms

Kingdom Archaebacteria

The organisms in this kingdom are single-celled prokaryotes.

Archaebacteria		
Group	**Examples**	**Characteristics**
Methanogens	*Methanococcus*	found in soil, swamps, the digestive tract of mammals; produce methane gas; can't live in oxygen
Thermophiles	*Sulpholobus*	found in extremely hot environments; require sulphur, can't live in oxygen
Halophiles	*Halococcus*	found in environments with very high salt content, such as the Dead Sea; nearly all can live in oxygen

Kingdom Eubacteria

There are more than 4,000 named species in this kingdom of single-celled prokaryotes.

Eubacteria		
Group	**Examples**	**Characteristics**
Bacilli	*Escherichia coli*	rod-shaped; free-living, symbiotic, or parasitic; some can fix nitrogen; some cause disease
Cocci	*Streptococcus*	spherical-shaped, disease-causing; can form spores to resist unfavorable environments
Spirilla	*Treponema*	spiral-shaped; responsible for several serious illnesses, such as syphilis and Lyme disease

Kingdom Protista

The organisms in this kingdom are eukaryotes. There are single-celled and multicellular representatives.

Protists		
Group	**Examples**	**Characteristics**
Sacodines	*Amoeba*	radiolarians; single-celled consumers
Ciliates	*Paramecium*	single-celled consumers
Flagellates	*Trypanosoma*	single-celled parasites
Sporozoans	*Plasmodium*	single-celled parasites
Euglenas	*Euglena*	single-celled; photosynthesize
Diatoms	*Pinnularia*	most are single-celled; photosynthesize
Dinoflagellates	*Gymnodinium*	single-celled; some photosynthesize
Algae	*Volvox*, coral algae	4 phyla; single- or many-celled; photosynthesize
Slime molds	*Physarum*	single- or many-celled; consumers or decomposers
Water molds	powdery mildew	single- or many-celled, parasites or decomposers

Kingdom Fungi

There are single-celled and multicellular eukaryotes in this kingdom. There are four major groups of fungi.

	Fungi	
Group	**Examples**	**Characteristics**
Threadlike fungi	bread mold	spherical; decomposers
Sac fungi	yeast, morels	saclike; parasites and decomposers
Club fungi	mushrooms, rusts, smuts	club-shaped; parasites and decomposers
Lichens	British soldier	symbiotic with algae

Kingdom Plantae

The organisms in this kingdom are multicellular eukaryotes. They have specialized organ systems for different life processes. They are classified in divisions instead of phyla.

	Plants	
Group	**Examples**	**Characteristics**
Bryophytes	mosses, liverworts	reproduce by spores
Club mosses	*Lycopodium*, ground pine	reproduce by spores
Horsetails	rushes	reproduce by spores
Ferns	spleenworts, sensitive fern	reproduce by spores
Conifers	pines, spruces, firs	reproduce by seeds; cones
Cycads	*Zamia*	reproduce by seeds
Gnetophytes	*Welwitschia*	reproduce by seeds
Ginkgoes	*Ginkgo*	reproduce by seeds
Angiosperms	all flowering plants	reproduce by seeds; flowers

Kingdom Animalia

This kingdom contains multicellular eukaryotes. They have specialized tissues and complex organ systems.

	Animals	
Group	**Examples**	**Characteristics**
Sponges	glass sponges	no symmetry or segmentation; aquatic
Cnidarians	jellyfish, coral	radial symmetry; aquatic
Flatworms	planaria, tapeworms, flukes	bilateral symmetry; organ systems
Roundworms	*Trichina*, hookworms	bilateral symmetry; organ systems
Annelids	earthworms, leeches	bilateral symmetry; organ systems
Mollusks	snails, octopuses	bilateral symmetry; organ systems
Echinoderms	sea stars, sand dollars	radial symmetry; organ systems
Arthropods	insects, spiders, lobsters	bilateral symmetry; organ systems
Chordates	fish, amphibians, reptiles, birds, mammals	bilateral symmetry; complex organ systems

Using the Microscope

Parts of the Compound Light Microscope

- The **ocular lens** magnifies the image 10×.

- The **low-power objective** magnifies the image 10×.

- The **high-power objective** magnifies the image either 40× or 43×.

- The **revolving nosepiece** holds the objectives and can be turned to change from one magnification to the other.

- The **body tube** maintains the correct distance between the ocular lens and objectives.

- The **coarse-adjustment knob** moves the body tube up and down to allow focusing of the image.

- The **fine-adjustment knob** moves the body tube slightly to bring the image into sharper focus.

- The **stage** supports a slide.

- **Stage clips** hold the slide in place for viewing.

- The **diaphragm** controls the amount of light coming through the stage.

- The light source provides a **light** for viewing the slide.

- The **arm** supports the body tube.

- The **base** supports the microscope.

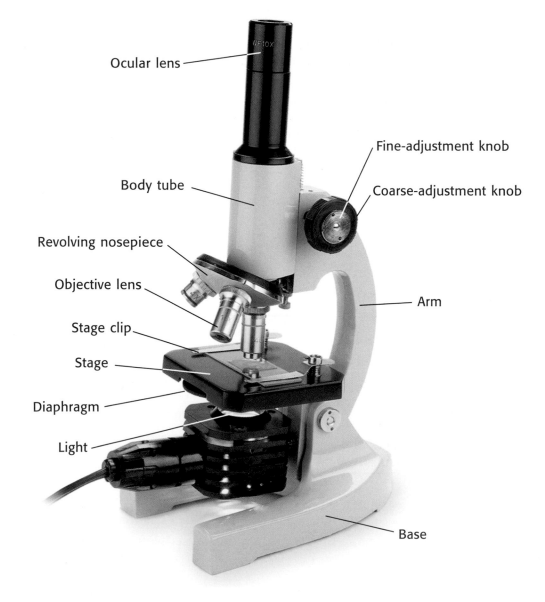

Ocular lens

Fine-adjustment knob

Body tube

Coarse-adjustment knob

Revolving nosepiece

Objective lens

Arm

Stage clip

Stage

Diaphragm

Light

Base

Proper Use of the Compound Light Microscope

1 Carry the microscope to your lab table using both hands. Place one hand beneath the base, and use the other hand to hold the arm of the microscope. Hold the microscope close to your body while moving it to your lab table.

2 Place the microscope on the lab table at least 5 cm from the edge of the table.

3 Check to see what type of light source is used by your microscope. If the microscope has a lamp, plug it in, making sure that the cord is out of the way. If the microscope has a mirror, adjust it to reflect light through the hole in the stage.
Caution: If your microscope has a mirror, do not use direct sunlight as a light source. Direct sunlight can damage your eyes.

4 Always begin work with the low-power objective in line with the body tube. Adjust the revolving nosepiece.

5 Place a prepared slide over the hole in the stage. Secure the slide with the stage clips.

6 Look through the ocular lens. Move the diaphragm to adjust the amount of light coming through the stage.

7 Look at the stage from eye level. Slowly turn the coarse adjustment to lower the objective until it almost touches the slide. Do not allow the objective to touch the slide.

8 Look through the ocular lens. Turn the coarse adjustment to raise the low-power objective until the image is in focus. Always focus by raising the objective away from the slide. *Never focus the objective downward.* Use the fine adjustment to sharpen the focus. Keep both eyes open while viewing a slide.

9 Make sure that the image is exactly in the center of your field of vision. Then switch to the high-power objective. Focus the image, using only the fine adjustment. *Never use the coarse adjustment at high power.*

10 When you are finished using the microscope, remove the slide. Clean the ocular lens and objective lenses with lens paper. Return the microscope to its storage area. Remember, you should use both hands to carry the microscope.

Making a Wet Mount

1 Use lens paper to clean a glass slide and a coverslip.

2 Place the specimen you wish to observe in the center of the slide.

3 Using a medicine dropper, place one drop of water on the specimen.

4 Hold the coverslip at the edge of the water and at a 45° angle to the slide. Make sure that the water runs along the edge of the coverslip.

5 Lower the coverslip slowly to avoid trapping air bubbles.

6 Water might evaporate from the slide as you work. Add more water to keep the specimen fresh. Place the tip of the medicine dropper next to the edge of the coverslip. Add a drop of water. (You can also use this method to add stain or solutions to a wet mount.) Remove excess water from the slide by using the corner of a paper towel as a blotter. Do not lift the coverslip to add or remove water.

Glossary

A

absolute dating   determining the age of an object or event in years, usually by measuring the amount of unstable atoms in the sample (133)

active transport   the movement of particles through proteins in the cell membrane against the direction of diffusion; requires cells to use energy (36)

adaptation   a characteristic that helps an organism survive in its environment (104)

adenine   (AD uh NEEN) one of the four bases that combine with sugar and phospate to form a nucleotide subunit of DNA; adenine pairs with thymine (80)

alleles   different forms of a single gene (61)

anaerobic   describes an organism that does not need oxygen (139)

Animalia   the classification kingdom containing complex, multicellular organisms that lack cell walls, are usually able to move around, and possess nervous systems that help them be aware of and react to their surroundings (171)

Archaebacteria   (AHR kee bak TIR ee uh) a classification kingdom containing bacteria that thrive in extreme environments (167)

australopithecine   (ah STRA loh PITH uh seen) an early hominid that evolved more than 3.6 million years ago (146)

B

bacteria   extremely small, single-celled organisms without a nucleus; prokaryotic cells (14, 167)

binary fission   the simple cell division in which one cell splits into two; used by bacteria (42)

C

cell cycle   the life cycle of a cell; in eukaryotes it consists of chromosome duplication, mitosis, and cytokinesis (42)

cell membrane   a phospholipid layer that covers a cell's surface and acts as a barrier between the inside of a cell and the cell's environment (11)

cell wall   a structure that surrounds the cell membrane of some cells and provides strength and support to the cell membrane (17)

cellular respiration   the process of producing ATP in the cell from oxygen and glucose; releases carbon dioxide and water (39)

Cenozoic era   the period in the geologic time scale beginning about 65 million years ago and continuing until the present day (143)

centromere   the region that holds chromatids together when a chromosome is duplicated (43)

chlorophyll   a green pigment in chloroplasts that absorbs light energy for photosynthesis (19)

chloroplast   an organelle found in plant and algae cells where photosynthesis occurs (19)

chromatids   identical chromosome copies (43)

chromosome   a coiled structure of DNA and protein that forms in the cell nucleus during cell division (42)

class   the level of classification after phylum; the organisms in all phyla are sorted into classes (161)

classification   the arrangement of organisms into orderly groups based on their similarities and presumed evolutionary relationships (160)

community   all of the populations of different species that live and interact in an area (8)

cytokinesis   (SIET oh ki NEE sis) the process in which cytoplasm divides after mitosis (45)

cytoplasm   (SIET oh PLAZ uhm) cellular fluid surrounding a cell's organelles (11)

cytosine   (SIET oh SEEN) one of the four bases that combine with sugar and phosphate to form a nucleotide subunit of DNA; cytosine pairs with guanine (80)

D

dichotomous key   (die KAWT uh muhs) an aid to identifying unknown organisms that consists of several pairs of descriptive statements; of each pair of statements, only one will apply to the unknown organism, and that statement will lead to another set of statements, and so on, until the unknown organism can be identified (164)

diffusion   the movement of particles from an area where their concentration is high to an area where their concentration is low (34)

DNA   deoxyribonucleic (dee AHKS ee RIE boh noo KLEE ik) acid; hereditary material that controls all the activities of a cell, contains the information to make new cells, and provides instructions for making proteins (11, 80)

dominant trait   the trait observed when at least one dominant allele for a characteristic is inherited (59)

E

ecosystem   a community of organisms and their nonliving environment (8)

endocytosis   (EN doh sie TOH sis) the process in which a cell membrane surrounds a particle and encloses it in a vesicle to bring it into the cell (37)

endoplasmic reticulum (EN doh PLAZ mik ri TIK yuh luhm) a membrane-covered cell organelle that produces lipids, breaks down drugs and other substances, and packages proteins for delivery out of the cell (18)

Eubacteria (YOO bak TIR ee uh) a classification kingdom containing mostly free-living bacteria found in many varied environments (167)

eukaryotic cell (eukaryote) (yoo KER ee OHT) a cell that contains a central nucleus and a complicated internal structure (15, 140)

evolution the process by which populations accumulate inherited changes over time (105)

exocytosis (EK soh sie TOH sis) the process used to remove large particles from a cell; during exocytosis, a vesicle containing the particles fuses with the cell membrane (37)

extinct describes a species of organism that has died out completely (135)

F

family the level of classification after order; the organisms in all orders are sorted into families (161)

fermentation the breakdown of sugars to make ATP in the absence of oxygen (39)

fossil the solidified remains or imprints of a once-living organism (106, 132)

fossil record a historical sequence of life indicated by fossils found in layers of the Earth's crust (106)

Fungi a kingdom of complex organisms that obtain food by breaking down other substances in their surroundings and absorbing the nutrients (170)

G

generation time the period between the birth of one generation and the birth of the next generation (118)

genes segments of DNA that carry hereditary instructions and are passed from parent to offspring; located on chromosomes (61)

genotype the inherited combination of alleles (61)

genus the level of classification after family; the organisms in all families are sorted into genera (161)

geologic time scale the division of Earth's history into distinct intervals of time (134)

Golgi complex the cell organelle that modifies, packages, and transports materials out of the cell (20)

guanine (GWAH NEEN) one of the four bases that combine with sugar and phosphate to form a nucleotide subunit of DNA; guanine pairs with cytosine (80)

H

heredity the passing of traits from parent to offspring (56)

hominid the family referring specifically to humans and several extinct, humanlike species, some of which were human ancestors (145)

homologous (hoh MAHL uh guhs) **chromosomes** chromosomes with matching information (43)

K

kingdom the most general of the seven levels of classification (161)

lysosome a special vesicle in a cell that digests food particles, wastes, and foreign invaders (22)

M

meiosis (mie OH sis) cell division that produces sex cells (65)

Mesozoic era the period in the geologic time scale beginning about 248 million years ago and ending about 65 million years ago (142)

mitochondria (MIET oh KAHN dree uh) cell organelles surrounded by two membranes that break down food molecules to make ATP (19)

mitosis nuclear division in eukaryotic cells in which each cell receives a copy of the original chromosomes (43)

multicellular made of many cells (7)

mutagen anything that can damage or cause changes in DNA (90)

mutation a change in the order of the bases in an organism's DNA; deletion, insertion, or substitution (90, 117)

N

natural selection the process by which organisms with favorable traits survive and reproduce at a higher rate than organisms without the favorable trait (116)

Neanderthal a species of hominid that lived in Europe and western Asia from 230,000 years ago to about 30,000 years ago (148)

nucleotide a subunit of DNA consisting of a sugar, a phosphate, and one of four nitrogenous bases (80)

nucleus the membrane-covered organelle found in eukaryotic cells; contains the cell's DNA and serves as a control center for the cell (14)

O

order the level of classification after class; the organisms in all the classes are sorted into orders (161)

organ a combination of two or more tissues that work together to perform a specific function in the body (5)

organ system a group of organs that works together to perform body functions (6)

organelle (OHR guh NEL) a structure within a cell, sometimes surrounded by a membrane (11)

organism anything that can independently carry out life processes (7)

osmosis the diffusion of water across a cell membrane (35)

P

Paleozoic era the period in the geologic time scale beginning about 570 million years ago and ending about 248 million years ago (141)

passive transport the diffusion of particles through proteins in the cell membrane from areas where the concentration of particles is high to areas where the concentration of particles is low (36)

pedigree a diagram of family history used for tracing a trait through several generations (92)

phenotype an organism's inherited appearance (61)

photosynthesis (FOHT oh SIN thuh sis) the process by which plants capture light energy from the sun and convert it into sugar (38, 140)

phylum the level of classification after kingdom; the organisms from all the kingdoms are sorted into several phyla (161)

Plantae the kingdom that contains plants—complex, multicellular organisms that are usually green and use the sun's energy to make sugar by photosynthesis (169)

plate tectonics the study of the forces that drive the movement of pieces of Earth's crust around the surface of the planet (137)

population a group of individuals of the same species that live together in the same area at the same time (7)

Precambrian time the period in the geologic time scale beginning when Earth originated, 4.6 billion years ago, and ending when complex organisms appeared, about 540 million years ago (138)

primate a type of mammal that includes humans, apes, and monkeys; typically distinguished by opposable thumbs and binocular vision (144)

probability the mathematical chance that an event will occur (62)

prokaryotic cell (prokaryote) (proh KER ee OHT) a cell that does not have a nucleus or any other membrane-covered organelles; also called a bacterium (14, 139)

prosimian the first primate ancestors; *also* a group of living primates that includes lorises and lemurs (146)

Protista a kingdom of eukaryotic single-celled or simple, multicellular organisms; kingdom Protista contains all eukaryotes that are not plants, animals, or fungi (168)

R

recessive trait a trait that is apparent only when two recessive alleles for the same characteristic are inherited (59)

relative dating determining whether an event or object, such as a fossil, is older or younger than other events or objects (133)

ribosome a small organelle in cells where proteins are made from amino acids (18, 89)

S

sediment fine particles of sand, dust, or mud that are deposited over time by wind or water (132)

selective breeding the breeding of organisms that have a certain desired trait (114)

sex cell an egg or sperm; a sex cell carries half the number of chromosomes found in other body cells (64)

sex chromosomes the chromosomes that carry genes that determine the sex of offspring (69)

speciation the process by which two populations of the same species become so different that they can no longer interbreed (120)

species the most specific of the seven levels of classification; characterized by a group of organisms that can mate with one another to produce fertile offspring (104, 161)

T

taxonomy the science of identifying, classifying, and naming living things (162)

thymine one of the four bases that combine with sugar and phosphate to form a nucleotide subunit of DNA; thymine pairs with adenine (80)

tissue a group of similar cells that work together to perform a specific job in the body (5)

trait a distinguishing quality that can be passed from one generation to another (114)

true-breeding plant a plant that always produces offspring with the same traits as the parent(s) (58)

U

unicellular made of a single cell (7)

V

vacuole (VAK yoo OHL) a large membrane-covered structure found in plant cells that serves as a storage container for water and other liquids (21)

vesicle a membrane-covered compartment in a eukaryotic cell that forms when part of the cell membrane surrounds an object and pinches off (21)

vestigial structure (ves TIJ ee uhl) the remnant of a once-useful anatomical structure (107)

Index

INDEX

Credits

Abbreviations used: (t) top, (c) center, (b) bottom, (l) left, (r) right, (bkgd) background

ILLUSTRATIONS

All illustrations, unless otherwise noted below by Holt, Rinehart and Winston.

Table of Contents: p. iv, Morgan-Cain & Associates; vi(b), John White/The Neis Group.

Chapter One Page 6 (br), Christy Krames; p. 6 (c), Michael Woods/Morgan-Cain & Associates; p. 7 (cl), Morgan-Cain & Associates; p. 7 (c), Morgan-Cain & Associates; p. 7 (cr), Christy Krames; p. 8 (br), Yuan Lee; p. 10 (bl), David Merrell/Suzanne Craig Represents Inc.; p. 12 (c), Morgan-Cain & Associates; p. 12 (tl), Terry Kovalcik; p. 13 (bc), Terry Kovalcik; p. 13 (cr), Morgan-Cain & Associates; p. 14 (br), Morgan-Cain & Associates; p. 15 (tr), Morgan-Cain & Associates; p. 16, Morgan-Cain & Associates; p. 17, Morgan-Cain & Associates; p. 18, Morgan-Cain & Associates; p. 19, Morgan-Cain & Associates; p. 20, Morgan-Cain & Associates; p. 21, Morgan-Cain & Associates; p. 22, Morgan-Cain & Associates; p. 23, Morgan-Cain & Associates; p. 29, Morgan-Cain & Associates.

Chapter Two p. 35 (tr), Stephen Durke/Washington Artists; p. 36 (bl,br), Morgan-Cain & Associates; p. 36 (tl), Terry Kovalcik; p. 37 (c), Morgan-Cain & Associates; p. 38 (bl), Morgan-Cain & Associates; p. 39, Morgan-Cain & Associates; p. 40 (tl), Robin Carter; p. 40 (cl), Morgan-Cain & Associates; p. 40 (bl), Morgan-Cain & Associates; p. 40 (cr), Morgan-Cain & Associates; p. 40 (br), Morgan-Cain & Associates; p. 44 (l), Alexander & Turner ; p. 51 (cr), Morgan-Cain & Associates.

Chapter Three Page 57 (b), Mike Weplo/Das Group; p. 58, John White/The Neis Group; p. 59, John White/The Neis Group; p. 60, John White/The Neis Group; p. 61, John White/The Neis Group; p. 65 (r), Alexander & Turner; p. 66 (l), Alexander & Turner; p. 67 (r) Alexander & Turner; p. 68, Alexander & Turner; p. 69 (bc), Alexander & Turner; p. 69 (br), Rob Schuster/Hankins and Tegenborg; p. 69 (cr), Blake Thornton/Rita Marie; p. 73 (cr), Blake Thornton/Rita Marie; p. 74, John White/The Neis Group; p. 75 (bl), John White/The Neis Group.

Chapter Four p. 80, Rob Schuster/Hankins and Tegenborg; p. 82 (c), Alexander & Turner; p. 82 (tl), Marty Roper/Planet Rep; p. 83 (cl), Alexander & Turner; p. 84, Morgan-Cain & Associates; p. 85 (r), Grey Geisler; p. 86 (cl), John White/The Neis Group; p. 88-89, Rob Schuster/Hankins and Tegenborg; p. 90 (tl), Rob Schuster/Hankins and Tegenborg; p. 91 (b) Rob Schuster/Hankins and Tegenborg; p. 96 Alexander & Turner; 97, Rob Schuster/Hankins and Tegenborg.

Chapter Five p. 105, Steve Roberts; p. 107 (tr), Ross, Culbert and Lavery; p. 107 (b), Rob Wood/Wood, Ronsaville, Harlin; p. 108-109, Rob Wood/Wood, Ronsaville, Harlin; p. 110, Christy Krames; p. 111 (c), Sarah Woods; p. 111 (tr), David Beck; p. 111 (cr), Frank Ordaz/Dimension; p. 113 (tl), Tony Morse/Ivy Glick; p. 113 (b), John White/The Neis Group; p. 115, Ross, Culbert and Lavery; p. 116 (r), Will Nelson/Sweet Reps; p. 118 (c), Carlyn Iverson; p. 118 (bl), Frank Ordaz/Dimension; p. 120 (c), Mike Weplo/Das Group; p. 120 (bl), Will Nelson/Sweet Reps; p. 121 (c), Carlyn Iverson; p. 124 (tc), Rob Wood/Wood, Ronsaville, Harlin; p. 124 (br), Christy Krames; p. 125, Carlyn Iverson; p. 127 (tr), Ross, Culbert and Lavery; p. 128 (tl), Carlyn Iverson.

Chapter Six p. 132 (b), Mike Weplo/Das Group; p. 133 (cr), Mike Weplo/Das Group; p. 133 (br), Rob Schuster/Hankins and Tegenborg; p. 134, Barbara Hoopes-Ambler; p. 135, John White/The Neis Group; p. 136, MapQuest.com; p. 137 (tr), MapQuest.com; p. 137 (br), Walter Stuart; p. 139, John White/The Neis Group; p. 140, Craig Attebery/Jeff Lavaty Artist Agent; p. 141, Barbara Hoopes-Ambler; p. 142, Barbara Hoopes-Ambler; p. 143 (tr), John White/The Neis Group; p. 144 (bl), Todd Buck; p. 144 (br), Will Nelson/Sweet Reps; p. 145, Christy Krames; p. 152, Barbara Hoopes-Ambler; p. 155 (tr), John White/The Neis Group; p. 155 (tr), John White/The Neis Group; p. 155 (tr), John White/The Neis Group; p. 155 (tr), John White/The Neis Group; p. 155 (tr), John White/The Neis Group; p. 156 (br), Greg Harris.

Chapter Seven p. 161 (bear, blue jay, earthworm), Michael Woods/Morgan-Cain & Associates; p. 161 (boy), Frank Ordaz/Dimension; p. 161 (whale), Graham Allen; p. 161 (lynx), David Ashby; p. 161 (cat, lion), Will Nelson/Sweet Reps; p. 162 (tl), Will Nelson/Sweet Reps; p. 162 (bear, platypus), Michael Woods/Morgan-Cain & Associates; p. 162 (cat, lion), Will Nelson/Sweet Reps; p. 163 (b), John White/The Neis Group; p. 163 (tr), Blake Thornton/Rita Marie; p. 164 (c), Marty Roper/Planet Rep; p. 164 (bl), John White/The Neis Group; p. 165 (br), Cy Baker/WAA; p. 165 (tl), John White/The Neis Group; p. 165 (tr), John White/The Neis Group; p. 174, John White/The Neis Group; p. 176 (cr), Marty Roper/Planet Rep; p. 177, (lemur), Will Nelson/Sweet Reps; p. 177 (baboon), Graham Allen; p. 177 (chimpanzee), Michael Woods/Morgan-Cain & Associates; p. 177 (human), Frank Ordaz; p. 178 (bl), John White/The Neis Group; p. 178 (tr), Barbara Hoopes-Ambler.Nelson/Sweet

LabBook p. 184 (tl), David Merrell/Suzanne Craig Represents Inc.; p. 184 (cr), Rob Schuster/Hankins and Tegenborg; p. 188 (bl), Kip Carter; p. 190 (bl), Keith Locke; p. 191 (cr), Keith Locke; p. 192, Rob Schuster/Hankins and Tegenborg; p. 193 (cr), Rob Schuster/Hankins and Tegenborg.

Appendix p. 196 (t), Terry Guyer; p. 200 (b), Mark Mille/Sharon Langley.

PHOTOGRAPHY

Cover and Title page: Dr. Dennis Kunkel/Phototake

Feature Borders: Unless otherwise noted below, all images copyright ©2001 PhotoDisc/HRW. "Across the Sciences" 30, 52, 156, all images by HRW; "Careers" 157, sand bkgd and Saturn, Corbis Images; DNA, Morgan Cain & Associates; scuba gear, ©1997 Radlund & Associates for Artville; "Eye on the Environment" 128, clouds and sea in bkgd, HRW; bkgd grass, red eyed frog, Corbis Images; hawks, pelican, Animals Animals/Earth Scenes; rat, Visuals Unlimited/John Grelach; endangered flower, Dan Suzio/Photo Researchers, Inc.; "Health Watch" 77, dumbbell, Sam Dudgeon/HRW Photo; aloe vera, EKG, Victoria Smith/HRW Photo; basketball, ©1997 Radlund & Associates for Artville; shoes, bubbles, Greg Geisler; "Scientific Debate" 100, 178, Sam Dudgeon/HRW Photo; "Science Fiction" 53, 101, 129, saucers, Ian Christopher/Greg Geisler; book, HRW; bkgd telescope, Dave Cutler Studio, Inc./SIS; "Science Technology and Society" 76, robot, Greg Geisler; "Weird Science" 179, mite, David Burder/Stone; atom balls, J/B Woolsey Associates; walking stick, turtle, EclectiCollection.

Table of Contents: p. iv(cl), Bonnie Jacobs/Southern Methodist University; p. v(t), Dr. Tony Brian & David Parker/Science Photo Library/Photo Researchers, Inc.; p. v(br), Runk/Schoenberger/Grant Heilman; p. v(bl), Sam Dudgeon/HRW Photo; p. iv(bl), Ken Lucas; p. vi(t) Robert Brons/BPS/Stone; p. vi(c), Visuals Unlimited/ Sherman Thomson; p. vii(tl), Visuals Unlimited/Doug Sokell; vii(tr), Visuals Unlimited/K. G. Murti; p. vii(cl), Visuals Unlimited/D. M. Phillips; p. vii(bl), Biophoto Associates/ Science Source/Photo Researchers, Inc.; p. vii(br), CNRI/Science Photo Library/Photo Researchers, Inc.

Chapter One: pp. 2-3 Dennis Kunkel/Phototake 3 HRW Photo; p. 4(cl), Image Copyright ©2001 Photodisc, Inc.; p. 4(bl, bcl, bcr), Dr. Yorgos Nikas/Science Photo Library/Photo Researchers, Inc.; p. 4(br), Lennart Nilsson; p. 5(tc), Visuals Unlimited/ Fred Hossler; p. 5(tl), National Cancer Institute/Science Photo Library/ Photo Researchers, Inc.; p. 5(tr), GW Willis/BPS/Stone; p. 5(cr), Visuals Unlimited/G. Shih and R. Kessel; p. 7(tc), Visuals Unlimited/Michael Abbey; p. 7(tr), Robert Brons/BPS/ Stone; p. 7(tl), David M. Phillips/Photo Researchers, Inc.; p. 7(b), E.S. Ross; p. 8(t), Joe McDonald/DRK Photo; p. 9(cl, c), C.C. Lockwood/DRK Photo; p. 9(b), Visuals Unlimited/Kevin Collins; p. 9(br), Leonard Lessin/Peter Arnold; p. 10(tl), Visuals Unlimited/Doug Sokell; p. 10(tr), Visuals Unlimited/K. G. Murti; p. 10(cl), Visuals Unlimited/D. M. Phillips; p. 11(b), Biophoto Associates/Science Source/Photo Researchers, Inc.; p. 11(tr), Dr. Petit/Rapho/Liaison International; p. 13 AP/Wide World Photos; p. 21(tr), Biology Media/Photo Researchers, Inc.; p. 24(tl, tc) Runk/ Schoenberger/Grant Heilman; p. 24(tr) Michael Abbey/Photo Researchers, Inc.; p. 24(bl) Runk/Schoenberger/Grant Heilmanp. 26(tr), Robert Brons/BPS/Stone; p. 26(c), Joe McDonald/DRK Photo; p. 28 Biophoto Associates/Science Source/Photo Researchers, Inc.; p. 30(l), Hans Reinhard/Bruce Coleman; p. 30(tr), Andrew Syred/ Stone; p. 31 Dr. Smith/University of Akron.

Chapter Two: pp. 32-33 Walker/Science Source/Photo Researchers, Inc.; p. 33 HRW Photo; p. 35(br), Visuals Unlimited/David M. Philips ; p. 37(tr), Photo Researchers, Inc.; p. 37(cr), Birgit H. Satir; p. 39 Runk/Schoenberger/Grant Heilman; p. 42 CNRI/ Science Photo Library/Photo Researchers, Inc.; p. 43(tr), L. Willatt, East Anglian Regional Genetics Service/Science Photo Library/Photo Researchers, Inc.; p. 43(br), Biophoto Associates/Photo Researchers, Inc.; p. 44(all), Ed Reschke/Peter Arnold; p. 45(cr), Visuals Unlimited/R. Calentine; p. 45(tr, cr), Biology Media/Photo Researchers, Inc.; p. 48(tc), Visuals Unlimited/Stanley Flegler; p. 48(cr) Runk Schoenberger/Grant Heilman; p. 49 Ed Reschke/Peter Arnold; p. 50 CNRI/Science Photo Library/Photo Researchers, Inc.; p. 51(cl, c), Biophoto Associates/Science Source/Photo Researchers, Inc.; p. 52 Lee D. Simons/Science Source/Photo Researchers, Inc.

Chapter Three: pp. 54-55 Carr Clifton/Mindon Pictures; p. 55 HRW Photo; p. 56(c), Frans Lanting/Minden Pictures; p. 56(br), Corbis; p. 57 Runk/Schoenberger/Grant Heilman Photography; p. 63(br), Image Copyright ©2001 Photodisc, Inc.; p. 63(tr), Gerard Lacz/Animals Animals; p. 64(cl), Phototake/CNRI/Phototake NYC; p. 64(bc), Biophoto Associates/Photo Researchers, Inc.; p. 69 Phototake/CNRI/Phototake NYC; p. 72 Frans Lanting/Minden Pictures; p. 76 Hank Morgan/Rainbow; p. 77(t, c), Dr. F. R. Turner, Biology Dept., Indiana University.

Chapter Four: pp. 78-79 Will & Deni McIntyre/Photo Researchers, Inc.; p. 79(t) HRW Photo; p. 79(bl) Leonard Lessin/Peter Arnold; p. 79(bc) Reprinted from "The Science of Fingerprints" courtesy of the FBI; p. 79(br) Archive Photos; p. 81(tr), Science Photo Library/Photo Researchers, Inc.; p. 81(br), Archive Photos; p. 83 Dr. Gopal Murti/Science Photo Library/Photo Researchers, Inc.; p. 84(cl), Phil Jude/Science Photo Library/Photo Researcher, Inc.; p. 85(cl), Biophoto Associates/Photo Researchers, Inc.; p. 85(tl), J.R. Paulson & U.K. Laemmli/University of Geneva; p. 85(bl), Dan McCoy/Rainbow; p. 86(br), Lawrence Migdale/Photo Researchers, Inc.; p. 91(br, cr), Jackie Lewin/Royal Free Hospital/Science Photo Library/Photo Researchers, Inc.; p. 93(cl), Remi Benali and Stephen Ferry/Gamma-Liaison; p. 93(tr), Visuals Unlimited/Science Visuals Unlimited/Keith Wood; p. 95 Victoria Smith/HRW Photo; p. 98 Kenneth Eward/Science Source/Photo Researchers, Inc.; p. 99 Remi Benali and Stephen Ferry/Gamma-Liaison; p. 100 Volker Steger/Peter Arnold

Chapter Five: pp. 102-103 Jeff Rotman/Stone; p. 103 HRW Photo; p. 104(cr), Gail Shumway/FPG International; p. 104(cl), Doug Wechsler/Animals Animals; p. 106(cl), Ken Lucas; p. 106(cr), John Cancalosi/ Tom Stack & Associates; p. 111(br), Visuals Unlimited/H.W. Robison; p. 112(b), Christopher Ralling; p. 112(bl), William E. Ferguson; p. 111(tr), Jeanne White/Photo Researchers, Inc.; p. 111(tl), [illegible] Photo; p. 114(bl), Robert Pearcy/Animals Animals; p. 114(cl), John Daniels/DANI2/Bruce Coleman, Inc.; p. 114(bc), Dennis and Catherine Quinn; p. 114(bl), Yann Arthus-Bertrand/Corbis; p. 114(cr), Fritz Prenzel/Animals Animals; p. 115(tl), Library of Congress/Corbis; p. 117(tr), Image Copyright ©2001 Photodisc, Inc.; p. 119(l, r), M.W. Tweedie/Photo Researchers, Inc.; p. 126 Ken Lucas; p. 127(bl), Breck P. Kent/Animals Animals; p. 127(bc), Pat & Tom Leeson/Photo Researchers, Inc.; p. 128(tr), Doug Wilson/Westlight.

continued on page 216

Self-Check Answers

Chapter 1—Cells: The Basic Units of Life

Page 11: Cells need DNA to control cell processes and to make new cells.

Page 14: 1. The surface-to-volume ratio decreases as the cell size increases. 2. A eukaryotic cell has a nucleus and membrane-covered organelles.

Page 18: Cell walls surround the cell membranes of some cells. All cells have cell membranes, but not all cells have cell walls. Cell walls give structure to some cells.

Chapter 2—The Cell in Action

Page 35: In pure water, the grape would absorb water and swell up. In water mixed with a large amount of sugar, the grape would lose water and shrink.

Page 43: After duplication, there are four chromatids—two from each of the homologous chromosomes.

Chapter 3—Heredity

Page 67: 1. four 2. two 3. They make copies of themselves once. They divide twice. 4. Two, or half the number of chromosomes in the parent, are present at the end of meiosis. After mitosis, there would be four chromosomes, the same number as in the parent cell.

Chapter 4—Genes and Gene Technology

Page 83: TGGATCAAC

Page 89: 1. 1000 amino acids 2. DNA codes for proteins. Your flesh is composed of proteins, and the way those proteins are constructed and combined influences much about the way you look.

Chapter 5—The Evolution of Living Things

Page 119: The population of light-colored moths would increase.

Chapter 6—The History of Life on Earth

Page 135: 5 g, 2.5 g

Page 141: b, c, d, a

Chapter 7—Classification

Page 168: 1. The two kingdoms of bacteria are different from all other kingdoms because bacteria are prokaryotes—single-celled organisms that have no nucleus. 2. The organisms in the kingdom Protista are all eukaryotes.

Credits (continued)

Chapter Six: pp. 130-131 Reuters Newmedia, Inc./CORBIS; p. 131 HRW Photo p. 132 Louie Psihoyos/Matrix; p. 138 SuperStock; p. 139 Visuals Unlimited/NMSM; p. 140 M. Abbey/Photo Researchers, Inc.; p. 144(cr), Daniel J. Cox/Stone; p. 144(c), Art Wolfe/Stone; p. 146(bl), John Reader/Science Photo Library/Photo Researchers, Inc.; p. 146(tl), Daniel J. Cox/Gamma-Liaison; p. 147(tr), David Brill; p. 147(br), John Gurche; p. 148(bl), John Reader/Science Photo Library/Photo Researchers, Inc.; p. 148(bl), E.R. Degginger/Bruce Coleman; p. 148(tl, br), Neanderthal Museum; p. 149 David Brill/National Geographic Society Image Collection; p. 153 Renee Lynn/Photo Researchers, Inc.; p. 154 John Reader/Science Photo Library/Photo Researchers, Inc.; p. 156(c), Thomas W. Martin, APSA/Photo Researchers, Inc.; p. 157(tl, b), Bonnie Jacobs/Southern Methodist University

Chapter Seven: pp. 158-159 Frans Lanting/Minden Pictures; p. 159 HRW Photo; p. 160 Ethnobotany of the Chacabo Indians, Beni, Bolivia, Advances in Economic Botany/The New York Botanical Gardens; p. 162(tl), Library of Congress/Corbis; p. 166 Biophoto Associates/Photo Researchers, Inc.; p. 167(tr), Sherrie Jones/Photo Researchers, Inc.; p. 167(bl, bc), Dr. Tony Brian & David Parker/Science Photo Library/ Photo Researchers, Inc.; p. 168(tl), Visuals Unlimited/M.Abbey; p. 168(cl), Visuals Unlimited/Stanley Flegler; p. 168(br), Chuck Davis/Stone; p. 169(c), Corbis Images; p. 169(b), Art Wolfe/Stone; p. 170(tl), Robert Maier; p. 170(c), Visuals Unlimited/Sherman Thomson; p. 170(br), Visuals Unlimited/Richard Thom; p. 171(cr), Telegraph Colour Library 1997/FPG; p. 171(tr), SuperStock; p. 171(cl), G. Randall/FPG; p. 171(c), SuperStock; p. 175 Robert Maier; p. 179 Peter Funch

Labook: "LabBook Header": "L", Corbis Images, "a", Letraset-Phototone, "b" and "B", HRW, "o" and "k", Images Copyright ©2001 PhotoDisc, Inc. 680(tc), Scott Van Osdol/HRW Photo; p. 181(cl), Michelle Bridwell/HRW Photo; p. 181(br), Image Copyright ©2001 Photodisc, Inc.; p. 182(bl), Stephanie Morris/HRW Photo; p.183(tr), Jana Birchum/HRW Photo; p. 183(b), Peter Van Steen/HRW Photo; p. 193(tr), Jana Burchum/HRW Photo; p. 193(b), Peter Van Steen/HRW Photo; p. 197(tl), Peter Van Steen/HRW Photo.

Appendix: p. 206 CENCO

Sam Dudgeon/HRW Photos: p,viii-1, 24(cl), 34, 41, 46, 70, 84, 87, 150, 151, 180(bl), 181(bc), 183(tl), 185, 186, 187, 193(tl), 197(br)

John Langford/HRW Photos: p. 39 ,48(cr), 8, 181(tr), p. 8(cr, br)

Acknowledgements continued from page iii.

Alyson Mike
Science Teacher
East Valley Middle School
East Helena, Montana

Donna Norwood
Science Teacher and Dept. Chair
Monroe Middle School
Charlotte, North Carolina

James B. Pulley
Former Science Teacher
Liberty High School
Liberty, Missouri

Terry J. Rakes
Science Teacher
Elmwood Junior High School
Rogers, Arkansas

Elizabeth Rustad
Science Teacher
Crane Middle School
Yuma, Arizona

Debra A. Sampson
Science Teacher
Booker T. Washington Middle School
Elgin, Texas

Charles Schindler
Curriculum Advisor
San Bernadino City Unified Schools
San Bernadino, California

Bert J. Sherwood
Science Teacher
Socorro Middle School
El Paso, Texas

Patricia McFarlane Soto
Science Teacher and Dept. Chair
G. W. Carver Middle School
Miami, Florida

David M. Sparks
Science Teacher
Redwater Junior High School
Redwater, Texas

Elizabeth Truax
Science Teacher
Lewiston-Porter Central School
Lewiston, New York

Ivora Washington
Science Teacher and Dept. Chair
Hyattsville Middle School
Washington, D.C.

Elsie N. Waynes
Science Teacher and Dept. Chair
R. H. Terrell Junior High School
Washington, D.C.

Nancy Wesorick
Science and Math Teacher
Sunset Middle School
Longmont, Colorado

Alexis S. Wright
Middle School Science Coordinator
Rye Country Day School
Rye, New York

John Zambo
Science Teacher
E. Ustach Middle School
Modesto, California

Gordon Zibelman
Science Teacher
Drexell Hill Middle School
Drexell Hill, Pennsylvania